From Head to Heart: High Quality Teaching Practices in the Spotlight

Nicholas D. Young

Elizabeth Jean

Teresa Allissa Citro

Series in Education

VERNON PRESS

www.vernonpress.com

In the Americas:	*In the rest of the world:*
Vernon Press	Vernon Press
1000 N West Street,	C/Sancti Espiritu 17,
Suite 1200, Wilmington,	Malaga, 29006
Delaware 19801	Spain
United States	

Series in Education

Library of Congress Control Number: 2018940485

ISBN: 978-1-62273-402-3

Cover design by Vernon Press, using elements selected by Kjpargeter / freepik

Table of Contents

Acknowledgment   *v*

Preface   *vii*

Chapter 1   **"This Is What I Am": The Evolving Landscape
             of Teacher Identity**   1

             David Bosso, Ed.D., *Berlin High School, Berlin,
             CT*

Chapter 2   **Using Student-Centered Teaching: Inspiring
             and Empowering Teachers and Learners**   21

             Erin K. Washburn, Ph.D., *Binghamton
             University - State University of New York* and
             Stefanie Olbrys, M.Ed., *Windsor Central School
             District, Windsor, NY*

Chapter 3   **The Love in the Lesson: How an Enthusiastic
             Teacher Improves Student Learning
             Outcomes**   45

             Nicholas Young, Ph.D, Ed.D, *American
             International College* and Aimee Dalenta, M.Ed.,
             Goodwin College

Chapter 4   **Response to Intervention: A Tool to Increase
             Student Comprehension**   59

             Nicholas D. Young, PhD, EdD, *American
             International College* and E. Marie McPadden,
             EdD, *Quinnipiac University*

Chapter 5   **Classroom Management: Strategies for All
             Teachers**   75

             Angela C. Fain, PhD, *University of West Georgia*
             and Ellen L. Duchaine, PhD, *Texas State
             University*

Chapter 6   **Daily Classroom Instruction: Embedding**
              Social-Emotional Skills for Optimal Learning   89

              Micheline Susan Malow, PhD, *Manhattanville*
              College

Chapter 7   **Penciling in Parents: Making Time for**
              Partnerships that Count   107

              Nicholas D. Young, PhD, EdD, *American*
              International College and Elizabeth Jean, EdD,
              Endicott College

Chapter 8   **Administrative Factors: Supporting Teachers**
              and Contributing to the Success of All
              Students   121

              Nicholas D. Young, PhD, EdD, *American*
              International College and Kristen Bonanno-
              Sotiropoulos, MS, *Bay Path University*

Chapter 9   **Stemming Teacher Shortages: A Community**
              Apprenticeship Model   131

              Dr. Tracey Benson, EDLD, *University of North*
              Carolina at Charlotte and Justin MacDonald,
              MA, *Digital Arts and Technology Academy*

Chapter 10   **"Physician, Heal Thyself:" A Guide to Wellness**
              as an Antidote to Teacher Burnout   147

              Vance L. Austin, PhD, *Manhattanville College*

List of Acronyms   165

About the Primary Authors   169

Acknowledgment

We would like to thank Sue Clark for her time and attention to this tome. In addition to being a valued member of our writing club, she has spent almost thirty years in the field of education where she has consistently modeled how to make others feel valued and special.

Preface

Head to Heart: High Quality Teaching Practices in the Spotlight was written for teachers and support staff, school leaders and school counselors, higher education faculty and pre-service teachers. This book represents a concerted effort to describe effective teaching practices that improve instruction and student outcomes while acknowledging that relationships are an important part of the educational equation. A great deal of research shows the connection between relationship building and educational outcomes for staff, students, and families; thus, teachers must be well-prepared to invest emotional currency in the classroom (Henderson & Mapp, 2002; Castro, Exposito-Casas, Lopez-Martin, Lizasoain, Navarro-Asencio, & Gaviria, 2015; Flamboyan Foundation, 2011; Wood, n.d.). *Head to Heart* recognizes the role teachers play in all aspects of the educational arena and, as such, delves into topics such as empowering teachers and engaging with families, promoting positive classroom management practices, and wellness recommendations to prevent teacher burnout. Other chapters discuss teacher identity, social-emotional skill building, and administrator support.

The motivation for writing this book comes from several concerns:

- *Our belief that teachers hold the power to create academic environments that support all students and benefit learning outcomes;*

- *Our knowledge that as the face of education changes, so too must our veteran and pre-service teachers and to do so, they need the assistance of school leaders and post-secondary faculty;*

- *Our heartfelt desire to share teaching practices that support not only the practical side of teaching but also the more heady, caring side;*

- *Our awareness that teachers are not in education for the money, rather gauge success as having made a difference and changing a life;*

- *Our years of experience as educators, administrators, counselors, and parents who have experienced, first-hand, the dedication of the profession and sought to support those who continued to work with children, and;*

- *Our interest in sharing effective teaching practices that have the potential to transform good educators into exemplary role models.*

Educators are a unique tribe committed to the advancement of young people. According to a study published in 2013, 88% of teachers surveyed agreed that the "rewards of teaching outweigh[ed] the challenges" (Primary Sources, 2013, n.p.), while 85% of the same group said they chose to teach to make a difference "in the lives of children" (Primary Sources, 2013, n.p.).

The teachers surveyed reported the five most critical factors for retaining top teachers as teacher collaboration (89%), access to teacher resources and high-quality curriculum (90%), more help for our most behaviorally needy students (91%), family engagement to enhance student outcomes (93%), while a supportive administration ranked at the top of the list (97%) (Primary Sources, 2012).

The average age of teachers in America is 42.3; however, the majority of teachers fall within the 21-34 age range (Primary Sources, 2013). There are almost equal numbers of men and women who teach high school, yet in PK-5, 74% are women (Primary Sources, 2013). And for those who question the work day of a teacher, a 2012 Primary Sources survey calculated that teachers worked 10 hour and 40 minutes a day - 13 hours more than a traditional 40-hour work week. Statistics such as these, point directly to the urgency of this tome, that is, that while teachers may use their heads to teach, they use their hearts to reach inside and extract the best qualities in each student.

How teachers connect with students provides the basis for all teaching and learning. Learning is not only a matter of how educators teach rather, it comes "from the identity and integrity of the teacher" (Parker, 1997). Stated another way, a teacher's identity is visible to students and often provides a picture of a caring individual who is willing to go the extra mile to ensure that quality learning takes place. Perhaps the most identifiable characteristic of an educator who teaches with heart is that they are compassionate, that is, they "have a feeling of deep empathy and respect" (Wolpow, Johnson, Hertel, & Kincaid, 2016, p.17) for their students and it is visible to the students as well. Educators who are compassionate are viewed by students as also being kind, empathetic, and positive (Alrubail, 2015). These are the same educators who inspire students and build relationships, and, in turn, students believe that their success matters (Alrubail, 2015; Hare, 2008).

In order to have meaningful change in student outcomes, educators need to make a connection through the heart, then the mind, of their students (Couros, 2015). They must build relationships and trust in order to build knowledge (Couros, 2015). An educator who teaches with heart may say hello to every student as they walk in the door, ensuring that each receives a warm smile and calm voice to start the day. It may be a teacher who, instead of reprimanding a student for a failed test, sits down to speak with him, learning about his likes and dislikes, abilities and struggles; thus, both the student and the teacher develop a connection that leads to learning (Delisio, 2009). It is this type of relationship that, once formed, allows the student to thrive within the classroom; it is this heart of a teacher that provides a solid base and safe haven for students. Teachers cannot fake teaching with heart, it is who they are, and it has a substantial impact on the student experience (Couros, 2015; Delisio, 2009). It is no surprise, then, that students who feel a connection to their teacher might be more inspired to perform better academically and work harder to reach and exceed their goals (Delisio, 2009; Hare, 2008).

Written by an experienced team of educational professionals, this text attempts to synthesize existing data while adding to the body of current and growing research. An examination of more personal educator topics shows the multiple roles teachers play as they work to provide students with a 'just-right' mix of academics, social-emotional stability, and family support, and that when this mix is in proper proportions, everyone wins. As a practitioner-oriented text, this book seeks to offer a comprehensive look at the literature, while offering strategies and tools to engage students through educator best practices.

The authors hope that all who teach or are preparing to teach the students of the 21st century will be reminded that the most personal qualities should be crafted and honed so that educators can provide budding scholars with the best they have to offer. In her famous TED Talk, Pierson (2013) eloquently reminded educators that "Teaching and learning should bring joy...Every child deserves a champion, an adult who will never give up on them, who understands the power of connection and insists that they become the best that they can possibly be" (Pierson, 2013, n.p.). We can ask for no more from our educators, and our students deserve no less.

References

Alrubail, R. (2015). *The heart of teaching: What it means to be a great teacher.* Retrieved from
https://www.edutopia.org/discussion/heart-teaching-what-it-means-be-great-teacher

Castro, M., Exposito-Casas, E., Lopez-Martin, E., Lizasoain, L., Navarro-Asencio, E., & Gaviria, J.L. (2015). *Parental involvement on student academic achievement: A meta-analysis.* Retrieved from
https://www.sciencedirect.com/science/article/pii/S1747938X15000032

Couros, G. (2015). *The innovator's mindset: Empower learning, unleash talent, and lead a culture of creativity.* San Diego, CA: Dave Burgess Consulting.

Delisio, E.R. (2009). *What students really think of their education, teachers.* Retrieved from
http://www.educationworld.com/a_issues/chat/chat239.shtml

Flamboyan Foundation. (2011). *Setting the stage: The family engagement field.* Retrieved from http://flamboyanfoundation.org/wp/wp-content/uploads/2011/06/Setting-the-stage-4-28-11.pdf

Hare, J. (2008). *Survey reveals what students really think of teachers.* Retrieved from http://teaching.monster.com/benefits/articles/7007-survey-reveals-what-students-really-think-of-teachers

Henderson, A. & Mapp, K.L. (2002). *A new wave of evidence: The impact of school, family, and community connections on student achievement.* Austin, TX: National Center for Family and Community Connections with Schools. Retrieved from https://www.sedl.org/connections/resources/evidence.pdf

Palmer, P.J. (1997). *The courage to teach: Exploring the inner landscapes of a teachers' life.* San Francisco, CA: Jossey-Bass.

Pierson, R. (2013). *Every kid needs a champion.* Retrieved from https://www.ted.com/talks/rita_pierson_every_kid_needs_a_champion/transcriptPrimary Primary Sources. (2012). *Primary Sources: 2012: America's teachers on the teaching profession.* Retrieved from http://www.scholastic.com/primarysources/pdfs/Gates2012_full.pdf

Primary Sources. (2013). *A portrait of America's teachers.* Retrieved from http://mediaroom.scholastic.com/files/PortraitofAmericasTeachers.jpg

Wolpow, R., Johnson, M.M. Hertel, R., & Kincaid, S.O. (2016). *The heart of learning and teaching: Compassion, resiliency, and academic success* (3rd printing). Retrieved from http://www.k12.wa.us/CompassionateSchools/Resources.aspx

Wood, L. (n.d.). *Promoting equity through family-school partnerships.* Retrieved from https://www.ed.gov/family-and-community-engagement/bulletin-board/promoting-equity-through-family-school-partnerships

Chapter 1

"This Is What I Am": The Evolving Landscape of Teacher Identity

David Bosso, Ed.D.,
Berlin High School, Berlin, CT

Teaching is complex. Working with children, classroom management, lesson design and implementation, policy mandates, responsibility to multiple stakeholders, and numerous other demands pose a unique set of challenges on a daily basis. It is at times stimulating, frustrating, inspiring, exhausting, and empowering. For many teachers, despite its many pressures, teaching is meaningful, fulfilling work, reflective of a sense of mission rooted in a service ethos and educational ideals. Perhaps because of this service orientation, the personal and professional identities of teachers are woven tightly together (Beijaard & Meijer, 2017; Downey, Schaefer, & Clandinin, 2014).

A few years ago, facing impending retirement, a teacher reflected on her life's work:

> This is what I am, and I cannot imagine putting myself in a situation where I can't say to people, "I'm a teacher." I don't know, this is the emotional version. I want to be remembered in the same way that I remember teachers I had. I hope that there are people out there who, when they think about me, kind of choke up because of the presence of teachers in their lives. And I think I probably have been that for a few kids.

For many teachers, their professional identity "is deeply embedded in…personal biography" (Bukor, 2015, p. 305) and teachers' vocational dispositions are a reflection of their goals, beliefs, aspirations, and motivations that guide them and shape them as professionals (Bukor, 2015).

The Uniqueness of Teacher Identity

Teacher identity is multifaceted, malleable, and fluid. It encompasses teachers' beliefs, values, views, experiences, thoughts, feelings, understandings, decisions, and actions (Mockler, 2011). Teacher identity is multi-dimensional and unique to each respective individual; thus, it is a difficult construct to define adequately. A teacher's self-identity evolves over the course of a career, responding to various personal and professional changes, as well as to larger cultural and political forces (Mockler, 2011). It reflects personal and professional beliefs situated in a cultural, political, and educational landscape that itself does not remain static. In response to these wide-ranging influences, teacher identity is "formed and constantly re-formed over the course of a career and mediated by a complex interplay of personal, professional, and political dimensions of teachers' lives" (Mockler, 2011, p. 518).

It is a generally accepted precept of education that the single most important factor in a child's academic experience is the quality of the teacher (Department of Education, 2006). The common interpretation of this view is largely grounded in the pedagogical effectiveness of the teacher as a practitioner. Often overlooked, is the less obvious, yet more intangible and more nuanced, complex synergy of behaviors, values, beliefs, perspectives, and experiences that comprise, influence, and reflect teachers' personal and professional identities (Frenzel, 2014).

Professional identity is not completely separate from personal sense of self; therefore, factors such as the emotional investment teachers make to their students, the moral purpose of teaching, and cultural and political contexts may exert a significant influence on teachers' views of themselves and their profession, as well as how they carry out their work (Fried, Mansfield, & Dobozy, 2015). They may encounter discrepancies between the goals that attracted them to the profession in the first place with the complicated realities of the work. When such goals are hindered, and dissonance arises for any number of reasons, teachers' professional and personal self-images may be challenged.

The Research Base

Since Lortie (1975) first elaborated on the social-emotional lives of teachers, more attention has been paid to better understand the work lives of teachers, particularly the development and expression of teachers' identities during an era of momentous changes in education (Beijaard & Meijer, 2017; González-Calvo & Arias-Carballal, 2017). Likewise, the work of Nias (1996) prompted increased consideration of the role of emotion as central to teachers' professional identity, most notably the research of Hargreaves (2001), and more recently a number of others (Frenzel, 2014; Fried, Mansfield, & Dobozy, 2015; Gill & Hardin, 2015). Other works have focused on the responses of teachers to perceived or real threats to their self-concepts, such as resilience and burnout (Mansfield, Beltman, Price, & McConney, 2012; Nagy & Takács, 2017).

Theoretical Underpinnings of Teacher Identity

According to the theory of self-determination, humans innately possess three main psychological needs: competence, autonomy, and relatedness (Ryan & Deci, 2017). Environmental conditions that cultivate and fulfill these needs are integral to personal growth, well-being, and positive sense of self (Ryan & Deci, 2017). Social contexts that are supportive of competence, autonomy and relatedness enhance intrinsic motivation, encourage the internalization of extrinsic motivators, and fortify personal goals related to the fulfillment of the basic needs (Ryan & Deci, 2017). When personal or environmental challenges prevent the needs from being adequately fulfilled, or external controlling behaviors are dominant, self-motivation and overall well-being decrease (Korthagen & Evelein, 2016; Roth, 2014; Ryan & Deci, 2017). Given the variables present in the social setting of schools and classrooms, traditional schooling attitudes and practices, and the exigencies of the educational policy landscape, the implications of self-determination theory on teachers' professional lives are significant (Ryan & Brown, 2005; Ryan & Weinstein, 2009).

Central to self-determination theory are the various types and sources of motivation, whether intrinsically or extrinsically derived. Intrinsic motivation refers to behaviors and activities that individuals engage in out of interest or passion, and from which feelings of enjoyment result, whereas extrinsic motivation compels people to seek rewards or avoid punishments associated with an activity (Hohnbaum, 2012). Engagement motivations and personal outcomes can range from "personal endorsement and a feeling of choice" to "compliance with an external regulation" (Ryan & Deci, 2000, p. 71).

Across the career continuum, teachers' feelings of accomplishment and efficacy are associated with intrinsic motivation and autonomy (Roth, 2014; Watt and Richardson, 2014). Teacher burnout, job dissatisfaction, lower levels of perceived efficacy, poor self-concept, and diminished morale and motivation are among the many negative consequences associated with these types of school climates. Conversely, high levels of morale, motivation, collegiality, trust, support, and collaboration are vital to enhanced intrinsic motivation, increased self-efficacy, and positive identity formation (Roth, 2014).

Another theoretical framework by which to better understand professional identity is an expectancy-value theory, which emphasizes the influence of cultural and social contexts on the formation of individuals' values, perceptions, and expectancies (Butler, 2017). From an expectancy-value perspective, professional identity is comprised of perceptions related to skills and characteristics, as well as personal values and goals (Eccles, 2009). The FIT-Choice Framework (Factors Influencing Teaching Choice), which incorporates expectancy-value theory, focuses on altruistic and intrinsic motivations, along with other factors that may lead one to a career in teaching (Richardson & Watt, 2016). It takes into account social influences, learning experiences, as well as self-perceptions and values. The altruistic motivation for teaching reflects a view of teaching as moral service, as a vocation or calling, as a social imperative, and as making a difference in students' lives (Gore, Holmes, Smith, & Fray, 2015; Richardson & Watt, 2016).

The Internal Architecture of Teacher Identity

Moral Purpose

An individual's motivation for choosing to teach as a career plays an important role in their ensuing professional engagement and identity development (Lauermann, Karabenick, Carpenter, & Kuusinen, 2017; Richardson & Watt, 2014). With the concepts of intrinsic motivation and altruistic motivation as pillars of teacher identity formation and reasons for entering the profession, a closer examination of other elements that comprise self-concept is warranted (Richardson & Watt, 2016). As a whole, teachers' self-identities reflect an intricate nexus of their professional activities and perspectives, their personal values and sense of self, and their overall life aspirations. Teachers often consider their work as a "calling" and moral purpose constitutes a powerful element of teachers' identities (Zembylas & Chubbock, 2014). The need to maintain a moral imperative for their work, relationships with others throughout the school community, professional autonomy, and overall pedagogical competence are vital to teachers' self-esteem, needs fulfillment, and intrinsic motivation (Richardson & Watt, 2016).

The moral principles and emotions involved in teaching as a profession are closely aligned with intrinsic and altruistic motivation, as well as basic needs fulfillment essential to self-determination theory. These ideals and values may be threatened by educational change efforts, bureaucratic forces, and controlling school environments. In the absence of intrinsic and altruistic motivation or when extrinsic motivators dominate, teachers may feel limited in their capacity to carry out their moral mission, and negative emotions, such as anxiety and frustration, and even guilt and anger, can emerge (Nias, 1999). When external forces erode their intrinsic motivation, feelings of low self-efficacy, stress, disengagement, and loss of morale may result. Indeed, teachers who may be most at risk of stress, demoralization, burnout, and attrition are often the ones who have the strongest sense of vocation about their work (Durr, Chang, & Carson, 2014; Richardson & Watt, 2016). Collaboration, support, emotion management, and resilience can counteract the detrimental effects of these tensions and reduce the potential for burnout and attrition (Hohnbaum, 2012). In other words, in educational settings, when the basic needs of self-determination theory are met, teacher morale, motivation, and efficacy can be bolstered, thereby positively affecting identity and growth (Hohnbaum, 2012).

Emotions and Beliefs

Teachers' emotions are central to their professional experiences, identities, and values. For most teachers, their identities and emotions "are inextricably related to each other" (Schutz & Mikyoung, 2014, p. 174), largely because of their deep emotional investment in their vocation and their students (Frenzel, 2014; Zembylas & Chubbock, 2014). Emotions shape, and are shaped by, teachers' values, beliefs, perspectives, and behaviors. As teachers' identities evolve, their attitudes, beliefs, and emotions change concomitantly, impacting and reflecting their sense of agency, efficacy, and commitment (Biesta, Priestley, & Robinson, 2015; Fives & Buehl, 2016).

The service orientation of teaching and working closely with children necessitates "emotional sensitivity [and] active emotional labor" (Hargreaves, 1998b, p. 560). Various factors within the classroom, the school environment, and the larger educational landscape influence emotional regulation, which includes balancing the appropriate expression of positive and negative emotions suitable for the context and the individuals within that setting (Taxer & Frenzel, 2015). Teachers typically experience positive emotion and feel a sense of self-worth and fulfillment when the pursuits in which they engage are intrinsically motivated, and when situational factors are congruent with one's goals and allow for the attainment of such goals (Hargeaves, 1998a). When teachers "lose their sense of purpose," influenced as it is by the moral imperatives of their profession, "they become literally demoralized" (Hargreaves, 1998a, p. 841).

It is difficult to disentangle teachers' personal and professional identities, their emotions, the moral purposes they ascribe to their vocation, and their capacities to pursue and attain those purposes. If prospective teachers are not prepared for the emotional demands of teaching, negative emotion, stress, and potential burnout can result (Frenzel, 2014; Schutz & Mikyoung, 2014). Since emotions and beliefs affect teachers' capacity "to thrive, not just survive in their professional life" (Fried et al., 2015, p. 416), it makes sense that emotional regulation may contribute to stronger professional commitment and lower attrition rates. Because teachers' moral principles, emotions, and beliefs are closely aligned with the intrinsic motivators, altruistic motivators, and basic needs fulfillment, how teachers navigate the emotional intricacies and changes to their beliefs are important variables to consider when addressing recruitment, retention, and support.

Self-Efficacy

Self-efficacy "refers to beliefs in one's capabilities to organize and execute the courses of action required to manage prospective situations, [thereby influencing] how people think, feel, motivate themselves, and act" (Bandura, 1997, p. 2). Teacher efficacy – derived from the perception that one's pedagogical skills, content knowledge, interactions with students, and other factors contribute to success in the teaching and learning environment – is a powerful force throughout an individual's teaching career (Kuther & Holberger, 2014). As such, teachers' sense of efficacy is closely intertwined with their agency, well-being, and professional identity (Day, 2017). Controlling environments, lack of connectedness, absence of supportive structures, and settings characterized by external motivators can impede the fulfillment of the basic needs of competence, autonomy, and relatedness and, subsequently, negatively impact the development of self-efficacy and, consequently, professional growth, motivation, morale, job satisfaction, and overall performance (Kuther & Holberg, 2014).

As the educators' career develops, teaching successes and failures inevitably will occur, and job-related confidence, competence, and satisfaction will grow or diminish, often as a result of, and in response to, interaction with colleagues, students, administration, parents, and the community; the overall workplace environment; opportunities for meaningful professional growth and career advancement; and larger educational policy pressures (Day, 2017). The ways by which teachers develop their sense of efficacy, navigate the school and policy environments, and simultaneously deal with the myriad challenges and complexities of their daily work will affect identity construction and evolution (Day, 2017).

Motivational and self-efficacy factors are closely related to commitment and/or burnout (Fernet, Guay, Senècal, & Austin, 2012). Given the potential for external forces to come into conflict with what intrinsically motivates many teachers, it is possible that educational reform measures and school-level policies can diminish self-efficacy and can contribute to higher levels of teacher workloads, stress, role conflict, role ambiguity, and possibly, burnout and attrition (Fernet, Guay, Senècal, & Austin, 2012). Nevertheless, despite the multifarious challenges confronted by teachers on a regular basis, there are many teachers who remain motivated, positive, enthusiastic, resilient, and efficacious.

Identity Development Across the Career Continuum

Formative Stages

A teacher's identity constantly evolves, as he or she engages in, and reflect upon, a multitude of tasks, decisions, and interactions on a daily basis (Buchanan, 2015). Personal and professional circumstances compel teachers to be "actively engaged in the process of creating themselves as teachers during their entire careers" (Bukor, 2015, p. 307), though the experiences of teachers in the formative stages of their professional lives are vital to positive identity development (Beijaard & Meijer, 2017). During the initial stages of one's career, "[f]inding a balance between personal views and experiences and the professional or cultural expectations of what it means to be a teacher is an important aspect of developing a professional identity as a teacher" (Beltman, Glass, Dinham, Chalk, & Nguyen, 2015, p. 226).

Although many individuals are drawn to teaching because of intrinsic and altruistic motivations, regrettably, many prospective teachers are often ignorant of the many demands, pressures, and challenges of everyday work in classrooms and schools, as well as the broader educational milieu as influenced by cultural and political attitudes (Beltman et al., 2015). For example, in a study of pre-service teachers, Beltman et al. (2015) found minimal evidence that study participants understood, or were prepared for, the rigors of the profession, the emotional labor it entails, and the realities present in their future work. The study also revealed confidence in their abilities and a generally positive representation of the work of teachers engaged in service to children and society (Beltman et al., 2015). Izadinia (2013) claims that much of the research on teacher identity construction tends to focus on positive, idealized, and simplistic views of the profession, leading teacher educators, and policymakers to underestimate the challenges of identity creation during the formative years. Since an individual's motivation for choosing teaching as a career and his/her self-efficacy beliefs contribute to nascent identity formation, providing positive, rich, and realistic experiences for prospective and beginning teachers that will affect their sense of professional commitment in ensuing career stages is a critical task for teacher trainers, policymakers, and school leaders (Izadinia, 2013).

Threats to Positive Identity Formation

Regardless of their views of their future profession, prospective teachers will face any number of challenges to their expectations and beliefs. As a result, "conflicts may emerge as tensions in the professional identity of (beginning) teachers and cause internal struggles" (Pillen, Beijaard, & den Brok, 2012, p. 2). Without supportive structures, colleagues, and leadership, and without ways to manage one's emotional response, conflict and tensions from various sources can have a substantial effect on the formation and evolution of one's teacher identity, particularly in the early years of one's teaching career (Beijaard & Meijer, 2017; Buchanan, 2015).

Such tensions, which are often accompanied by negative emotions and feelings of inadequacy, underscore the importance of self-efficacy and environments that foster feelings of competence (Beijaard & Meijer, 2017). Beginning teachers often unduly focus on classroom management and the acquisition of content knowledge, often to the detriment of other pedagogical and affective aspects of their work. Failure to mitigate these numerous tensions can result in increased anxiety, constrained efficacy, negative self-concepts, and possibly burn out, causing some to leave the profession altogether. Teachers, especially during the formative and early stages of their careers, need to reconcile personal and professional beliefs so as to develop and sustain "a realistic teacher identity" (Beijaard & Meijer, 2017). For new teachers, supportive and collaborative cultures characterized by trust, respect, and strong leadership, among other factors, can facilitate the development of self-efficacy and the positive identity construction (Beijaard & Meijer, 2017).

Later Career Stages

The evolving nature of teacher identity means that positive identity development remains a challenge even after the initial years of one's teaching career (Day, 2017). It is never a completely smooth progression from novice teacher to master teacher, there are always going to be some trials and hindrances along the way. Teachers do not usually experience steady upward growth trends reflective of efficacy, agency, and pedagogical mastery. It is, more often than not, an uneven progression where "At different times and in different personal, workplace, and policy contexts, they may experience uncertainty about who they are, what is expected of them, and how they are perceived as professionals" (Day, 2017, p. 44), and it is during these times that educators may find it difficult to be their best self.

Disequilibrium results from not only professional challenges and changes within one's school, district, or broader educational setting, but also from personal pressures and transformations over the career span (Day, 2017). In such instances, teacher identity evolution can be for better or for worse, as well as subtle and private or momentous and conspicuous. Such developments can reflect changes in teacher practice, beliefs, emotions, and attitudes that govern interactions with students, colleagues, administrators, curriculum, and other stakeholders, as well as perceptions toward, and implementation of, pedagogy and policy (Day, 2017).

Day (2017) suggests that more years of experience usually parallel increased responsibilities, the result of which impacts, and perhaps even complicates, ongoing identity formation. It is not uncommon for many veteran teachers to struggle with "work-life tensions" (Day, 2017, p. 54) that are accompanied by increasing workloads and challenges to their sense of efficacy, energy, resilience, and self-image. Importantly, the "emotional resilience" (Day, 2017, p. 78) of teachers is crucial for their professional commitment and sustained moral purpose. From a self-determination perspective, Roth (2014) suggests that a robust sense of autonomy "may enable teachers to withstand periodic disturbances and obstacles, and may prevent deleterious experiences leading to low vitality and exhaustion" (p. 39). Regardless of career stage, the vital components that comprise a teacher's identity will be shaped by various forces, thereby impacting sense of self, beliefs, behaviors, responses, and interactions with others throughout the educational environment across the span of one's career.

External Influences on Teacher Identity Development

Situational Influences: The Cultural, Historical, and Political Context

The mutable, unique nature of teacher identity as the expression of personal and professional self-concepts is influenced by individual personality traits in combination with cultural, historical, and political factors (Buchanan, 2015; Day, 2017). Teachers' personal traits, beliefs, and expectations, themselves molded by external forces reflective of a particular zeitgeist, color how educators interpret situations affecting their identities and work (Fried et al., 2015).

Teachers are shaped by, and respond to, personal, local, and broader forces; thus, the evolution of teacher identity is "a dynamic, career-long process of negotiating the teacher-self in relation to personal and emotional experiences, the professional and social context, and the micro and macro political environment" (Zembylas & Chubbuck, 2014, p. 177). Common, often monolithic, views of the teaching profession can be challenged by the very fact that teachers' self-identities are uniquely comprised of multiple personal and contextual variables (Zembylas & Chubbuck, 2014). Failure to appreciate these forces causes a myopic view of teachers and teaching and further constrains societal and political views toward the teaching profession and education as a whole.

Traditional views. Views of the teaching profession and the status of teachers affect teacher identity. Although teaching meets the "classic" criteria of semi-professions, it is also unique in many ways (Hargreaves & Fullan, 2012). In short, teachers occupy the world of children. As opposed to the characteristics typically used to define other professions, the professional orientation of teachers reflects more intangible characteristics such as dedication to students and moral purpose. It is perhaps these very qualities that make teaching such a noble endeavor in the minds of many, but that also limits the prestige and status of the profession (Hargreaves & Fullan, 2012).

These fundamental conditions distinguish teaching from traditional professions like medicine and law, but also many other service-oriented professions. Moreover, the "feminine caring ethic" of teaching "is trapped within a rationalized and bureaucratized structure" (Hargreaves, 2001, p. 1069) of the corporate and policy-making spheres. Accordingly, traditional stereotypes of teachers continue to affect views towards the profession, as well as the perceptions that educators hold of themselves and their work. These entrenched attitudes undermine professionalization efforts that might otherwise enhance teachers' professional identities, further perpetuating views of teachers and education.

International comparisons. International comparisons also affect the way teachers feel about their work, as well as the commonly held perceptions of teachers and schools by the public and policymakers. Over the past several decades, international rankings of student performance on assessments such as PISA and TIMSS have been used to scrutinize teachers and their work, and international comparison rhetoric has amplified concerns about American education and its teaching corps (OECD, 2014). Of course, major educational shifts related to foreign competition and heightened apprehension over American global standing are not new. Public perception of schools and teachers has eroded, and federal involvement in schools has increased in response to, for example, the launching of Sputnik in the 1950s, the economic growth of Japan during the 1980s, and more recently, the rise of China and India (OECD, 2014). In spite of these inclinations to criticize U.S. teachers and schools, it is worth noting that in countries where teachers report feeling valued and supported, PISA results are better (OECD, 2014).

Education reform. Sahlberg (2015) refers to this worldwide shift toward standardization, accountability, testing, and privatization as the Global Education Reform Movement (GERM). Educational changes wrought by GERM can have potentially damaging effects on teachers, students, and school communities (Sahlberg, 2015). Inherent in this approach is an overarching emphasis on measurable results and accountability; the more nuanced aspects of everyday life in schools, teacher-student interactions, and other intangible dynamics carry minimal weight (Sahlberg, 2015). The dilemma emerging from accountability and standardization on the one hand, and educators' understandings of the complex forces at work in school environments on the other, has become a tremendous source of stress and conflict for educators, impacting motivation, morale, and professional identities in negative ways. Invariably, failure to demonstrate expected performance outcomes, as measured by high-stakes test results, further contributes to the public perception of deteriorating schools and teacher inefficacy, and, as such, it is not surprising that teacher identity would be affected (Sahlberg, 2015).

Extrinsic motivators. The extrinsic motivators of high stakes testing, standardization, and accountability, from a self-determination theory point of view, reflect the controlling nature of top-down policies (Ryan & Deci, 2017). As such, the extrinsic motivation approach endemic to many reform efforts can undermine the intrinsic motivators necessary for the cultivation of autonomy, relatedness, competence, and genuine learning and growth (Ryan & Deci, 2017). The dissonance resulting from teachers' beliefs, values, moral purpose, and intrinsic and altruistic motivations for teaching in conflict with external demands and pressures can impair self-efficacy and autonomy, and generate considerable tensions in teachers' work lives and identities (Day, 2017; Frenzel, 2014). In doing so, teachers' "reserves of resilience (emotional energy) [may be depleted and their] sense of motivation, moral purpose, and job fulfillment [diminished, offering a significant] challenge to teachers' substantive identity" (Day, 2017, p. 32). While fulfilling their professional duties and managing increasing responsibilities, teachers must also possess the emotional and pedagogical wherewithal to cope with this incongruence.

Response to change. Educational reforms represent change, and change is often associated with loss. Various conditions may affect teacher resilience, or the capacity to navigate challenges, handle setbacks, and to maintain enthusiasm for one's work. Because resilience and motivation to teach are closely connected, teachers' sense of moral purpose might be severely challenged by potential changes (Day, 2017). Despite the difficulty reconciling the disparity between educational ideals and daily realities, an ability to cope with change and its attendant emotions is a reflection of the resilience that many teachers exhibit.

Teachers, particularly those with many years of experience, may regard reform endeavors as a challenge to their expertise, efficacy, professional identity, and moral and emotional connection to their work (Day, 2017). The time and energy that they have invested and their experiences with previous iterations of education reform may influence how they view and contend with, new policies, expectations, and changes to their working lives. In many instances, reform measures generate negative reactions, particularly when teachers perceive their identities, integrity, motivations, autonomy, and agency to be questioned or challenged (Roth, 2014). In other words, when external forces, often with minimal appreciation for the intricacies of teachers' work lives and educational environments, attempt to impose policies and demands, teachers – who, as a result of their accumulated expertise and experiences, have a keen understanding of their craft – may react with justifiable suspicion and concern (Roth, 2014).

Situational Influences: The Local Context

While large-scale reform efforts have an effect on teachers' work lives, and thus, their professional identities, the realm of policymaking is often distant and abstract (Buchanan, 2015). The local educational environment, at the classroom, school, and district levels, is likely to have a more perceptible, perhaps even more immediate impact, on teacher motivation, morale, and identity. In either case, school environments consist of a wide range of complex dynamics, and "[t]eacher identity is constantly being embedded in power relations, ideology, and culture" (Salifu & Agbenyega, 2013, p. 62). Accordingly, the evolution of teachers' professional identities reflects how "teachers use their cultural tools to make sense of and interact with their local working context" (Buchanan, 2015, p. 704).

School climate and relatedness. In school settings, leadership, relationships, and support are essential factors related to teacher morale, motivation, self-efficacy, professional commitment, self-concept, and job satisfaction (Salifu & Agbenyega, 2013). Environmental factors can support or undermine the three basic psychological needs of autonomy, relatedness, and competence (Salifu & Agbenyega, 2013). School culture, therefore, plays a significant role in positive identity development, professional commitment, and overall well-being (Roth, 2014). Within school settings, teachers' relationships with others are among the most important variables that shape professional identity. For teachers in the early years of their careers, relationships affect their capacity to cope with daily stressors, develop self-efficacy and agency, regulate emotions, and construct positive self-image (Le Cornu, 2013). Moreover, the positive feelings associated with strong relationships in the professional setting "have been linked to the powerful emotion of hope, which many would argue underpins resilience" (Le Cornu, 2013, p. 9).

The affective nature of teaching means that "teacher emotions are almost inextricably linked to the relationships they form with their students" (Frenzel, 2014, p. 503). Teachers' sense of obligation to cultivate students' academic, social, and emotional growth is instrumental to their professional identities. Not only do teachers feel a responsibility to prepare students for the next phases of their academic careers, but they also feel that they are important contributors to their development as productive, capable, and engaged citizens in society (Frenzel, 2014). Teachers who find the most enjoyment in their work often rely on the positive emotions associated with relatedness with students, as well as student performance and growth, leading to greater efforts and engagement, more sustained professional commitment, and better results (Kunter & Holzberger, 2014). For those later in their careers, "the immense value and self-worth that they derive from their pupils' growth serves to reinforce and fulfill their original call to teach, enhances their morale, and builds their psychological, intellectual, social and professional resources" (Day, 2017, p. 57).

Importance of school leadership. The attitudes, actions, and core philosophies of school leaders have a significant influence on teachers' emotions, motivation, morale, job satisfaction, and professional identity (Day, 2017). By nurturing a school environment that remains responsive to teachers' basic needs of competence, autonomy, and relatedness, school leaders nurture teachers' positive identity development and self-efficacy. While this is true for beginning teachers, it is also imperative for mid- and late-career teachers, especially if they are afforded opportunities for leadership roles, distributive decision-making, and sharing of expertise and knowledge (Day, 2017). In the absence of such supportive structures and practices, coupled with any number of personal and professional challenges, it may be difficult for teachers to sustain their sense of moral purpose and professional commitment (Day, 2017).

The overlapping influence of school climate, relatedness, and leadership on teacher motivation, morale, and identity formation cannot be overstated. Controlling leadership styles and behaviors are related to job-related stresses, constrained autonomy, burnout, and attrition (Eyal & Roth, 2011). If administrators adopt a top-down, bureaucratic orientation characterized by lack of trust and autonomy, opportunities for empowerment, renewal, job satisfaction, and ongoing improvement to teaching and learning will be jeopardized (Eyal & Roth, 2011). In school settings, leadership styles, policies, and expectations "that ignore, destabilize, or erode core beliefs and values and threaten existing practices...can destroy teachers' sense of efficacy and agency, and destabilize and diminish their sense of stable professional identity" (Day, 2017, p. 38). Conversely, when teachers feel trusted as professionals and are able to go about their work in an autonomous way, they are more likely to exhibit behaviors and feelings associated with commitment, satisfaction, and collaboration (Eyal & Roth, 2011; Kunter & Holzberger, 2014). In turn, teachers' self-efficacy, positive emotions, and self-determinism increase contributing to a healthy sense of self.

Final Thoughts

Given the salient characteristics of teachers' identities, coupled with external forces at play in the educational, political, and cultural landscapes, it is unsurprising that teachers feel a strong sense of moral purpose for the work they do. Teachers tend to talk of teaching as a calling, and they feel that they are making a difference in the lives of their students and in society as a whole. Motivation, morale, and sense of self seem to be strongest when teachers are able to act in accordance with their values, have agency within the environment, and are able to sustain their intrinsic and altruistic motivation, though the presence of demanding external pressures often results in the opposite outcome. In response to educational change and accompanying stressors that often conflict with teachers' views of what is important in education and best for students, school cultures can either mitigate or intensify threats to teacher identity.

For many teachers, their initial idealism and enthusiasm upon entering the profession is difficult to maintain, and they are challenged with balancing the joys of the profession with its frustrations and pressures. Unmediated stress, role conflict and ambiguity, excessive demands, and work overload associated with extrinsic motivators, exacerbated by societal perceptions of schools and teachers, can negatively impact teacher identity, performance, morale, motivation, commitment, and efficacy. In light of these trends, it is no wonder that teachers' job satisfaction has dropped to its lowest level in two decades, and the percentage of teachers who report that they are likely to leave the profession has increased (Metropolitan Life Insurance, 2012). Among other developments, the American teaching corps is becoming grayer, greener, and less stable, even as teachers emphasize and exemplify the social and moral imperatives with which their work is suffused (OECD 2014).

Despite often negative or erroneous attitudes, many teachers remain motivated by forces that are often difficult to quantify, chief among which are the connections they have with their students. Guided by moral purpose, teachers feel a sense of obligation for, and develop a sense of efficacy from, their students' successes and growth. Knowing that they have made, and can continue to make, a perceptible and substantial difference in students' lives is fundamental to teachers' sense of efficacy, morale, motivation, and professional identity. Although the daily demands and emotionality of teaching produce a fair amount of tension in teachers' work lives, teachers' intrinsic and altruistic motivations, and a strong sense of moral purpose are sources of strength in the face of many challenges.

Points to Remember

- *Teacher identity is dynamic, contextual, and evolves over the course of the career.*

- *The early stages of a teaching career are vital to identity development.*

- *The vocational, affective, and moral dimensions and demands of teaching strongly influence teachers' motivation, sense of efficacy, and professional identities.*

- *Expectations of teachers, daily demands, and policy pressures impact teacher motivation, sense of efficacy, and professional identity.*

- *School culture, structures, and leadership can be a source of empowerment or disillusionment.*

- *Teachers are most effective, motivated, and committed when their identities and educational environments are aligned.*

- *Teachers' sense of moral purpose is reflected in their sense of obligation to their students' success, well-being, and growth.*

References

Bandura, A. (1997). *Self-efficacy in changing societies.* Cambridge, UK: Cambridge University Press.

Beijaard, D. & Meijer, P. C. (2017). Developing the personal and professional in making a teacher identity. In D. J. Clandinin & J. Husu (Eds.), *The SAGE Handbook of Research on Teacher Education* (pp. 177-192). Thousand Oaks, CA: SAGE Publications.

Beltman, S., Glass, C., Dinham, J., Chalk, B. & Nguyen, B. (2015). Drawing identity: Beginning pre-service teachers' professional identities. *Issues in Educational Research*, 25(3), 225-. Retrieved from http://www.iier.org.au/iier25/beltman.htm

Biesta, G., Priestley, M. & Robinson, S. (2015). The role of beliefs in teacher agency. *Teachers and Teaching*, 21(6), 624-640. doi:10.1080/13540602.2015.1044325

Buchanan, R. (2015). Teacher identity and agency in an era of accountability. *Teachers and Teaching*, 21(6), 700-719. doi:10.1080/13540602.2015.1044329

Bukor, E. (2015). Exploring teacher identity from a holistic perspective: reconstructing and reconnecting personal and professional selves. *Teachers and Teaching*, 21(3), 305-327.doi:10.1080/13540602.2014.953818

Butler, R. (2017) Why choose teaching, and does it matter? In H. M. G. Watt, P. W. Richardson & K. Smith (Eds). *Global Perspectives on Teacher Motivation*, (pp. 377-388). New York: Cambridge University Press.

Day, C. (2007). School reform and transitions in teacher professionalism and identity. In T. Townsend and R. Bates (Eds.), *Handbook of Teacher Education: Globalization, Standards and Professionalism in Times of Change*, (597–612). Dordrecht, The Netherlands: Springer.

Day, C. (2017). *Teachers' worlds and work: Understanding complexity, building quality.* New York: Routledge.

Department of Education. (2006). *Highly qualified teachers for every child.* Retrieved from https://www2.ed.gov/nclb/methods/teachers/stateplanfacts.html

Downey, C. A., Schaefer, L., & Clandinin, D. J. (2014). Shifting teacher education from "skilling up" to sustaining beginning teachers. *Teacher Education:
Learning From Experiences*, 8(1), pp. 15-19. Retrieved from
https://mafiadoc.com/teacher-education-learning-from-experiences-
learning-landscapes_598074051723ddeb5639ffb1.html

Durr, T., Chang, M., & Carson, R. L. (2014). Curbing teacher burnout: The
transactional factors of teacher efficacy and emotion management. In P. W.
Richardson, S. A. Karabenick & H. M. G. Watt (Eds.), *Teacher Motivation:
Theory and Practice*, (pp. 198-213). New York: Routledge.

Eccles, J. (2009). Who am I and what am I going to do with my life? Personal
and collective identities and motivators of action. *Educational Psychologist*,
44(2). 78-89.doi:10.1080/00461520902832368

Eyal, O. & Roth, G. (2011). Principals' leadership and teachers' motivation:
Self-determination theory analysis. *Journal of Educational Administration*,
49(3), 256-275. doi:10.1108/09578231111129055

Fernet, C., Guay, F., Senècal, C., & Austin, S. (2012). Predicting intraindividual
changes in teacher burnout: The role of perceived school environment and
motivational factors. *Teaching and Teacher Education*, 28, 514–525. doi:
10.1016/j.tate.2011.11.013

Fives, H. & Buehl, M. M. (2016). Teachers' beliefs, in the context of policy
reform. *Policy Insights from the Behavioral and Brain Sciences*, 3(1), 114-121.
doi:10.1177/2372732215623554

Frenzel, A. C. (2014). Teacher emotions. In E. A. Linnenbrink-Garcia & R.
Pekrun (Eds.), *International Handbook of Emotions in Education*, (pp. 494-
519). New York, NY: Routledge.

Fried, L., Mansfield, C. & Dobozy, E. (2015). Teacher emotion research: Introducing a conceptual model to guide future research. *Issues in Educational
Research*, 25(4), 415-441. Retrieved from
http://www.iier.org.au/iier25/fried.pdf

Gill, M.G. & Hardin, C. (2015). A "hot" mess: Unpacking the relation between
teachers' beliefs and emotions. In H. Fives & M.G. Gill (Eds.), *International
Handbook of Research on Teachers Beliefs* (pp. 230-246). New York: Taylor &
Francis

González-Calvo, G., & Arias-Carballal, M. (2017). A Teacher's personal-
emotional identity and its reflection upon the development of his professional identity. *The Qualitative Report*, 22(6), 1693-1709. Retrieved from
http://nsuworks.nova.edu/tqr/vol22/iss6/14

Gore, J., Holmes, K., Smith, M. & Fray, L. (2015). *Investigating the factors that
influence the choice of teaching as a first career: A report commissioned by the
Queensland College of Teachers*. Retrieved from
http://www.qct.edu.au/pdf/WhyChooseTeachingReport.pdf

Hargreaves, A. (1998a). The emotional practice of teaching. *Teaching and
Teacher Education*, 14(8), 835-854. doi:10.1016/S0742-051X(98)00025-0

Hargreaves, A. (1998b). The emotions of teaching and educational change. In
A. Hargreaves, A.

Lieberman, M. Fullan, & D. Hopkins (Eds.), *International Handbook of Educational Change*, (558-575). Boston, MA: Kluwer Academic Publishers. doi:10.1007/1-4020-4453-4_14

Hargreaves, A. (2001). Emotional geographies of teaching. *Teachers College Round*, 103(6).

1056-1080. Retrieved from https://ww2.faulkner.edu/admin/websites/jfarrell/emotional%20geographies%20of%20teaching.pdf

Hargreaves, A. & Fullan, M. (2012). *Professional capital: Transforming teaching in every school*. New York: Teachers College Press.

Hohnbaum, B. (2012). *Intrinsic and extrinsic motivation of teachers*. Retrieved from https://www.slideshare.net/breeellen22/intrinsic-and-extrinsic-motivation-of-teachers

Izadinia, M. (2013). A review of research on student teachers' professional identity. *British Educational Research Journal*, 39(4), 694–713. doi:10.1080/01411926.2012.679614

Korthagen, F. A. J. & Evelein, F. G. (2016). Relations between student teachers' basic needs fulfillment and their teaching behavior. *Teaching and Teacher Education*, 60 (p. 234-244). doi:10.1016/j.tate.2016.08.021

Kunter, M. & Holzberger, D. (2014) Loving teaching: Research on teachers' intrinsic orientations. In P. W. Richardson, S. A. Karabenick & H. M. G. Watt (Eds.), *Teacher Motivation: Theory and Practice*, (pp. 83-99). New York: Routledge.

Lauermann, F., Karabenick, S. A., Carpenter, R. & Kuusinen, C. (2017). Teacher motivation and professional commitment in the United States: The role of motivations for teaching, teacher self-efficacy and sense of professional responsibility. In H. M. G. Watt, P. W. Richardson & K. Smith (Eds). *Global Perspectives on Teacher Motivation*, (pp. 322-348). New York: Cambridge University Press.

Le Cornu, R. (2013). Building early career teacher resilience: The role of relationships. *Australian Journal of Teacher Education*, 38(4). 1-16. doi:10.14221/ajte.2013v38n4.4

Mansfield, C.F., Beltman, S., Price, A., & McConney, A. (2012) Don't sweat the small stuff: Understanding teacher resilience at the chalkface. *Teaching and Teacher Education*, 28(3), 357-367. doi: 10.1016/j.tate.2011.11.001

Metropolitan Life Insurance (2012). The MetLife survey of the American teacher: Teachers, parents, and the economy. *New York: MetLife*. Retrieved from https://www.metlife.com/assets/cao/foundation/MetLife-Teacher-Survey-2012.pdf

Mockler, N. (2011). Beyond 'what works': Understanding teacher identity as a practical and political tool. *Teachers and Teaching: Theory and Practice*, 17(5), 517-528. doi:10.1080/13540602.2011.602059

Nagy, E.& Takács, I. (2017). The road to teacher burnout and its possible protecting factors – A narrative review. *Review of Social Sciences*, 2(8), 9-15. doi:10.18533/rss.v2i8.107

Nias, J. (1999). Teachers' moral purpose: Stress, vulnerability, and strength. In R. Vandenberghe & A. M. Huberman (Eds.), *Understanding and Preventing Teacher Burnout: A Sourcebook of International Research and Practice* (223-237). New York: Cambridge University Press.

OECD (2014). *Teachers love their job but feel undervalued, unsupported and unrecognised, says OECD.* Retrieved from http://www.oecd.org/newsroom/teachers-love-their-job-but-feel-undervalued-unsupported-and-unrecognised.htm

Pillen, M., Beijaard, D. & den Brok, P. (2012). Tensions in beginning teachers' professional identity development, accompanying feelings and coping strategies. *European Journal of Teacher Education*, 36(3), 1-20. doi:10.1080/02619768.2012.696192

Richardson, P. W. & Watt, H. M. G. (2014). Why people choose teaching as a career: An expectancy –value approach to understanding teacher motivation. In P. W. Richardson, S. A. Karabenick & H. M. G. Watt (Eds.), *Teacher motivation: Theory and Practice* (pp. 3-19). New York: Routledge.

Richardson P.W. & Watt H.M.G. (2016) Factors influencing teaching choice: Why do future teachers choose the career? In: Loughran J., Hamilton M. *International Handbook of Teacher Education.* Springer, Singapore DOI:10.1007/978-981-10-0369-1-8

Roth, G. (2014). Antecedents and outcomes of teachers' autonomous motivation: A self-determination theory analysis. In P. W. Richardson, S. A. Karabenick & H. M. Watt (Eds.), *Teacher Motivation: Theory and Practice*, (pp. 36-51). New York: Routledge.

Ryan, R. M. & Brown, K. W. (2005). Legislating competence: The motivational impact of high stakes testing as an educational reform. In A. E. Elliot & C. Dweck (Eds.), *Handbook of Competence* (354-374). New York: Guilford Press.

Ryan, R. M. & Deci, E. L. (2017). *Self-determination theory: Basic psychological needs in motivation, development, and wellness.* New York: The Guilford Press.

Ryan, R. M. & Weinstein, N. (2009). Undermining quality teaching and learning: A self-determination theory perspective on high-stakes testing. *Theory and Research in Education*, 7(2), 224-233. doi:10.1177/1477878509104327

Sahlberg, P. (2015). *Finnish lessons 2.0: What can the world learn from educational change in Finland?* New York: Teachers College Press.

Salifu, I. & Agbenyega, J.S. (2013). *Teacher Motivation and Identity Formation: Issues Affecting Professional Practice.* MIER Journal of Educational Studies, Trends & Practices 3(1), 58-74.

Schutz, P. A. & Mikyoung, L. (2014). Teacher emotion, emotional labor and teacher identity. *Utrecht Studies in Language & Communication*, 27, 169-186.

Taxer, J. L. & Frenzel, A. C. (2015). Facets of teachers' emotional lives: A quantitative investigation of teachers' genuine, faked, and hidden emotions. *Teaching and Teacher Education*, 49, 78-88. doi: 10.1016/j.tate.2015.03.003

Watt, H. M. G. & Richardson, P. W. (2014). A motivational analysis of teacher beliefs. In H. Fives & M. G. Gill (Eds.), *International Handbook of Research on Teachers' Beliefs* (pp. 191-211). New York: Routledge.

Zembylas, M. & Chubbuck, S. (2014). The intersection of identity, beliefs, and politics to conceptualizing "teacher identity." In H. Fives & M. Gill (Eds.), *International Handbook of Research on Teachers' Beliefs*, (pp. 173-190). New York: Routledge.

Chapter 2

Using Student-Centered Teaching: Inspiring and Empowering Teachers and Learners

Erin K. Washburn, Ph.D.,
Binghamton University - State University of New York
and
Stefanie Olbrys, M.Ed.,
Windsor Central School District, Windsor, NY

Arianna, a 3rd-grade student, was becoming disengaged with school. Though she was reading and writing on grade level and appeared to have the skills needed to be successful in school, she seemed bored and often acted out during whole group instruction. Further, Arianna was starting to voice her opinion about her disengagement with school by responding to Ms. Williams, her teacher, and other adults in the school with "Why do we have to do this?" and "I really don't want to do this." Ms. Williams, Arianna's teacher, knew that she needed to intervene before school, and more importantly, learning became completely obsolete to Arianna. Additionally, Ms. Williams knew that Arianna wasn't her only student who wasn't fully engaged in her classroom. Being a reflective practitioner, Ms. Williams thought about how she could change her instruction to heighten engagement for all of her students. Ms. Williams started to talk to her colleagues and read more about changing her approach to teaching, which had been more traditional and teacher-driven, to be more student-centered. In this chapter, we discuss approaches to student-centered teaching and provide practices and principles for a student-centered approach to teaching. As we do so, we will return to Ms. Williams and share aspects of her journey in creating a learning environment and experience where her students find relevance in what they were learning and feel empowered to make a difference in their school and community.

A Need for "Future Ready" Students

Educators, like Ms. Williams, join the education field to make a difference and prepare students for their future. Unfortunately, the current educational system "was built for an economy and society that no longer exists" (National Education Association, 2012, p. 5). According to Berger (2014) young children, generally speaking, enter kindergarten with high levels of curiosity, a strong inclination towards questioning, and are excited to learn; however, as a child's experience with school progresses, curiosity and engagement wanes (p. 44). This can be attributed to traditional classroom structures, where the teacher is viewed as the expert and where there is only one right answer; a setting that not only leads students to disengage but is likely to stifle the development of 21st-century skills (Berger, 2014). This model worked well in the 20th century when the United States was an industrial nation in need of workers but does not support the needs of current students who must be able to find "success in college, career, and citizenship in the 21st century" (National Education Association, 2012, p. 3).

Today's workplace, and that of the future, requires individuals to be creative, critical thinkers and have strong communication and collaboration skills (Partnership for 21st Century Learning, 2015). Due to the tremendous amount of readily accessible information, a need to be digitally literate and tech-savvy is also more important than ever before. In addition to these "future ready" skill sets, a need exists to inspire and empower students to become active and engaged citizens who believe that their voice and societal contributions matter now and, in the future (Phillips, 2015). The reality is "if we want our students to change the world, we'll have to take a good look at how we can change our classrooms to support inquiry and innovation" (Juliani, 2015, p. xxiii).

Educators believe that each and every student that crosses their path is unique and all have immeasurable capabilities that should be awakened (Juliani, 2015). When teachers engage that uniqueness, rather than expecting every student to say, do, and act the same, educators empower and inspire them--making a lasting impact (Juliani, 2015). It is an exhilarating time to be a teacher as the opportunity to place students at the center of their learning is not only ideal but essential.

As exciting as a student-centered approach to teaching and learning can be, an implementation may be intimidating, particularly if an educator has little knowledge or experience of the approaches associated with student-centered learning (Ertmer & Simons, 2005). It is necessary, then, to define and illustrate common evidence-based approaches to student-centered learning, describe principles, practices, and strategies for implementing student-centered learning in the K-12 classroom, and offer current resources to support the implementation process.

Defining Student-Centered Teaching and Learning

Student-centered teaching is an umbrella term that encompasses a variety of instructional approaches that are all focused on student ownership of learning, to include, inquiry-based learning, problem-based learning, and project-based learning. More specifically, a student-centered approach is aimed at providing students with authentic learning experiences that are designed to: (a) promote deep understanding of content in conjunction with the development of higher-order thinking skills such as analysis and/or synthesis, (b) ensure active engagement, (c) provide student choice and voice, and (d) sustain inquiry and innovation (Cattaneo, 2017). Therefore, student-centered approaches truly engage students as researchers and producers of information rather than passive receivers.

Student-centered teaching is rooted in constructivist pedagogy and dates back to the work of John Dewey (1916) and progressivism. Over a century ago, Dewey (1916) envisioned schools to be environments where education began with the curiosity of the learner and learning occurred *by* and *from* experience, meaning that learning should be based on student inquiry, discovery, and experience, as opposed to teacher-centered delivery of content, such as the traditional lecture. This changes the role of the teacher from the 'sage on the stage' to that of the 'guide on the side' and encourages the development of 21st-century skills, as opposed to looking to one person for all the answers. (Morrison, 2014). This approach to teaching does not dismiss the teacher's expertise but rather uses his/her expertise to design and facilitate the learning experience and provide consultation throughout the learning process (Morrison, 2014). In fact, without thoughtful design and teacher guidance and support, well-intended student-centered activities can go awry (Ertmer & Glazewski, 2015; Krahenbuhl, 2016). Purposeful planning allows students to form their own conclusions and in doing so, they become empowered as learners.

In the past century, several approaches to student-centered learning have been coined and examined for efficacy and classroom utility, specifically inquiry-based learning, problem-based learning, and project-based learning (Cattaneo, 2017). These popular approaches have many similarities and depending upon the source, it can be difficult to tell the approaches apart; however, a careful review of the literature defines each learning approach (Krauss & Boss, 2013; Larmer, 2015; Larmer, Mergendoller & Boss, 2015).

Inquiry-Based Learning

Inquiry-based learning (IBL) is often "the most favored and useful instructional model" (Oguz-Unver & Arabacioglu, 2011, p. 304) in science, and has long been advocated for as the way in which historians' study history (Monte-Sano, 2012). In a research review of the effectiveness of IBL, Barron and Darling-Hammond (2008) reported that an IBL approach to teaching held "positive changes for teachers and students in motivation, attitude toward learning, and skills, including work habits, critical thinking skills, and problem-solving abilities" (p. 12). Recent research has highlighted the efficacy of using an IBL approach with K-12 learners, and it has been reported as effective for striving learners as well as academically strong learners (Abdi, 2014; Duran & Dökme, 2016; Frieson & Scott, 2013). Students in the IBL classroom not only see the value in it academically – they have identified leadership as a learning outcome of this type of teaching (Olbrys & Strahley, 2015).

Central to all student-centered approaches is an inquiry, often described as the personal path of questioning, investigating, and reasoning that leads a student from not knowing to deep understanding (Krauss & Boss, 2013). IBL begins with a question and a period of investigating possible solutions where experiences and discoveries lead to new knowledge that is then internalized through deep reflection (Krauss & Boss, 2013). IBL is designed to spark curiosity and results in intrinsic motivation and deeper personal inquiry, possibly even innovation (Juliani, 2015). This approach is not loose, but rather, it is a result of purposeful planning (Daniels, 2017).

Constructing questions that peak student interest, drive and sustain inquiry, and require higher order thinking skills such as to analyze, synthesize, and evaluate, are essential in IBL (Daniels, 2017). These questions are often referred to as essential questions, and they are designed to, "stimulate ongoing thinking and inquiry, raise more questions, spark discussion, and answers to them may change as understanding deepens" (McTighe & Wiggins, 2013, p. 14). There are several variations and names given to the question that will initiate the inquiry, including the compelling question, driving question, and overarching question (McTighe & Wiggins, 2013).

Teachers ask questions every day, but an overarching question is different in that it could be used to initiate an inquiry in a middle school social studies classroom where students are learning about America during the Great Depression: "Was the Great Depression a Tragedy or Triumph?" whereas a traditional question may be "What was the Great Depression?" The first question requires students to take on the role of a researcher to investigate multiple information sources and consider various viewpoints before constructing an answer or claim (McTighe & Wiggins, 2013). Even more impressive is that it is a question that could be answered today, given current context and impact as opposed to the second question that has a finite conclusion and does not require higher order thinking skills to answer. Overarching questions are alive, "if we really engage with it, if it seems genuine and relevant to us, and if it helps us to gain a more systematic and deep understanding of what we are learning" (McTighe & Wiggins, 2013, p. 8). Asking the right questions is critical to keeping the inquiry alive far beyond lesson, unit, and school walls.

Depending on content/subject matter, student skills, and background knowledge, the teacher may choose to design the inquiry with more or less scaffolding. MacKenzie (2016) shared four types of inquiry based on the work of Dana, Thomas, & Boynton (2011) that describes the amount of teacher scaffolding needed: (a) structured, (b) controlled, (c) guided, and (d) free. In each of these types of inquiry, the teacher releases more and more control of the inquiry process to students and MacKenzie (2016) used the metaphor of a swimming pool and its deepness to describe the four types. The deeper one is into the swimming pool, the more student-driven the inquiry becomes. When first experimenting with inquiry most teachers begin, "with short, well-structured lessons that they used to test the kids' capabilities--and their own comfort level" (Daniels, 2017, p. xv). Some educators start the year with a more structured approach and end the year more towards the deep end, where other educators aim to move from structured to free within a given lesson or unit and some educators stick to one type for the whole year (MacKenzie, 2016).

On the shallow end of the pool are structured inquiry and controlled inquiry. In a structured inquiry, there is a high level of teacher support because the inquiry is a whole class learning experience and the teacher directs the inquiry process (MacKenzie, 2016). The educator provides an overarching question and controls the specific learning activities, guides the entire class through the research process of predetermined resources at the same time, and all students demonstrate learning in the same summative assessment. It is important to note, however, that while this approach seems similar to traditional teaching, it is still centered on inquiry through an overarching question and teachers are leading and modeling inquiry but not lecturing (MacKenzie, 2016).

In keeping with the pool metaphor, a controlled inquiry is in a slightly deeper part of the pool. Similar to the structured inquiry, a controlled inquiry is when the teacher provides several essential questions, and predetermined resources and students demonstrate their learning in a similar way (MacKenzie, 2016). Controlled inquiry differs from structured in that students (often working in small groups) are given the freedom to unpack the resources with the goal of gaining insight, build understandings, and ultimately construct claims to the essential questions (Oguz-Unver & Arabacioglu, 2011). These two approaches may be a starting point for incorporating IBL and is likely to help learners become more familiar with the process of inquiry. A structured or controlled inquiry could also provide teachers the opportunity to integrate the teaching of specific skills, such as research skills needed for later, more student-driven inquiries.

Closer to the deep end of the pool is guided inquiry, and it is a more student-driven approach than the previous two. The teacher chooses the topic and/or overarching question; however, students are tasked with finding relevant sources and resources and choosing how they will demonstrate their learning (Oguz-Unver & Arabacioglu, 2011). At the deepest end of the pool (with the diving board) is a free inquiry. In free inquiry, students choose their topics, craft an overarching question, find their own sources and resources, and decide how they will demonstrate their learning (Barron & Darling-Hammond, 2008).

Inquiry brings the classroom to life and puts students center stage, leaving teachers as inspired guides. Daniels (2017), reports that educators enjoy teaching more when they do so with the inquiry and that the process of inquiry transfers to other aspects of their professional and personal life. Those who embark on the inquiry journey state, "we don't do inquiry; we live it every day" (Daniels, 2017, p.184).

Problem-Based Learning

Problem-based learning (PBL) and IBL are similar but not the same. In PBL, learning is generated through student investigation of a real-world problem with the goal of explaining and solving the problem. Problems in PBL, however, are ill-structured and conduits for free inquiry (Savery, 2015). Students often follow a predetermined six-step problem-solving process: (a) students are presented with the ill-structured problem, (b) students define the problem by constructing a problem statement, (c) students generate a "knowledge inventory" (a list of "what we know about the problem" and "what we need to know"), (d) students generate possible solutions, (e) students engage in self-directed and/or scaffolded researching of sources and/or through hands-on experimentation, and (f) share findings and solutions to the problem (Larmer, 2015).

Other researchers have recommended that, after findings and solutions are shared, students should reflect on the problem-solving process and evaluate their solution (Ertmer & Simons, 2006; Savery, 2015). Asking students targeted questions such as "What went well during the process?" "How did your ideas about the problem and solution change over the course the process?" "What will you do differently next time?" Other educators have provided guidance on how to structure the PBL process (see McConnell et al., 2008, for a sequence specific to science).

Though PBL follows a more prescriptive process, the role of the teacher is by no means lockstep and like IBL, PBL requires thoughtful planning. Teachers must first plan the process by identifying a content-relevant problem and then decide the amount of support given during the research and investigation phase of the process. If students have had little experience researching, for example, then the teacher may decide to provide resources for students and pre-teach how to find credible sources and extract relevant information, both of which are Common Core aligned skills, prior to PBL (Savery, 2015; Common Core State Standards Initiative, 2018). If students have strong research skills and have had previous experience with a PBL approach, then the teacher may have students find relevant resources on their own.

When implementing PBL, particularly the first PBL experience, teachers act as models, thinking aloud with students and practicing the behavior they want their students to use (Oguz-Unver & Arabacioglu, 2014). Specifically, teachers need to model the use of metacognitive questions such as "What's going on here?" "What do we need to know more about?" "How do you know?" "What is your evidence?" "What did we do during the problem that was effective?" As students become self-regulated and self-directed learners, teacher modeling and metacognitive questioning should move to occasional prompting and then fade completely over the progression of the PBL experience (English & Kitsantas, 2013).

PBL was initially used in medical schools to move beyond the acquisition of knowledge to the application of knowledge in a realistic context (Savery, 2015). The approach was so successful in medical schools that PBL quickly spread to other professional schools, such as business and law, and throughout higher education (Savery, 2015). Therefore, it is no surprise that PBL has been particularly successful in K-12 science context and other STEM related fields (Lee & Bae, 2008; Rehmat, 2015). Research reports the efficacy of PBL in early childhood and elementary settings as well as in the visual arts and in interdisciplinary contexts such as math and science (Merritt, Lee, Rillero & Kinanch, 2017).

Problems are inevitable and "through problem-based learning, students learn how to use an iterative process of assessing what they know, identifying what they need to know, gathering information, and collaborating on the evaluation of hypotheses in light of the data they have collected" (Stepien & Gallagher, 1993). Moreover, through this student-centered teaching approach, 21st-century skills are developed and fostered resulting in future-ready empowered problem solvers (Larmer, 2015).

Project-Based Learning

Project-based learning (PjBL) is a teaching method in which students gain knowledge and skills by working for an extended period of time to investigate and respond to an authentic, engaging and complex question, problem, or challenge (Buck Institute for Education, 2018a.). PjBL, like IBL and PBL, is focused on student investigation of a problem or overarching question (often referred to as a "driving question" in PjBL). The original model has been refined and updated to include seven essential project design elements as well as seven project-based teaching practices and has been dubbed the "Gold Standard PBL" (Mergendoller, & Larmer, 2015, n.p.). Both the design elements and the teaching practices share key knowledge, understanding, and success skills (Larmer, Mergendoller, & Boss, 2015). The essential project design elements include: (a) challenging problem or question, (b) sustained inquiry, (c) authenticity, (d) student voice and choice, (e) reflection (f) critique and revision, and (g) a publicly presented product (Larmer & Mergendoller, & Boss, 2015). Teachers who use PjBL have always had a set of teaching practices that they adhered to; however, it had never been specifically stated. With Gold Standard PBL, Larmer, Mergendoller, and Boss (2015), added an explicit set of teaching practices that include (a) design and plan, (b) align to standards, (c) build the culture, (d) manage the activities, (e) scaffold student learning, (f) assess student learning, and (g) engage and coach.

PjBL is often done over extended time periods, and one specifically unique component is that students are required to publicly present their project work by explaining, displaying and/or presenting their answer/solution to an audience beyond the classroom. It is important to note the differences between projects and PjBL. Projects, generally speaking, are tasks that are assigned by a teacher, often at the end of the unit (or another segment of learning) and have been described as the "dessert" at the end of a meal (Larmer & Mergendoller, 2011, p. 2). A traditional end of unit project is often done in a prescriptive fashion, for example – 'based on directions, create a diorama of the solar system,' not necessarily done to solve a problem that is pressing and relevant, and can be completed by a student or group of students at home or during classroom time. Projects are then displayed or shared, but assessment of student learning is still likely to be completed through a summative assessment of student recall of factual knowledge. PjBL, however, is "the main course" (Larmer & Mergendoller, 2011, p. 1) where learning and assessment are intertwined as students seek to solve real-world issues, thus learning of material is accomplished through the project.

To illustrate the differences between assigning a project and PjBL, we share what one of Ms. Williams' colleagues at the middle school, Mr. Duncan, did to change a unit on tobacco use in his 8th-grade health class. Prior to learning about PjBL, Mr. Duncan taught the unit through teacher-directed lecture, student small group activities, and independent reading of the topic. He also assigned an independent student project as the summative assessment at the end of the unit: Create an informative pamphlet on the dangers of tobacco use. To turn this traditional teaching unit into a PjBL experience, Mr. Duncan posed the following driving question to his students with the expectation that they present their findings publicly to groups of 6th and 7th grade students during a homeroom period: Are electronic cigarettes good? In order to gain the insight and information his students needed to take a stance, they embarked upon small group research to find out about the effect of traditional tobacco use as well as current understandings about smoking electronic cigarettes (a timely and relevant topic).

Though PjBL is not a new approach, it has gained popularity in the past decade, and the current research base is growing (Larmer, 2015). Specifically, researchers have reported a positive impact on student content learning, attitude, and motivation (Karaçalli & Korur, 2014). PjBL has been reported as effective for students of varying academic abilities (Han, Capraro, & Capraro, 2015). Because PjBL is often interdisciplinary in nature, several recent studies have been conducted on the usefulness of the approach in multidisciplinary contexts and across content areas (Selmer, Rye, Malone, Fernandez, & Trebino, 2014; Verma, Dickerson, & McKinney, 2011). Furthermore, using a PjBL approach can empower students to be active and engaged citizens and change agents in their communities (Remijan, 2017).

As discussed throughout, student-centered teaching is not dismissive of the crucial role the teacher plays in crafting learning experiences that are both content-rich and engaging (Krauss & Boss, 2013). The processes of planning and implementing a student-centered approach to teaching is a thoughtful one; one that requires careful consideration of what content could best be learned through inquiry and discovery (Daniels, 2017). A teacher working with early readers (preschool, kindergarten, 1st grade) and/or striving readers (below grade level expectations), for example, would want to take a more teacher-directed approach to teaching foundational reading skills such as phonological awareness and phonics. The same primary school teacher could use a student-centered approach when learning about force, motion, and interactions or when exploring roles of community helpers.

A student-centered approach to teaching is possible in any learning context; however, there are factors and classroom conditions that can help maximize student learning (Larmer, Mergendoller & Boss, 2015). Teachers should consider specific principles and practices when building a student-centered classroom environment as well as planning and implementing a student-centered approach to teaching.

Principles and Practices for Planning and Implementing Student-Centered Teaching

Principle One: Create a Student-Centered Learning Environment

A successful student-centered learning environment looks and feels very different than a traditional learning environment. In a successful student-centered learning environment, engagement mimics that which we would desire from our citizenry, where speaking as well as listening are critical and learning never ceases (Daniels, 2017). This classroom environment is not one that should be left to chance, and intentional steps should be put in place to ensure that a collaborative culture that is in pursuit of growth is established (Daniels, 2017).

It is important to recognize that it is not one person, but rather the collective efforts of all, that can turn a classroom into a community of learners. Successful student-centered learning environments aim to create democratic communities where all student voices are recognized and appreciated (Ginsberg, 2015). In an ideal student-centered learning environment, students, as well as the teacher, play a role in the development of the classroom norms (Ginsberg, 2015). Norms should be a collectively agreed upon set of standards that "create an environment in which everyone feels respected and able to participate comfortably in learning" (Ginsberg, 2015, n.p.) ultimately setting the stage for student-centered teaching.

In the student-centered learning environment teachers and students are in pursuit of continual growth, and both realize there is so much they don't know and learning never ceases. The teacher steps into the role of facilitator and learner, continually modeling their curiosities and lifelong learning skills (Daniels, 2017). Much of the work on the teacher's part is done before stepping into the classroom. Careful planning and crafting of lessons that spark curiosity and cultivate student's voice allow students to discover their learning rather than being told it. This means allowing the students in the classroom to become historians, mathematicians, scientists, and such (Ritchart, Church, & Morrison, 2011). In the history classroom, for example, this may mean crafting lessons with the same primary source documents that historians would have looked at and then asking them to tell the story (Ritchart, Church, & Morrison, 2011).

To further illustrate the planning process of student-centered teaching we return to Ms. Williams, who, understanding the importance of a student-centered learning environment, seeks guidance from Ms. Smith, a high school social studies teacher, who has experienced success with inquiry and student's voice. Ms. Smith describes her launch to the school year, in which she has her students develop classroom norms through an inquiry seeking to answer, "What makes the best possible classroom environment?" In this inquiry she has students dive into the power of choices, where they come to the realization that they have a choice every day to make her classroom a place where others do or do not want to be. Through her activities around the power or choices, they see that all it takes is a second and a sarcastic comment or a snide laugh, to make it a place where others do not want to be. It is a choice the students make when they step foot into the classroom (Urban, 2008). In this inquiry she also has students as well as teacher define, describe, and evaluate the best possible classroom. She explains how during this she models life-long learning and curiosity, as she wants to know more about how she can create the best possible classroom for them. Collaboratively, they picture the best possible classroom and then examine the roles of the teacher and students in that classroom. With a vision of the best possible classroom in mind, she then has students craft their own personal mission statements. In it, they write their promise to themselves and the class (Urban, 2008). Once a collective vision of the best possible classroom environment has been established she uses it as a launching point to collaboratively develop classroom norms. Each norm works to ensure that this vision is continually developed and fostered. Ms. Smith explains that at the completion of creating the norms, not only have they collaboratively envisioned the perfect learning environment, they have also collaboratively set norms to ensure this environment is maintained. Even more impressive is that the process has instilled in each and every student that his/her voice matters and plays a vital role in the learning.

Principle Two: Plan with Purpose

Purposeful planning is essential for student-centered teaching; however, it ought to be noted that planning for a student-centered learning experience is not lock-step procedure but rather a recursive process. If this is the first endeavor, teachers, who are new to designing this approach, should begin by creating a short-term learning experience or renovating an existing unit/project/lesson (Miller, 2015). Thinking back to MacKenzie's (2016) pool analogy, it is important to begin where you are most comfortable. That may mean stepping into the shallow end with a small structured inquiry versus diving right into the deep end of a free inquiry. Regardless of the desired time frame for the learning experience, there are certain components or steps in the planning process to consider, such as:

- *Step 1*: Identify desired **learning outcomes** for the unit

- *Step 2*: Craft an **overarching question** that hooks the students and encompasses the desired outcomes

- *Step 3*: Plan **activities** that allow students to form their own conclusions on the desired outcomes
  (Miller, 2015)

The first part of the planning process is identifying the desired learning outcomes (Ritchhart, Church, & Morrison 2011). What is it that students need to know and be able to do? Being clear on the desired learning outcomes provides a focus for planning as well as the lesson execution. These outcomes should be rich and should aim for students to gain a true understanding of the content. True understanding typically results from deep learning through a more active and constructive practice rather than surface learning, which focuses on memorization (Ritchhart, Church, & Morrison, 2011).

Student-centered teaching gets at the deeper understanding as it allows students to form their own conclusions, rather than being told them. Moreover, learning outcomes should not be limited and should include application, analysis, evaluating, and creating. These deeper learnings are what truly lead to understanding, and at the end of a student-centered unit, students should be able to walk away with an understanding that allows them to form an argument or claim around their learning and thinking. Similar to Backwards Design (McTighe & Wiggins, 2013), it is most important to determine the expected outcomes first.

Once the desired outcomes for the unit have been determined, the overarching question can be crafted. This question should encompass all the learning, answers to it should be able to vary and change from day to day or as new learning is happening (McTighe & Wiggins 2013). It should look to make the learning relevant for the students. If that question can, "flip on that "curiosity switch" in the brains of our students, we empower them to grapple, persist and build knowledge" (Daniels, 2017, p. 142). The question is critical as it hooks the students and makes them want to know more. Developing this question can come at any point in the planning process, and many times throughout the planning process this question may evolve to be bigger and better (Daniels, 2017). A good point to initially reflect on it is after the outcomes have been established and collaborative discussion about the question with peers is always helpful.

Below are questions for reflection to test the overarching question, adapted from Essential Questions (McTighe & Wiggins, 2013, p. 3):

- Is it open-ended? (It doesn't have a single or final answer)

- Is it thought-provoking and intellectually engaging? (It sparks discussion or debate.)

- Does it call for higher-order thinking? (It cannot be answered based off of recall alone.)

- Does it point toward important and transferable ideas? (It can sometimes connect to other disciplines and today.)

- Does it raise additional questions? (It sparks further inquiry.)

- Can it be asked again and again?

The next step is planning the activities that will ensure students reach the desired learning outcomes and can work to continually answer the overarching question (Ritchhart, Church, & Morrison, 2011). In this stage of the planning process, it is important to be purposeful in planning activities that allow students to form their own conclusions. This deep understanding comes from engaging students in authentic intellectual activities such as problem-solving, and decision making. A good base for planning these activities is to reflect on activities that are authentic to the discipline, for example, "What do scientists, artists, historians, etc... do?" (Ritchhart, Church, & Morrison, 2011). These activities should be planned with student success in mind, both for today and the future. Students should work to develop and foster the twenty-first-century skills of communication, collaboration, creativity, and critical thinking.

While constructing questions and activities to ensure and sustain inquiry, considering how to incorporate student choice and voice is key. According to Rainer and Matthews (2002) student "choice, voice, and shared authority are critical elements in most definitions of ownership" (p. 25), and this is essential for student-centered learning to take place. Therefore, thinking about how and when students are given choices in the learning experience and how individual and collective voices will be shared and valued is an essential part of student-centered teaching (Rainer & Matthews, 2002). One of the main aims for student-centered teaching should be to instill in each and every student that their voice matters through intentional questioning and activities that allow students to find success. Strategies that, despite being well-intentioned, can stifle student critical thinking and opportunities for communication include asking closed-ended questions and/or evaluating their questions with generic feedback, such as 'good job.' Activities such as the "Question Formulation Technique" or QFT (Rothstein & Santana, 2012) can be a helpful framework for fostering student questioning, creating a safe space for student's voice, and sustaining inquiry. The QFT consists of four principles: (a) students can ask as many questions as they can, (b) do not stop to discuss, critique, or answer any question, (c) Write down every question exactly as it is stated, and (d) change any statement into a question (Rothstein & Santana, 2012).

To further illustrate the planning process of student-centered teaching we return to Ms. Williams, who as a newcomer to the inquiry, decides to incorporate a controlled inquiry at the beginning of the year to model for students how to think like scientists and how to engage in inquiry. She starts with the end in mind and reflects on her desired learning outcomes. Using her district's curriculum for 3rd-grade science and the Next Generation Science Standards (NGSS, 2013), she has identified the essential content of plant and animal life cycles. She wants students to know the components and function of plant and animal life cycles, as well as the differences between the two and she, wants students to be aware of the impact humans have on plants and animals. Ms. Williams also wants students to feel inspired by their learning and empowered to make a change in their environment. To help organize her thoughts and tease out what and when to assess, Ms. Williams used the "Project Assessment Map" which was designed using the principles of Backward Design (Wiggins & McTighe, 2005; Buck Institute for Education, 2018a).

With clearly defined learning outcomes, Ms. Williams dives into thinking about a question that will engage students in a meaningful way with this curriculum. She knows that she needs to take the previously used, close-ended and overarching unit question of "What are the similarities and differences between plants and animals?" and change it to be a question that is compelling. She uses suggestions established by McTighe and Wiggins (2013) in that the essential question she drafts needs to be provocative, open-ended, and content-aligned and at the same time allow for exploration. After many iterations, Ms. Williams crafts an overarching question that she believes will spark curiosity and launch the inquiry: Do we affect the environment or does the environment affect us? Now, she must consider what follow-up questions, resources, and activities will help sustain the inquiry and the class formulate an answer the compelling question.

As it is the first time incorporating IBL, Ms. Williams uses a model that she discovered during a professional development workshop for teaching social studies: the Inquiry Design Model (IDM) Blueprint (Grant, Swan, & Lee, 2017). The IDM Blueprint is a format that can be used to design any learning experience where inquiry is central and is formatted to help teachers structure inquiries beginning with a compelling question, what will be done to launch the question, and then what follow-up questions, sources, and resources will be used to sustain inquiry (Grant, Swan, & Lee, 2017). This model supports her in further planning and organizing activities that will facilitate the learning.

When thinking about the activities that will achieve the desired learning outcomes, she works to plan activities that allow students to assume the role of scientist and form their own conclusions time and time again. She decides to kick off the inquiry with a nature walk, where students seek to answer the big question, 'Do I affect the environment or does the environment affect me?'. In doing so, they are looking for evidence much like scientists do. The students will record their observations, and she has anticipated that there will be a variety of claims. She knows students will not only see leaves falling from the trees, as the weather is getting colder, but they will also see bird houses and bird feeders. Critical thinking, collaboration, communication, and creativity are integral to student-centered learning. As Ms. Williams continues to engage in the planning process, she thinks about the learning outcomes and how she can be intentional about incorporating these 21st-century skills.

While constructing questions and activities to ensure and sustain inquiry, considering how to incorporate student choice and voice is key and critical to maintaining a successful-student-centered learning environment. With regard to student's voice, Ms. Williams sees this concept in two different, but related realms: (a) speaking and listening skills within the classroom walls and (b) providing a platform for collective and individual voices to be heard within and beyond the classroom walls (Smyth, 2006). In the first realm, Ms. Williams wants to make sure that students are working on their speaking and listening skills throughout the inquiry and continuing to build a healthy and positive classroom culture. One of the classroom norms in Ms. Williams room is to "share your thoughts and to listen to others' thoughts with your whole body." The class created this norm because they want to value each other's ideas and thoughts. In planning, Ms. Williams thinks about how and when she will incorporate short listening and speaking activities such as 'turn and talk' and 'think-pair-share' and when she will have students engage in small group activities and use strategies such as 'Chalk Talk' or 'Say Something to read and discuss sources (Connell, 2016; Lemov, 2015; EL Education, 2014). In the second realm, Ms. Williams thinks about how her students' voices will be shared after the learning experience and beyond her classroom.

Ultimately, Ms. Williams wants her students to be aware of the ways in which humans impact plants and animals and that as citizens of their community they can make choices to impact their living environments positively. Therefore, she wants to make sure that she also provides time and space for students to think about and plan ways to impact the environment they live in positively. Student-centered teaching not only aims to engage students in the classroom. Ideally, the inquiry is sustained beyond the school walls and the twenty-first-century skills that have been developed in the classroom allow students to be and do more as citizens in their community.

Principle Three: Recursive Reflection

When Dewey (1916) envisioned student-centered schools, he advocated that learning is a result of discovery, doing and reflection. As such reflection needs to be built into any student-centered learning experience. Teachers who use student-centered learning should provide opportunities for students to reflect periodically during and after a learning experience (Boss, 2012). Equally important, teachers reflect with their students as well as with other colleagues not as a one-time activity but as a habit of mind (Heick, 2014). Using simple reflection activities provides students with a way to communicate their learning with one another to become a stronger community of learners, provides a space to make their learning concrete and supports growth mindset (Dweck, 2007). The Buck Institute (2018) has catalogued several materials including planning tools, templates, and reflection surveys to help teachers plan and implement reflection.

Ms. Williams is already a reflective practitioner - that is, she thinks about her own practice and how it impacts student learning. We saw this with Arianna; however, Ms. Williams hasn't always built in opportunities for students to reflect on their own learning in a systematic way nor has she reflected with her students. When thinking about how and when she will have her students reflect, Ms. Williams first thinks about how she can have students reflect on a daily basis about their growth as learners. She builds in time during morning meeting for the group as a whole to reflect on what they have learned during their IBL process. During the morning meeting, she has the students turn and talk with one another about what they have learned, what they have yet to find out, and how they are growing as learners and scientists. Ms. Williams can record this information on a flip chart and return to that information throughout the IBL process. She also believes that checking in with specific students, particularly students she is concerned about (e.g., Arianna), about how they are growing as learners will help support engagement and ownership. Ms. Williams also creates a short reflection survey to give her students at the end of the IBL experience. She designs the survey using the "Self-Reflection on Project Work" template (Buck Institute for Education, 2018b).

Ms. Williams also thinks about setting time aside during her week to keep a log of her own reflections about student learning, engagement, and her teaching. She realizes that in order to grow in the process, she needs to be open to sharing what she is learning; therefore, she is also cognizant of sharing with her colleagues that are also using a student-centered approach to teaching. She sees her sharing as an opportunity to learn from other teachers as well.

After thoughtful planning, Ms. Williams is enthusiastic about implementing this new approach. She has a newfound excitement for the content, and she is looking forward to seeing how learning transpires with students at the helm. Ms. Williams is also a bit anxious about the unknown; however, she realizes that her students, especially Arianna, need this new approach. With that un-

derstanding, Ms. Williams acknowledges that this will be a learning curve for both her students and herself.

Resources for Planning and Implementing Student-Centered Teaching and Learning

Planning and implementing a student-centered approach is no doubt a thoughtful and thought-filled undertaking. Ertmer and Simons (2006) have suggested that as teachers embark on this process that they seek out the support of other educators who have had experience with student-centered teaching to help teachers plan, reflect, and evolve student-centered learning classrooms and experiences. Ideally, this could be a fellow colleague and/or instructional coach.

The internet has a wealth of resources for implementing student-centered teaching; however, navigating the hundreds, if not thousands, of potential resources can be daunting. To reduce the frustration that may be involved in this task, a limited list of resources for the three most common student-centered teaching approaches follows.

Inquiry-based learning

- Daniels, S. (2017). *The curious classroom: 10 structures for teaching with student-directed inquiry.* Portsmouth, NH: Heinemann.

- Juliani, A. (2015). *Inquiry and Innovation in the Classroom.* New York: Routledge.

- MacKenzie, T. (2016.) *Dive into inquiry.* Irvine, CA: EdTechTeam Press.

- Wiggins, J., & McTighe, G. (2013). *Essential questions: Opening doors to student understandings.* Alexandria, VA: ASCD.

- Edutopia (Inquiry-based learning)
  _https://www.edutopia.org/topic/inquiry-based-learning

- Annenberg Teacher as Learner Professional Development Video Series: *Learning Science Through Inquiry*
  https://www.learner.org/workshops/inquiry/resources/faq.html

Problem-based learning

- Thorp, L. & Sage, S. (2002). *Problems as possibilities: Problem-based learning for K-12 education* (2nd ed.). Alexandria, VA: ASCD.

- McConnell, T. J., Parker, J., & Eberhardt, J. (2017). *Problem-Based Learning in the Earth and Space Science Classroom, K–12.* Arlington, VA: NSTA.

- McConnell, T. J., Parker, J., & Eberhardt, J. (2016). *Problem-Based Learning in the Life Science Classroom, K–12.* Arlington, VA: NSTA.

- Problem-based Learning at the University of Delaware: http://www1.udel.edu/inst/resources/institutions.html

Project-based learning

- Bender, W. (2012). *Project-based learning: Differentiating instruction for the 21st century.* Thousand Oaks, CA: Sage Corwin.

- Boss, S., & Krauss, J. (2014). *Reinventing project-based learning: Your field guide to real-world projects in the digital age.* Arlington, VA: International Society for Technology in Education.

- Larmer, J., Ross, D., & Mergendoller, J. (2009). *Project-based learning starter kit.* Novato, CA: Buck Institute for Education.

- Larmer, J., Mergendoller, J., & Boss, S. (2015). *Setting the standard for project-based learning.* Alexandria, VA: ASCD.

- The Buck Institute: http://www.bie.org/

- Edutopia (Project-based learning): https://www.edutopia.org/project-based-learning

- The Teaching Channel, PjBL videos: https://www.teachingchannel.org/videos?q=ProjectBasedLearning

Final Thoughts

The 21st century requires future ready students who have a skill and knowledge base that is different from ever before. In order to ensure students are ready, teachers would be well advised to implement student-centered learning in their classrooms. This shift in learning is time-consuming and sometimes arduous; however, the benefits outweigh any difficulties. The classroom comes to life, student voices are at the heart, and students are engaged in meaningful work that inspires them to be and do more.

Inquiry-based learning, problem-based learning, and project-based learning all share some common student outcomes such as (a) offering authentic experiences (b) promoting deep understanding of content in conjunction with the development of higher-order thinking skills such as analysis and/or synthesis, (c) ensuring active engagement, (d) providing student choice and voice, and (e) sustaining inquiry and innovation (Cattaneo, 2017). Inquiry-based learning is a basic model where there is a question, a period of investigation, and a period of reasoning (Oguz-Unver & Arabacioglu, 2011). Project-based learning is the most authentic and offers a specific trajectory that is totally student driven, while problem-based learning offers real-world problems with a slightly more teacher directed outcome (Lamer, 2015; Lamer, Mergendoller, & Boss, 2015).

Regardless of the type, all student-centered learning options engage students and require them to be independent learners. In order to ensure success, teachers must create a student-centered environment, plan with a purpose, and engage in recursive reflection along with their students. Although this method of teaching sometimes requires a reset of teaching style, the benefits to students are numerous and provide the proper ingredients to ensure 21st-century college and career readiness.

Points to Remember

- *The 21st century demands future ready students who are independent learners. The best way to prepare them is to engage them in student-centered learning where they are responsible for the final product and learning that is attached to it.*

- *Student-centered learning encompasses a number of instructional approaches that are focused on student ownership of learning and take their cue from John Dewey's (1916) constructivist pedagogy.*

- *There are three main types of student-centered learning: inquiry-based, problem-based, and project-based. All provide similar outcomes; however, project-based learning offers students the most authentic learning experience.*

- *Similar to Backwards Design (McTighe & Wiggings, 2013) it is important to begin with the end in mind. Determine the desired learning outcomes, carefully craft an overarching question, then prepare for the remainder of student learning.*

- *Project-based learning has undergone a transformation and now includes seven essential project design elements for students as well as seven project-based teaching practices for educators.*

- *When preparing to teach using one of the student-centered approaches, it is necessary to create a specific type of environment, plan with a purpose, and consistently use reflection to improve the practice. Students should also use reflection in their learning.*

References

Abdi, A. (2014). The effect of inquiry-based learning method on students' academic achievement in science course. *Universal Journal of Educational Research, 2*(1), 37-41.

DOI: 10.13189/ujer.2014.020104

Barron, B., & Darling-Hammond, L. (2008). How can we teach for meaningful learning? In L. Darling-Hammond (Ed.), *Powerful learning: What we know about teaching for understanding* (pp. 11-70). San Francisco, CA: Jossey-Boss.

Berger, W. (2014). *A More Beautiful Question.* New York: Bloomsbury USA.

Boss, S. (2012). Teachers need time to reflect, too. Retrieved from https://www.edutopia.org/blog/project-learning-teacher-reflection-suzie-boss

Buck Institute for Education. (2018a). *Project assessment map.* Retrieved from http://www.bie.org/object/document/project_assessment_map

Buck Institute for Education. (2018b). *Self-reflection on project work.* Retrieved from https://www.bie.org/object/document/self_reflection_on_project_work

Cattaneo, K. H. (2017). Telling Active Learning Pedagogies Apart: from theory to practice. *Journal of New Approaches in Educational Research, 6*(2), 144-152. Retrieved from https://naerjournal.ua.es/article/download/v6n2-8/369

Connell, G. (2016). *Chalk talks to engage all students.* Retrieved from https://www.scholastic.com/teachers/blog-posts/genia-connell/chalk-talks-engage-all-students/

Common Core State Standards Initiative. (2018). *Preparing America's students for success.*
Retrieved from http://www.corestandards.org/

Dana, N. F., Thomas, C., & Boynton, S. (2011). *Inquiry: A districtwide approach to staff and student learning.* Thousand Oaks, CA: Corwin Press.

Daniels, H. (2017). *The curious classroom.* Portsmouth: Heinemann.

Dewey, J. (1916). *Education and democracy.* New York: Macmillian.

Duran, M., & Dökme, İ. (2016). The effect of the inquiry-based learning approach on student's critical-thinking skills. *Eurasia Journal of Mathematics, Science & Technology Education, 12*(12). Retrieved from https://eric.ed.gov/?id=EJ1117272

Dweck, C.S. (2007). *Mindset: The new psychology of success: How we can learn to fulfill our potential.* New York, NY: Ballentine Books.

EL Education. (2014). *Common Core ELA curriculum: Appendix: Protocols and strategies.*
Retrieved from http://commoncoresuccess.eleducation.org/sites/default/files/curriculum/grades/ela-3/eledappendixprotocolsandresources0616.pdf

English, M. C., & Kitsantas, A. (2013). Supporting student self-regulated learning in problem-and project-based learning. *Interdisciplinary Journal of*

Problem-Based Learning, 7(2), 128-150. Retrieved from http://docs.lib.purdue.edu/ijpbl/vol7/iss2/6/

Ertmer, P. A., & Glazewski, K. D. (2015). Essentials for PBL implementation: Fostering collaboration, transforming roles, and scaffolding learning. In A. Walker, H. Leary, C.E. Hmelo-Silver, & P.A. Ertmer. *Essential Readings in Problem-Based Learning,* (1st ed), pp. 89-106. West Lafayette, IN: Purdue University Press

Ertmer, P. A., & Simons, K. D. (2005). Scaffolding teachers' efforts to implement problem-based learning. *International Journal of Learning, 12*(4), 319-328. Retrieved from https://pdfs.semanticscholar.org/765d/c0a57dc7376d4eb9b9db726ccaf76d5a4a5a.pdf

Friesen, S., & Scott, D. (2013). *Inquiry-based: A review of the research literature.* Retrieved from http://galileo.org/focus-on-inquiry-lit-review.pdf

Ginsberg, M. (2015). Making Diverse Classrooms Safer for Learning. *Educational Leadership.* Retrieved from http://www.ascd.org/publications/educational-leadership/mar15/vol72/num06/Making-Diverse-Classrooms-Safer-for-Learning.aspx

Grant, S. G., Swan, K., & Lee, J. (2017). *Inquiry-Based Practice in Social Studies Education: Understanding the Inquiry Design Model.* New York, NY: Routledge

Han, S., Capraro, R., & Capraro, M. M. (2015). How science, technology, engineering, and mathematics (STEM) project-based learning (PBL) affects high, middle, and low achievers differently: The impact of student factors on achievement. *International Journal of Science and Mathematics Education, 13*(5), 1089-1113. Retrieved from https://eric.ed.gov/?id=EJ1074282

Heick, T. (2014). *Reflecting on reflection: A habit of mind.* Retrieved from https://www.edutopia.org/blog/reflecting-on-reflection-habit-of-mind-terry-heick

Juliani, A. (2015). *Inquiry and innovation in the classroom.* New York: Routledge.

Karaçalli, S., & Korur, F. (2014). The effects of project-based learning on students' academic achievement, attitude, and retention of knowledge: The subject of "electricity in our lives." *School Science and Mathematics, 114*(5), 224–235. DOI: 10.1111/ssm.12071

Krahenbuhl, K. S. (2016). Student-centered education and constructivism: challenges, concerns, and clarity for teachers. *The Clearing House: A Journal of Educational Strategies, Issues and Ideas, 89*(3), 97-105. Retrieved from https://eric.ed.gov/?id=EJ1106715

Krauss, J., & Boss, S. (2013). *Thinking through project-based learning: Guiding deeper inquiry.* Thousand Oaks, CA: Corwin Press.

Larmer, J. (2015). Project-based learning vs. problem-based learning vs. X-PBL. Retrieved from https://www.edutopia.org/blog/pbl-vs-pbl-vs-xbl-john-larmer

Larmer, J. & Mergendoller, J.R. (2011). *The main course, not dessert: How are students reaching 21st century goals? With 21st century project-based learning.* Retrieved from http://www.bie.org/object/document/main_course_not_dessert

Larmer, J., Mergendoller, J. & Boss, S. (2015). *Setting the standard for project-based learning: A proven approach to rigorous classroom instruction.* Alexandria, VA: ASCD.

Lee, H., & Bae, S. (2008). Issues in implementing a structured problem-based learning strategy in a volcano unit: A case study. *International Journal of Science and Mathematics Education, 64*(6), 655-676. DOI: 10.1007/s10763-007-9067x

Lemov, D. (2015). *Teach like a champion: 62 techniques that put students on thee path to college* (2nd ed). San Francisco, CA: Wiley.

MacKenzie, T. (2016). *Dive into inquiry.* Irvine, CA: EdTechTeam Press.

McConnell, T. J., Eberhardt, J., Lundeberg, M. A., Parker, J. M., Koehler, M. J., Urban-Lurain, M., & Stanaway, J. C. (2008). The PBL project for teachers: Using problem-based learning to guide K-12 science teachers' professional development. *MSTA Journal, 53*(1), 16-21. Retrieved from http://www.academia.edu/4339070/The_PBL_Project_for_Teachers_Using_problem-based_learning_to_guide_K-12_science_teachers_professional_development

McTighe, J., & Wiggins, G. (2013). *Essential Questions.* Alexandria, VA: ASCD.

Mergendoller, J.R. & Larmer, J. (2015). *Why we changed our model of the "8 essential elements of PBL."* Retrieved from https://www.bie.org/blog/why_we_changed_our_model_of_the_8_essential_elements_of_pbl

Merritt, J., Lee, M., Rillero, P., & Kinach, B. M. (2017). Problem-Based Learning in K–8 Mathematics and Science Education: A Literature Review. *Interdisciplinary Journal of Problem-Based Learning, 11*(2). Retrieved from http://docs.lib.purdue.edu/ijpbl/vol11/iss2/3/

Miller. A. (2015). *Using assessment to create student-centered learning.* Retrieved from https://www.edutopia.org/blog/assessment-create-student-centered-learning-andrew-miller

Monte-Sano, C. (2012). What makes a good history essay? Assessing historical aspects of argumentative writing. *Social Education, 76*(6), 294-298. Retrieved from http://mdk12.msde.maryland.gov/instruction/ccr_conferences/resources/S106/Secondary_Social%20Studies_Historical%20Investigations_5of9_v1.pdf

Morrison, C.D. (2014). From 'Sage on the Stage' to 'Guide on the Side': A Good Start. *International Journal for the Scholarship of Teaching and Learning:* Vol. 8: No. 1, Article 4. Retrieved from https://digitalcommons.georgiasouthern.edu/cgi/viewcontent.cgi?article=1011&context=ij-sotl

National Education Association. (2012). *Preparing 21st Century Students for a Global Society*. National Education Association. Retrieved from http://www.nea.org/assets/docs/A-Guide-to-Four-Cs.pdf

NGSS. (2013). *Next Generation Science Standards: For States, By States*. Washington, DC: The National Academies Press.

Oğuz Ünver, A., & Arabacioğlu, S. (2011). Overviews on inquiry based and problem based learning methods. *Western Anatolia Journal of Educational Sciences*, (WAJES), 303-310. Retrieved from http://webb.deu.edu.tr/baed/giris/baed/ozel_sayi/303-310.pdf

Olbrys, S., & Strahley, L. (2015, June). *The Deliberative Classroom*. Action research presented at the American Democracy Project, Indianapolis, IN.

Partnership for 21st Century Learning. (2015). *P21 framework Definitions*. Retrieved from http://www.p21.org/storage/documents/docs/P21_Framework_Definitions _New_Logo_2015.pdf

Phillips, J. (2016). *9 steps to a future-ready education: Initiatives are about more than just adopting technology*. Retrieved from https://edtechmagazine.com/k12/article/2016/07/9-steps-future-ready-education

Rainer, J.D. & Matthews, M.W. (2002). Ownership of learning in teacher education. *Action in Teacher Education, 23* (10), 22-30. DOI: 10.1080/01626620.2002.10463264

Rehmat, A. P. (2015). *Engineering the path to higher-order thinking in elementary education: A problem-based learning approach for STEM integration*. Retrieved from https://pdfs.semanticscholar.org/49f3/5a2bd818aa5a4361a13fcc4fec494b61 e376.pdf

Remijan, K. W. (2017). Project-Based Learning and Design-Focused Projects to Motivate Secondary Mathematics Students. *Interdisciplinary Journal of Problem-Based Learning, 11*(1), 1-15. Retrieved from https://docs.lib.purdue.edu/cgi/viewcontent.cgi?article=1520&context=ijpb l

Ritchhart, R., Church, M., & Morrison, K. (2011). *Making Thinking Visible*. San Francisco, CA: Jossey-Bass.

Rothstein, D. & Santana, L. (2012). *Make just one change: Teach students to ask their own questions*. Cambridge, Massachusetts: Harvard Education Press.

Savery, J.R. (2015). Overview of problem-based learning: Definitions and distinctions. In A. Walker, H. Leary, C. Hmelo-Silver, & P. Ertmer. *Essential Readings in Problem-Based Learning* (pp.357-368). West Lafayette, IN: Purdue Press.

Selmer, S.J., Rye, J.A., Malone, E, Fernandez, D., & Trebino, K. (2014). *What should we grow in our school garden to sell at the Farmers' Market? Initiating statistical literacy through science and mathematics integration*. Retrieved from https://eric.ed.gov/?id=EJ1024644

Smyth, J. (2006). Educational leadership that fosters 'student voice'. *International Journal of Leadership in Education, 9*(4), 279-284. DOI: 10.1080/13603120600894216

Stepien, W. J., & Gallagher, S. A. (1993). Problem-based learning: As authentic as it gets. *Educational Leadership, 50*(7), 25–28. Retrieved from http://www.ascd.org/publications/educational_leadership/apr93/vol50/num07/Problem-Based_Learning@_As_Authentic_As_It_Gets.aspx

Urban, H. (2008). *20 Lessons from the Classroom*. Saline, Michigan: Great Lessons Press.

Verma, A.K., Dickerson, D., & McKinney, S. (2011). *Engaging students in STEM careers with project-based learning: Marine tech project.* Retrieved from https://eric.ed.gov/?id=EJ941852

Wiggins, G., & McTighe, J. (2005). *Understanding by design* (2nd ed.). Alexandria, VA: ASCD.

Chapter 3

The Love in the Lesson:
How an Enthusiastic Teacher Improves
Student Learning Outcomes

Nicholas Young, Ph.D, Ed.D,
American International College
and
Aimee Dalenta, M.Ed.,
Goodwin College

The benefits of an enthusiastic teacher go far beyond helping a student to be more engaged in the classroom learning environment. There are many ways in which teachers can express enthusiasm for a particular topic or content area. The manner in which students respond to this perceived enthusiasm can, in fact, have a direct correlation to their academic and behavioral learning outcomes, as well as several other benefits (Rosenshine, 1970; Bettencourt, Gillett, Gall, & Hull, 1983). In this modern era of education, much has changed in the way students consume information. Educators, therefore, must recognize this shift and adapt their methods to address their varied learning styles successfully. Although change is difficult for some teachers, and updating their personal teaching style requires thoughtful reflection and examination, the fact remains that in order to reach this generation of learners, some elements in the presentation of academic material must be altered to allow students to access content area information effectively. Current research suggests that teachers who present subject matter in an enthusiastic and engaging way inspire students to achieve highly in a number of different academic, social, and behavioral criteria (Kunter, Frenzel, Nagy, Baumert, & Pekrun, 2011; Keller, Neumann, & Fischer, 2013; Keller, Goetz, Becker, Morger, & Hensley, 2014; Keller, Hoy, Goetz, & Frenzel, 2015).

Over the course of the past century, numerous researchers have studied the effects of teacher enthusiasm on specific student indicators (Kunter et al., 2011; Keller et al., 2014; Keller et al., 2015). These indicators have ranged from intrinsic motivation, student interest, student engagement, and many others.

These studies themselves have also ranged significantly, studying students from preschool through graduate school and teachers at the very beginning of their careers through seasoned, veteran educators (Kunter et al., 2011; Keller et al., 2014). Much of the information garnered through years of research points to the notion that an enthusiastic teacher has a positive effect on student academic, social, and behavioral outcomes. Broadly stated, an overwhelming majority of the research has found that there are links between teacher engagement and positive student behaviors in the classroom (Mitchell, 2013; Keller et al., 2015).

One of the most challenging aspects regarding this particular area of interest is the vagueness and ambiguity of the term "teacher enthusiasm." Enthusiasm is an extremely subjective behavior or set of behaviors, and there is not universal agreement throughout the field regarding how to define and explore the topic. There are many deviations of the term "enthusiasm," as well as a number of different lenses that educational leaders have used to quantify expectations over the past several decades (Alsharif & Qi, 2014; Orosz et al., 2015). Although this divide presents challenges, countless studies have nonetheless been conducted in an attempt to help leaders in the field understand exactly how and why teacher enthusiasm affects students (Mitchell, 2013; Alsharif & Qi, 2014; Orosz et al., 2015; Keller, 2015). There is still much work to be done and the information yet to be discovered will help to unlock the potential of an enthusiastic teacher further.

Defining Enthusiasm

The topic of teacher enthusiasm has been studied in depth over the past century, with most of the prominent research occurring in the early 1970s and 1980s. Significant studies conducted by Rosenshine (1970) and Bettencourt et al. (1983) laid the foundation for modern theories pertaining to teacher enthusiasm and its effect on students. Broadly, these studies asserted definitively that teacher enthusiasm can, in fact, be interconnected to student learning outcomes (Rosenshine, 1970; Bettencourt et al., 1983). The new millennium ushered in a reinvigorated interest in the topic, and experts in the field began investigating the subject through varied lenses. Early on, one particular intensive study correlated teacher enthusiasm with academic achievement, while more recent studies focus on the topic of student engagement (Patrick, Hisley, & Kempler, 2000; Keller et al., 2015, Kunter et al., 2011, Zhang, 2014). Collectively, one thing has remained relatively constant: teacher enthusiasm is a fairly subjective entity, and therefore difficult to conclusively define (Patrick et al., 2000; Keller et al., 2015; Kunter et al., 2011, Mitchell, 2013).

Researchers have attempted to place confines on the definition with moderate success (Mitchell, 2013; Kunter et al., 2011; Keller, 2015). The most notable researchers in this area of study agree that enthusiasm can be broken into two distinct categories: the teacher's enthusiasm for subject matter during instruction, and the teacher's overall behavioral affect denoting pleasure during teaching (Keller et al., 2014). Teacher behaviors, such as non-verbal cues and more, allow the student to infer the teacher's enjoyment for a subject or in the act of teaching, which, in turn, correlates to an overall improved academic experience (Alsharif & Qi, 2014). In both of these categories, teacher enthusiasm is associated with student enjoyment, motivation, and attention during class. Within these constructs, enthusiasm can also be further broken down into displayed enthusiasm and experienced enthusiasm. (Keller et al., 2015).

Specific Behavioral Mannerisms Associated with Enthusiasm

Displayed enthusiasm has a number of mannerisms associated with it, including an energetic effect, use of humor, gesticulation, and facial expressions (Keller et al., 2015). Teachers who are perceived as enthusiastic vary the pitch and speed of their speech, use an uplifting cadence, and have intense vocal inflection (Keller et al., 2014). These teachers are articulate communicators, using highly descriptive adjectives and a variety of descriptors to convey their subject matter (Mitchell, 2013). The use of eye and facial expressions convey excitement, and it has been noted that their eyes light up, often wide, with eyebrows raised (Kunter et al., 2011). Teachers' body movements are quick and sweeping, utilizing all extremities to gesture, including nodding their heads and clapping their hands (Kunter et al., 2013). Furthermore, the most enthusiastic teachers enhance their lessons with humor, smile frequently, and engage in a dialogue with students during the lesson (Kunter et al., 2013).

Patrick et al. (2000) noted other descriptors of teacher enthusiasm including the teacher appearing to have vitality, the teacher helping the student to understand why the material is important, and the teacher clearly presenting the material during lessons. This research supports the notion that teachers who are comfortable with and encourage a hands-on learning approach are more likely to appear enthusiastic to students (Patrick et al., 2000). Research has also uncovered a link between perceived enthusiasm and sense of humor (Collins 1976). When a teacher has a good sense of humor, engages students in friendly banter, laughs, and makes light of situations in the classroom, he or she is often seen by students as being more enthusiastic than their counterparts who do not engage in these activities (Collins, 1976).

How Teacher Enjoyment Conveys Enthusiasm

Whether or not an educator appears to be fully devoted to the teaching craft has been linked to the perceived level of enthusiasm (Alsharif & Qi, 2014).

Teacher enjoyment is conveyed to students through their teaching behaviors; if behaviors are excited and positive, this is transferred to students (Frenzel et al., 2009) Animated teaching begins even before the onset of the lesson as the educator, introducing a topic of study to students enthusiastically, thus avoiding the pitfalls of apathetic behavior. Mitchell (2013) cited a situation in which a teacher began a lesson using a statement akin to "I know you don't like this activity, and I don't like it much either. But we will get through this together." He argues that this is, perhaps, one of the most detrimental ways to present information to students. While teacher enthusiasm is in no way the most important variable as it pertains to student achievement, educators should value the merits of the research. To engage students most effectively, teachers must begin a lesson with authentic excitement for the topic. When teachers are not authentic in their enthusiasm, this is often recognized by students and impacts success (Cui, Yao, & Zhang, 2017).

When educators are invested and content in their professional work environments, they are often able to portray genuine enthusiasm for their subject area more successfully than colleagues who are not content in their professional lives. Kunter et al. (2011) linked occupational well-being to teacher enthusiasm; however, other studies have suggested that for this enthusiasm to transfer positively to student achievement, it must be genuine (Zhang, 2014). If teachers force excitement or enthusiasm for a topic, their rate of burnout increases and their overall perception towards education can decline (Zhang, 2014). Research indicates that while enthusiasm can actually be taught to pre-service teachers, there must be a foundational love of teaching and education for the enthusiasm to be considered genuine (Frenzel et al., 2009). Teacher enjoyment plays a major role in the lives of both students and teachers alike. Excitement, positive mannerisms, and overall gratification for the profession can lead to higher student achievement (Frenzel et al. 2009)

Kunter et al. (2013) assert that the teaching profession requires teachers to present themselves positively to students, and that teacher enthusiasm (as part of teachers' overall professional aptitude) determines the quality of the learning experience for students and plays a large role in student motivation. Teachers who convey higher levels of enthusiasm for their profession report higher levels of satisfaction both personally and professionally (Kunter et al. 2013). Conditions that are known to affect teacher enthusiasm at the school level are teaching autonomy and positive mentoring programs, amongst other factors (Kunter et al. 2013). Often, these factors are beyond the control of the educators themselves, such as whether or not they are in a school with administrators who support autonomy. Research shows a correlation between positive classroom conditions and school structure with teacher enthusiasm (Kunter et al., 2013).

Reciprocal Effects

Teacher enthusiasm positively affects students' behaviors and level of achievement (Keller et al., 2015). This elevated behavior and achievement can also reciprocally influence the teacher. "Not only does teacher enthusiasm positively affect students, but the level of student achievement and motivation likely impacts the teachers' enthusiasm as well" (Keller, 2015, p. 32). Kunter et al. (2011) demonstrated that student motivation levels and academic achievement levels were linked to teachers' experienced enthusiasm; therefore, it can be broadly stated that the concept of teacher enthusiasm can be viewed as cyclical. When students perceive that their teacher is enthusiastic, they are in turn motivated to succeed both academically and behaviorally Kunter et al., 2011). It stands to reason, then, that when the academic achievement and behaviors of students increase or improves, teachers are more likely to feel genuine enthusiasm for their classroom environments, the field of education as a whole, as well as their students' abilities (Kunter et al., 2011). This, in turn, elevates their enthusiasm level, which reciprocally motivates their students even further. The effects of this phenomenon have not been fully studied, but research indicates that this is a promising link towards influencing both teacher and student successes (Kunter et al., 2011; Mitchell, 2013).

Planning an Enthusiastic Lesson

Mitchell (2013) suggests that various behaviors will convey enthusiasm to students during a lesson and that the most detrimental behavior a teacher can convey is apathy. First, teachers must communicate a genuine pleasure to be in the company of their students and begin to develop a rapport (Mitchell, 2013). This can be done by warmly welcoming students into the classroom and continuing with both verbal and nonverbal communication during the lesson. Teachers can smile, nod, shake hands with students, or make eye contact with them to let them know that they are openly invited into the learning space (Kunter et al., 2013). Teachers must find immediate ways to welcome all ideas and backgrounds of their students, as well as provide positive reinforcement when they have achieved something notable. One-to-one interaction is key to building an enthusiastic relationship with students, concurrently making students of all backgrounds and beliefs feel safe in their learning environment (Mitchell, 2013).

During the lesson, students must be actively engaged in activities, have an open dialogue with the teacher and peers, and have differentiated access to the subject matter (Mitchell, 2013). Adequate preparation is paramount for the enthusiastic teacher. Pre-planning materials and technology, gathering anecdotes and personal stories about a particular topic to share with stu-

dents, and arranging details of a thorough lesson are all important in conveying enthusiasm (Mitchell, 2013). Students both young and old are often savvy
enough to ascertain whether or not a teacher has spent a satisfactory amount
of time preparing to teach given content. It is, therefore, paramount for
teachers to adequately prepare for lessons and units. This not only helps
teachers to deliver high-quality lessons in an effective way, but it also conveys
the message to students that teachers find the material important, valuable,
and important enough to prepare for thoroughly (Mitchell, 2013). This perception lends itself to student learning.

At the conclusion of a lesson, enthusiastic teachers share a common strategy of ending the lesson by previewing what will be taught next (Kunter et al.,
2013; Mitchell, 2013). An educator who is excited and enthusiastic about content will leave the students wondering what is to come next. Students should
be provided with enough information to pique their interest, allowing them to
make an assumption that their teacher is extremely invested (enthusiastic)
about the upcoming subject matter (Mitchell, 2013).

Connections between teacher enthusiasm and test performance, information recall, on-task behavior, student attitude toward learning, and student
interest have been studied over the past several decades (Alsharif & Qi, 2014;
Zhang, 2014). The positive associations linked between these indicators clearly support the notion that teacher enthusiasm is more meaningful than research may have previously believed (Alsharif & Qi, 2014). It would be extremely difficult for an educator to present a dynamic and powerful lesson if
he or she had not fully committed and prepared for the lesson. Research indicates that teachers must devote themselves to thorough lesson planning to
assure that their passion and enthusiasm is conveyed to students making it
more likely for students to achieve socially, academically, and behaviorally
(Alsharif & Qi, 2014; Zhang, 2014).

Teacher Enthusiasm Elevates Student Interest, Academic Self-Efficacy, and Engagement

When teachers are enthusiastic, they convey to their students that they are
experiencing enjoyment and finding personal value in the subject matter
being taught. Keller et al. (2014) indicate that students will draw on this level
of perceived interest by their teacher, and subsequently, experience elevated
enjoyment and interest themselves. Students perceive higher enthusiasm
from a teacher who is emotionally expressive and who displays pride, excitement, or humor (Keller et al., 2014). Students find these behaviors to be relat-
able and understand them as teacher excitement and authenticity; thus, they
internalize them and become more interested in the subject matter being
taught (Keller et al., 2014).

Patrick et al. (2000) found that teacher enthusiasm and positive affect are among the most important variables related to students' intrinsic motivation and that there is a direct correlation between these and the intrinsic motivation of students. Although intrinsic motivation is a personal and self-directed behavior within a given student, many students may have motivation hidden deep within themselves, lying dormant and awaiting inspiration; thus, Patrick et al. (2000) filled a gap in the literature.

The researchers (Patrick et al., 2000) designed a controlled experiment in which teacher enthusiasm was manipulated and measured to ascertain the effect on student motivation. The hypothesis was that "students who were taught subject material by a highly enthusiastic teacher would be more intrinsically motivated to learn about that material and related material, whereas students with apparently unenthusiastic teachers would be less intrinsically motivated" (Patrick et al., 2000). Results of this study indicated that there was a relationship between teachers' nonverbally expressed enthusiasm and students reporting intrinsic motivation and also indicated that when a lesson was presented with high energy, students experienced the learning with more enjoyment and vigor, and were intrinsically motivated to learn the subject matter (Patrick et al., 2000).

Teacher enthusiasm also has an effect on students' academic self-efficacy, classroom engagement, and learning goal orientation. According to a major study conducted by Zhang (2014), teachers who exhibit characteristics of enjoyment and enthusiasm in classroom teaching are more likely to foster a classroom environment where students feel empowered and capable academically. It has also been hypothesized that this self-efficacy transfers into positive classroom behaviors, motivation, and performance. The results of the study by Zhang indicate that "teacher enthusiasm is an effective predictor of student behavioral, cognitive, and emotional engagement, intrinsic goal orientation, and academic self-efficacy, (and) the power of teacher enthusiasm in predicting positive student behavior in the classroom." (Zhang, 2014, p. 51) The results very clearly articulate that the more enthusiastic and dynamic a teacher is, the more engaged students are behaviorally, cognitively, and emotionally.

Enthusiastic Teaching May Lower Academic Cheating

Behavioral engagement in the classroom can be outwardly displayed by a student in several different ways, such as appropriate classroom conduct, rule following, and willingness to engage in academic or social activities within the classroom (Orosz et al., 2015). It can also manifest itself as deeper self-regulation and a willingness to go above and beyond the regular academic requirements. Although a strong direct correlation is difficult to prove for many reasons, including the subjectivity of the term "enthusiasm", enthusiastic teachers often spark excitement and curiosity within their students as well as motivate them to practice on-task behaviors during lessons (Bettencourt et al., 1983; Patrick et al., 2000).

One unexpected benefit to high teacher enthusiasm is its impact on student engagement in terms of academic cheating (Orosz et al., 2015; Hohnbaum, 2012). Academic cheating is a social phenomenon that dates back to ancient times and presents itself at every level of education, from young students to students at high levels of education (Orosz et al., 2015). This study explored cheating through several lenses, including intrinsic and extrinsic motivating factors and results showed that the rate of cheating was lower when a teacher presented information in an engaging way and was perceived as friendly and caring (Orosz et al., 2015). If teachers are viewed as capable, inspired, welcoming, fair-minded, engaged, kind, and interesting, students tend to cheat less, and, in addition, the more respect students have for their teachers, the less likely they are to cheat in their class (Hohnbaum, 2012; Orosz et al., 2015). Although more research is needed in the area to make further conclusive connections, the information garnered from the study determined that students of enthusiastic teachers cheat less (Orosz et al., 2015).

Enthusiastic Teaching to Combat Classroom Boredom

Boredom in the classroom is a common emotion experienced by students at all levels of education. A body of research indicates that when students perceive that academic tasks in the classroom have low value, boredom increases (Frenzel et al., 2009; Kunter et al. 2013). As a result, much emphasis has been placed on understanding how teachers can increase positive teaching practices to inspire students (Frenzel et al., 2009). Enthusiastic teaching behavior was linked to improving task value perception by students, has been identified as one of the most important qualities that an educator can possess, and has the potential to positively affect students' learning outcomes (Frenzel et al., 2009; Keller et al., 2015). Daschmann, Goetz, and Stupnisky (2014) revealed that interest in a specific task was negatively correlated with boredom; therefore, when teachers are able to spark an interest in their students, they can inspire their learning process. Evidence now supports the notion that if a teacher is enthusiastically presenting information regarding a certain academic topic, the students are less likely to be bored than if the teacher were presenting the same information in an unenthusiastic manner (Daschmann et al., 2014).

Teachers who are described as being passionate and invested in their area of study are more likely to engage students in their classrooms, and thus combat boredom (Cui et al., 2017). Students need to believe that there is high value in the tasks that they are being asked to perform by their teachers on a daily basis. By conveying this message to students, teachers are essentially getting their students to 'buy into' their own learning. When students feel this sense of personal investment, they are significantly less likely to feel the negative emotion of boredom during their school day (Cui et al., 2017).

Student boredom levels are also lowered when there is perceived autonomy in the classroom (Cui et al., 2017). Students who perceive more teacher enthusiasm may also perceive more autonomy support from their teachers; thus, students who believe that autonomy is a core component of their classroom learning environment are likely to report lower levels of boredom (Cui et al., 2017). These students are also more likely to be interested in a given topic of study, which may translate into higher academic achievement (Cui et al., 2017).

High-quality teachers who are focused on student understanding will work diligently to appear more passionate, enthusiastic, and inspired by the subject matter that they teach. The perceived level of teacher enthusiasm has an effect on students (Zhang, 2014; Harden & Laidlaw, 2017). This is an important distinction to make, as the way students perceive the enthusiasm level is not necessarily the level of enthusiasm that the teacher is actually feeling (Zhang, 2014). Regardless, the expression of enthusiasm, it is now clear, is one of the most influential factors in determining various levels of student successes. Specifically, when a student perceives that their teacher is enthusiastic, research supports the notion that this student will experience less boredom within the classroom Frenzel et al., 2009; Kunter et al., 2013).

Teacher Enthusiasm and Intrinsic Motivation

Intrinsic motivation can be defined as an energizing behavior that comes from within an individual, out of will and interest for the activity at hand (Kunter et al., 2013). No external rewards are required to incite the intrinsically motivated student into action rather, the reward is the behavior itself (Hohnbaum, 2012; Patrick et al., 2000). There is a correlation between a highly enthusiastic teacher and a student's intrinsic motivation to do well in a given academic subject (Hohnbaum, 2012; Patrick et al., 2000). Intrinsically motivated students perform tasks for the natural benefit of the task itself, without the expectation or need for external factors such as rewards or positive reinforcements (Hohnbaum, 2012). For centuries, philosophers of education such as Maria Montessori have heralded the benefits of intrinsic student motivation; however, questions have always remained as to how teachers can inspire this virtue in their students (Fitch, 2013).

The art of teaching is an endless journey on the path towards finding the best personal blend of pedagogy, strategies, and procedures in the classroom. In higher education, student evaluation is a critical instrument used to measure students' perception of their professor's style and classroom environment. A constantly reoccurring theme of student evaluations is how the behaviors, attitude, and demeanor of the educator affect student learning (Alsharif & Qi, 2014). A relationship exists between instructor enthusiasm and students' intrinsic motivation to learn and the teacher who can foster a positive relationship may be able to help students engage in the learning process to the fullest extent (Alsharif & Qi, 2014). Students are more successful when teachers create classrooms that are student-centered, challenging, and engaging (Harden & Laidlaw, 2017). When students have ownership of classroom activities, their attitudes improve, they are more engaged in learning, and their level of self-motivation increases (Harden & Laidlaw, 2017).

It is clear that when teacher enthusiasm is high "students are more likely to be interested, energetic, curious, and excited about learning" (Patrick et al., 2000, p. 10); however, this alone is not enough to maintain intrinsic student motivation; rather, it is one important component in a great variety of skills that a teacher must possess in order to activate the best outcomes for their students (Patrick et al., 2000; Harden & Laidlaw, 2017). This is yet another critical component to successful student learning engagement that teacher enthusiasm can positively affect.

Words to Action: How to Teach with Enthusiasm

Teaching with enthusiasm is one of the key elements of effective instruction and although it can be argued that there are many other influencing factors pertaining to student learning, teacher enthusiasm is potentially even more meaningful than a teacher's knowledge of subject matter, their pedagogical strategies employed, and their technological savviness (Hobbs, 2012). For these reasons, passion is the epicenter of the best examples of teaching.

One of the biggest challenges to fostering enthusiastic teachers is that enthusiasm is often seen as a personality trait that cannot be taught (Harden & Laidlaw, 2017; Fried, 2001). On the contrary, enthusiasm can, in fact, be taught; however, one teacher may display enthusiasm differently than another (Fried, 2001). Teachers do not necessarily need to be extroverted and showy to convey their passion for a subject or for teaching in general. Specific ways teachers can practice being enthusiastic and passionate educators include working in partnership with students, allowing students to see their teacher being vulnerable, i.e., caring deeply about student successes and missteps, and being sincerely invested in the curriculum planning of their subject area (Hobbs, 2012). Above all, an enthusiastic teacher will be intensively reflective about their own practice - thinking about the teaching process before, during, and after lessons to increase the level of satisfaction and self-esteem (Fried, 2001; Harden & Laidlaw, 2017). It allows the educator to contemplate what is working within the classroom and make changes accordingly and, equally important, it conveys the high level of enthusiasm for the content area and for teaching as a profession (Harden & Laidlaw, 2017).

Final Thoughts

In the ever-changing landscape of modern education, expectations placed on teachers have never been higher. Many educators feel an inordinate amount of pressure every day from administrators, districts, and parents. This pressure is directly linked to academic performance standards and student outcomes, which often becomes the central focus of conversations, with little emphasis placed on how specific teacher behaviors can be a part of the solution.

Teaching is an art, a science, and a calling for many, and their level of enthusiasm is one of the most under-discussed solutions for the many issues that exist surrounding academic, social, and behavioral success within the classroom. Students with enthusiastic teachers perform higher on academic tests, are more intrinsically motivated, have higher genuine interest in the subject matter, and are less likely to cheat, amongst many other benefits (Hohnbaum, 2012). Furthermore, researchers now know that some of the behaviors denoting enthusiasm in educators can actually be taught (Hobbs, 2012).

Educational leaders must assist teachers in understanding how emphasizing their own enthusiastic behaviors will impact student learning and behavioral outcomes positively (Keller et al., 2015). Districts and schools need to foster the type of environments that are conducive to teachers feeling respected and autonomous within their classroom walls. It is these feelings that lead to higher teacher satisfaction and more genuine enthusiasm about the field of education, which in turn positively influence student outcomes (Kunter et al., 2015).

Points to Remember

- *The topic of teacher enthusiasm is complex and subjective. Defining the characteristics of an enthusiastic teacher has proved to be difficult, but most agree that it involves the overall behavioral effect of passion during teaching.*

- *Teacher enthusiasm has been studied for decades and supports the notion that teacher enthusiasm is directly linked to positive student outcomes (Patrick et al., 2000; Frenzel et al., 2009; Keller, 2015).*

- *Teacher enthusiasm must be genuine; however, aspects of the behavior can be taught to educators, and supported by administrators who foster positive school communities for their teachers.*

- *Enthusiastic teachers can positively influence classroom engagement, student interest, intrinsic motivation, and academic self-efficacy.*

- *Although there are many other components of effective teaching methods that affect student academic and behavioral outcomes, teacher enthusiasm plays an important role in overall teacher effectiveness.*

References

Alsharif, N.Z. & Qi, Y. (2014). A Three-Year Study of the Impact of Instructor Attitude, Enthusiasm, and Teaching Style on Student Learning in a Medicinal Chemistry Course. *American Journal of Pharmaceutical Education*: Volume 78, Issue 7, Article 132. DOI:10.5688/ajpe787132.

Bettencourt, E. M., Gillett, M. H., Gall, M. D., & Hull, R.E. (1983). Effects of teacher enthusiasm training on student on-task behavior and achievement. *American Educational Research Journal*, 20(3), 435-450. DOI: 10.3102/00028312020003435

Collins, M. L. (1976). *The effects of training for enthusiasm on the enthusiasm displayed by preservice elementary teachers.* DOI: 10.1177/002248718702900120

Cui, G., Yao, M., & Zhang, X. (2017). The Dampening Effects of Perceived Teacher Enthusiasm on Class-Related Boredom: The Mediating Role of Perceived Autonomy Support and Task Value. *Frontiers in Psychology*, v. 8 400. DOI: 10.3389/fpsyg.2017.00400

Daschmann, E. C., Goetz, T., and Stupnisky, R. H. (2014). Exploring the antecedents of boredom: do teachers know why students are bored? Teach. Teach. Educ. 39, 22–30.

Finch, V.A. (2013). *Further fostering intrinsic motivation in the Montessori elementary classroom.* Retrieved from https://eric.ed.gov/?id=ED540068

Frenzel, A. C., Goetz, T., Lüdtke, O., Pekrun, R., & Sutton, R. E. (2009). Emotional transmission in the classroom: exploring the relationship between teacher and student enjoyment. *Journal of Educational Psychology.* 101, 705–716. DOI: 10.1037/a0014695

Fried, R.L. (2001). The Passionate Teacher: A Practical Guide. Boston: Beacon Press.

Harden, R. & Laidlaw, J. (2017). *Essential Skills for a Medical Teacher.* Laguna Hills, CA: Elsevier.

Hobbs, L. (2012). Examining the aesthetic dimensions of teaching: Relationships between teacher knowledge, identity, and passion. *Teaching and Teacher Education: An International Journal of Research and Studies, 28*(5), 718-727. DOI:10.1016/j.tate.2012.01.010.

Hohnbaum, B. (2012). *Intrinsic and extrinsic motivation of teachers.* Retrieved from https://www.slideshare.net/breeellen22/intrinsic-and-extrinsic-motivation-of-teachers

Keller, M. M., Goetz, T., Becker, E. S., Morger, V., & Hensley, L. (2014). Feeling and showing: a new conceptualization of dispositional teacher enthusiasm and its relation to students' interest. *Learning and Instruction.* doi: 10.1016/j.learninstruc.2014.03.001

Keller, M. M., Hoy, A. W., Goetz, T., & Frenzel, A. C. (2015). Teacher enthusiasm: reviewing and redefining a complex construct. *Educational Psychology Review.* 28, 743–769. DOI: 10.1007/s10648-015-9354-y

Keller, M. M., Neumann, K., & Fischer, H. E. (2013). Teacher enthusiasm and student achievement. In J. Hattie & E.M. Andermann, *International Guide to Student Achievement* (p. 247-249). New York, NY: Routledge

Kunter, M., Frenzel, A. C., Nagy, G., Baumert, J., & Pekrun, R. (2011). Teacher enthusiasm: dimensionality and context specificity. *Contemporary Educational Psychology.* 36, 289 301. doi: 10.1016/j.cedpsych.2011.07.001

Kunter, M., Klusmann, U., Baumert, J., Richter, D., Voss, T., & Hachfeld, A. (2013).
Professional competence of teachers: effects on instructional quality and student development. J. *Educational Psychology.* 105, 805–820. doi: 10.1037/a00 32583

Mitchell, M. (2013). Teacher Enthusiasm: Seeking Student Learning and Avoiding Apathy. *Journal of Physical Education, Recreation, and Dance.* DOI: 10.1080/0733084.2013.779536

Orosz, G., Tóth-Király, I., Bőthe, B., Kusztor, A., Kovács, Z. Ü., & Jánvári, M. (2015). Teacher enthusiasm: a potential cure of academic cheating. *Frontiers in Psychology,* 6, 318. http://doi.org/10.3389/fpsyg.2015.00318

Patrick, B. C., Hisley, J., and Kempler, T. (2000). *"What's everybody so excited about?": the effects of teacher enthusiasm on student intrinsic motivation and vitality.* doi: 10.1080/00220970009600093

Rosenshine, B. (1970). Enthusiastic teaching: a research review. doi: 10.1086/442929

Zhang, Q. (2014). Assessing the Effects of Instructor Enthusiasm on Classroom Engagement, Learning Goal Orientation, and Academic Self-Efficacy. *Communication Teacher.* Volume 28: p. 44-56. Retrieved from https://eric.ed.gov/?id=EJ1026830

Chapter 4

Response to Intervention:
A Tool to Increase Student Comprehension

Nicholas D. Young, PhD, EdD,
American International College
and
E. Marie McPadden, EdD,
Quinnipiac University

Effective scientific research-based intervention has long been a subject of professional learning targets to improve instruction (Allington, 2012). Classroom teachers are responsible for providing effective instruction, including differentiated interventions to all students in need. Researchers have long studied what instructional methods work as best practices in the classroom (Allington, 2012). Teacher effectiveness aligns with using best instructional practices for students who need intervention and through a comprehensive understanding of proven instructional strategies "teachers are better able to put them to use. Effective teaching requires understanding not only what to do but also how to do it" (Goodwin, 2011, p. 26). What teachers do when the classroom door closes matters and, as such, strategy selection should be deliberate and purposeful. Marzano, Pickering, & Pollock (2001) refer to nine effective strategies that can be used as tools with the understanding that "they should not be expected to work in all situations" (p. 8).

Research studies have cited a variety of factors that contribute to school improvement and student achievement (Stronge & Hindman, 2003; Leithwood, Anderson, & Wahlstrom, 2004). School improvement is very much a matter of teacher excellence, and understanding scientific-based interventions is a large part of that (Stronge & Hindman, 2003). Stronge and Hindman (2003) cite studies that quantify why teacher quality has a lasting effect on student learning, especially negative effects when students have an ineffective teacher. Although the word 'effective' has been defined by Merriam-Webster Dictionary (2018) as "producing a decided, decisive, or desired effect" (n.p.); those who describe elite educators often use "words such as caring, competent, humorous, knowledgeable, demanding, and fair" (Stronge & Hindman, 2003, p. 50).

As interesting as it is that effective teachers are the most important factor contributing to student achievement, the "principal is second only to the teacher in terms of impact on student learning" (Leithwood et al., 2004, p. 5). The daily role of the principal has changed to include many more teacher observations with the role of an instructional leader taking front stage. New teacher evaluation plans are largely responsible for this shift (Leithwood et al., 2004).

Since high stakes testing has become a national obsession of research and discussion, it is important to revisit the instructional strategies that are effective in the classroom (Long, 2014). In addition to the nine strategies, effective facilitation of other strategies such as summarizing, use of nonlinguistic visuals, classifying, similarities and differences, feedback, homework and practice, feedback, and generating and testing hypothesis (Marzano et al., 2001, p. 146).

Response to Intervention (RTI) is used in public school districts nationwide and is mandated by the federal government as a way to decrease the need for more extensive special education services (National Center for Learning Disabilities, n.d.). RTI is a three-tiered model where Tier I focuses on effective classroom instruction and interventions as well as behavioral strategies and interventions (National Center for Learning Disabilities, n.d.). RTI has been the standard for "identifying and assisting struggling students" (Terrill, 2017, p. 41) for more than a decade. The other tiers address more intensive issues, and after tier III, students are typically referred for a battery of tests to see if they qualify for special education services (Terrill, 2017).

Assessing Tier I Students

Tier I has been described as "a universal level of instruction that emphasizes the use of high quality, research-based core curriculum and teaching methods that have been shown to promote learning and limit learning difficulties" (Whitten, Esteves, & Woodrow, 2009, p. 14). Tier I should include eight factors for all students:

- Research-based curricula;
- Research-based instructional methods;
- Assessment of student learning strengths, interests, and academic performance;
- Teaching strategies targeted toward individual academic needs, interests, and strengths;
- Differentiated instruction within the classroom;

- Flexible groupings;

- Screening of student achievement; and

- Ongoing professional development.

  (Whitten et al., 2009, p. 14)

A clearly articulated schoolwide RTI plan can usually be found at the elementary level, less so at the middle grades level, and is sometimes nonexistent at the secondary level (Buffum, Mattos, & Malone, 2018). Creating a plan that not only identifies instructional and or behavioral practices at each tier but also tracks progress using today's technology, is relatively easy and there are several types of assessments that a classroom teacher can use to track and monitor student progress over time (Buffum et al., 2018). Examples of progress monitoring tools include:

- AIMSweb: A Web-based formative assessment system (Pearson, 2014);

- Accelerated Reading and Math: a computerized program that also generates individualized quizzes and provides immediate feedback (Rosen, 2018);

- Developmental Reading Assessment: a set of criterion-referenced reading (McCarthy & Christ, 2010);

- Reading A-Z Assessments: a website that contains various forms of progress monitoring tools such as running records, quick comprehension checks, and rubrics (LAZEL, 2018).

The classroom teacher will conduct baseline data assessment and ongoing data collection that shows student struggles and successes in the academic arena. It is through this six to eight-week cycle of monitoring that student reading progress, or lack of, that the journey of RTI begins (Buffum et al., 2018). In an RTI model, students are not expected to stay in intervention forever.

RTI is a combination of early intervention, assessment, and ongoing progress monitoring to inform instruction, and personalized learning based on student need (Buffum, 2018; National Center for Learning Disabilities, n.d.). Each of the aforementioned services can be instrumental in allowing students to succeed early on thereby reducing the chance of being labeled for special services before given ample opportunity to succeed in the regular classroom. Whitten et al. (2009), confirm this concept by indicating that "RTI can improve students' academic opportunities and help reduce costs associated with addressing learning disabilities" (p. 3). Once the student has been identified as struggling, it is the classroom teacher that must try scientific research-based strategies to combat the weak areas.

Although RTI emerged from special education legislation, the model is a general education initiative whereby the classroom teacher is the first line of defense in supporting student success (Buffum et al., 2018; National Center for Learning Disabilities, n.d.). With each new strategy tried over a period of six to eight weeks, progress monitoring with short formative or computer adaptive assessments defines if the instructional path has led to progress and release from support or if another instructional strategy needs to be facilitated (Buffum et al., 2018). As the classroom teacher exhausts the implementation of specific strategies to support the student in succeeding, the student may be recommended for Tier II interventions that will be facilitated by a tutor or reading specialist along with more time spent on direct reading instruction (National Center for Learning Disabilities, n.d.). That is not to say that the classroom teacher is no longer responsible for continuing to support the student, rather, the educator and the tutor/specialist work in tandem. Tier II does not replace Tier I instruction by the classroom teacher, it is in addition to the classroom strategies being used daily (Buffum, 2018). Everyone is responsible for effective instruction for all students.

Understanding the Three-Way Plan

In a study (Marzano et al., 2001) conducted to identify effective instructional strategies for classroom teachers, nine strategies were described as effective. Three of those strategies, when combined, become a powerful, yet simple, plan that educators can teach to students, that offers three distinct opportunities to comprehend more deeply. An additional focus includes the design of lessons using the same simple three-way plan and specifically integrates 21st-century skills. These skills are often referred to as a new set of literacies and are sometimes condensed into four categories; creativity and innovation, critical thinking and problem solving, communication, and collaboration (Beers, 2011, p. 4). While the goal is to create a toolbox of effective strategies and learning opportunities, "not every instructional plan has to include every skill" (Beers, 2011, p. 28).

Effective Instructional Strategies

Literacy is the basis for all learning, and all students can learn when exposed to a daily diet of high-quality instruction; thus, it is vital that reading and writing instruction be on target and include best practices. Without proper instruction, students suffer through an educational process that quickly becomes frustrating and unmotivating and, as such, several reading strategies rise to the top.

Close Reading and the Importance in Instructional Practice

As students move through the grades, the Common Core State Standards (CCSS) become increasingly more complex for reading both fiction and non-fiction texts (Common Core State Standards Initiative, 2018). The strategy of close reading creates a higher bar for students to synthesize, analyze, and evaluate reading content (Lehman & Roberts, 2014). Close reading requires rereading text more than once, in fact, it is recommended that a text be read at least three times, in order to build a deeper understanding for interpretation and comprehension (Burke, n.d.). Students don't generally like to reread, especially struggling readers, yet close reading is "something we should teach students to do, rather than something we just do to them" (Lehman & Roberts, 2014, p. 4).

Close reading allows the student three chances to comprehend the material and each time through the passage has a specific purpose. During the first reading, the reader looks for key ideas and details, while the second time through the passage the reader focuses on craft and structure (Burke, n.d.). The final reading provides the student an opportunity to integrate or synthesize knowledge and ideas from several texts (Burke, n.d.).

When the reading material becomes complex, rereading, readjusting reading rate, and focusing on the reading with deliberation are all necessary components to becoming a successful reader. Put nicely, "To read something closely is to get to know the text intimately, to hold it close, to cherish its details, to return for more. It is falling in love. It is a ritual for reading and living" (Lehman & Roberts, 2014, p. 125).

The Common Core State Standards require the reader to analyze and evaluate two or more primary sources in each content area, a task that becomes increasingly difficult for the struggling reader (Ciercierski, 2017). This is the primary reason why texts must be connected, and educators need to ensure they consider "discourse, linguistics and semiotics, a textual stance, and writing" (Ciercierski, 2017, p. 285) when looking for multiple texts selections.

When teachers connect texts to each other, students "can tailor their thinking in a manner that will aid in their success at deconstructing the texts for meaning" (Ciercierski, 2017, p. 289). Making sense of texts and the connection to self, world, and other texts will support students in deeper comprehension.

The Reciprocal Teaching Model

Regardless of being developed over 30 years ago, the Reciprocal Teaching Model (Palincsar & Brown, 1986) remains a popular reading model to facilitate comprehension. There are three types of readers: those who can decode and comprehend; those who can decode and don't comprehend; and, those who cannot decode and therefore, don't comprehend (Palincsar & Brown, 1986). The Reciprocal Teaching Model focuses on the use of four specific strategies: predicting, clarifying, student-generated questioning and summarizing (National Behavior Support Service, n.d.). Reciprocal teaching can be used during whole group instructional meetings, or in small group instruction, it becomes a Reciprocal Circle (Palincsar & Brown, 1986).

Planning is critical to the success of implementing this model. The teacher models and teaches each of the four strategies across a select piece of text and the instruction is carefully scaffolded to engage students in the process of comprehending text (Fountas & Pinnell, 2001). The teacher then helps the student practice independently, thus providing the reciprocal aspect – that of a shared process (Fountas & Pinnell, 2001). This technique has been effectively used with students who can decode, but do not comprehend while reading, as such, students begin to use their language as inquiry (Fountas & Pinnell, 2001).

A reciprocal circle or small guided reading group provides an optimal place for implementation; however, the strategies can be taught through teacher modeling for several whole group mini-lessons and later reinforced in the small groups that need to develop better comprehension skills. Once again, students are given several opportunities to improve their comprehension of text. The strategies can be taught as single strategies over the course of several lessons until students demonstrate their understanding of the strategy. Palincsar and Brown (1986) indicate that the "hallmark of this form of instruction is its interactive nature" (p. 773).

The teacher plays a critical role in supporting students to understand when to use each strategy as well as why to use that particular strategy (Palincsar & Brown, 1986). The four strategies each serve a very specific purpose for before, during, and after reading a section of text. Once the strategies are fully understood, the teacher models how students will eventually become the facilitator of the group. Reciprocal teaching is an excellent way to engage students in reading and thinking about a text in that it includes the skills of prediction, clarification, questioning, and summarizing; thus, the four strategies provide a way to connect the ideas together (Palincsar & Brown, 1986).

The power of prediction. Predicting is the first strategy taught in the Reciprocal Teaching Model and is typically done prior to reading a new section of text; however, it can also be ongoing during and after the reading (Palincsar & Brown, 1986). Predicting what the class may learn about is a typical use of prediction before reading. During reading, predicting based on what has been read will inform the teacher if the students are comprehending or not. It is important that the teacher values the predictions that students make; however, when a student predicts something absolutely off base, the teacher should ask, "Based on what we have just read, why do you think so?" The power of prediction can be used across all grades PK-12.

The prediction strategy can also support teaching text structure such as compare and contrast, time sequence, cause and effect as important features of nonfiction text (Palincsar & Brown, 1986). This becomes extremely critical during content area instruction for students who, once again, can decode but are not comprehending, especially in upper elementary grades and beyond.

Focus on clarifying. Clarifying is the second strategy in the Reciprocal Teaching Model and is an important self-monitoring strategy (Fountas & Pinnell, 2001). Good readers monitor their reading by recognizing when something doesn't make sense and taking some action to correct their confusion. They stop and think about what they are reading, and if something doesn't make sense, their impulse takes them back a sentence, paragraph, or page to understand and make sense of the reading (Fountas & Pinnell, 2001). Struggling readers do not usually monitor their reading behaviors; thus, teaching students to think about what they need to be clarified while they are reading is teaching them to self-monitor. Self-monitoring is a taught skill that often is unnoticed once students' progress to silent reading as opposed to oral reading. At this point, without formative assessment measures in place, it becomes difficult to know that the student is "reading", but not comprehending (Fountas & Pinnell, 2001).

This behavior is best described as the aforementioned type of reader, that is, one who can decode, but does not comprehend. Unfortunately, if undiagnosed the student will start to fail across all content areas; after all, reading is the basis of all content areas. According to Palincsar and Brown (1986):

> These students very likely believe that the purpose of reading is saying the words correctly; they may not be particularly uncomfortable with the fact that the words and, in fact, the passage are not making sense. When students are asked to clarify, their attention is called to the fact that there may be many reasons why text is difficult to understand (p. 772).

The classroom teacher may choose to model the reading and suggest that some of the reasons why the text is difficult to understand may include "unfamiliar vocabulary, unclear referent words, new and perhaps difficult concepts" (Palincsar & Brown, 1986, p.772).

The importance of questioning. Questioning is the third strategy taught in the Reciprocal Teaching Model. Here, it is important that the questioning be generated solely by the student (Palincsar & Brown, 1986) as teachers who constantly ask the question are not allowing for students to think independently. Comprehension is dependent on reading for meaning and understanding, yet, readers who can decode and not comprehend will not be reading for meaning and understanding. A student will be hard-pressed to develop a question about the reading if they are not comprehending the material. In order to engage students in the process of wonder and inquiry and produce critical thinkers, students must be allowed to ask questions that are important to them as then the educator will have a better understanding of student comprehension (Tovani, 2015). Once student questions are known, teachers can make instructional decisions that are in the best interest of the student.

Rothstein and Santana (2012) developed a Question Formulation Technique (QFT) that teachers can share with students to "produce their own questions, to improve their questions, and to prioritize their questions" (p. 15) as a way to promote divergent thinking, convergent thinking, and metacognition. Inferential and analytic questions modeled to students show the difference between literal questions, those with the answers directly in the text, and questions that inspire deeper critical thinking (Dean, Hubbell, Pitler, & Stone, 2012). Students can usually answer simple text-based questions, but inference and analytic questions require more higher-level thinking within and beyond the text, as such, when teachers not only ask questions but also had students generate their own questions, students became much more engaged in reading (Dean et al., 2012).

Beers and Probst (2016) incorporate three questions across all text reading: "What surprised you? What did the author think you already knew? What challenged, changed, or confirmed what you already knew?" (p. 108). In a different twist to student-generated questions, asking these three specific questions, students engage in self-reflection and deep thinking in order to answer the questions as a simple yes or no will not suffice.

Beyond memorization tactics, questioning is critical to making meaning for deeper understanding. Beers and Probst (2016) acknowledge that nonfiction is more demanding than fiction and as such students "must question the text, question the author, question their own understanding of the topic, and accept the possibility that our views will change as a result of the reading we're doing" (p. 19)." Clearly, deliberate questioning and student-generated questioning support a deeper understanding of the text.

Summarizing: The most difficult strategy of all. The fourth strategy in the Reciprocal Teaching Model is summarizing, which is "an excellent tool for integrating the information presented in the text" (Palincsar & Brown, 1986, p. 772). Summarizing is typically facilitated after reading a paragraph, a page, several pages, or a chapter. Students often have a difficult time summarizing;

thus, students often work together to identify the main points of the text reading (Palincsar & Brown, 1986). Young students may confuse summarizing with the retelling. While summarizing is an overview, retelling recalls every single detail of a story or nonfiction passage.

Marzano et al. (2001) grouped summarizing and note-taking as one of nine research-based strategies for improving student achievement. One well used summarizing strategy is referred to as "a rule-based summary strategy" (Marzano et al., 2001, p. 34). Following this rule-based summary strategy, an easy way to teach summarizing vs. retelling is to have students read a section of text. There are two columns on the board or on chart paper: retell and summary. First, students identify all the details sequentially from the reading. Second, the educator crosses out any details that are trivial, redundant and or repetitive. Some substitutions of subordinate terms may be made according to the rules (Marzano et al., 2001). Lastly, take the statements that are left and bullet them under the heading summary. The organized chart will create a visual for the students to understand better that summarizing requires less, not more.

Graphic Organizers Create a Visual to Support Comprehension

A student-centered contemporary classroom that facilitates a workshop literacy model serves as a strong basis for developing self-monitoring, self-regulated, and self-directed learners in all subject areas. One strategy that Marzano (2007) found particularly effective was comparing and contrasting across a variety of texts; as such, graphic organizers help students provide a visual representation of what they read. The most common compare and contrast graphic organizer is a Venn Diagram (McKnight, 2018). Creating a Venn Diagram after reading a section or chapter of the text supports deeper comprehension and a second chance for reflection. Students are able to see the similarities and differences of specific topics or ideas related to the text reading. Marzano (2001) refers to using nonlinguistic representations a "powerful aspect of learning – generating mental pictures to go along with information, as well as creating graphic representations for that information" (p. 72). Equally important, there are at least six specific graphic organizers that can be used based on how text information is organized (Marzano et al., 2001, p. 75). Text organization is something that struggling readers grapple with to understand. By facilitating the use of specific graphic organizers that match the patterns of organization for the text, that is, descriptive, time sequence, process/cause-effect, problem/solution, episode patterns, and concept patterns, students have the opportunity to understand better, and learn the importance of, identifying text organization (Marzano, 2001, p. 75).

Information is "stored in memory in two ways: as words (linguistic) and as images (nonlinguistic)" (Dean et al., p. 63). Students are "better able to process, organize and retrieve information from memory [when they use these strategies to] produce a nonlinguistic representation of knowledge" (Dean et al., 2012, p. 64). The reason this strategy works is that students are able to create a video or picture in their head that represents the "knowledge at a deeper level and recall it more easily" (p. 66). Examples of nonlinguistic representations of various graphic organizers, including but not limited to, semantic feature analysis maps, compare and contrast charts, and cause and effect diagrams along with student-created models of construction, pictures, illustrations, and pictographs are meaningful to deepening comprehension (Dean et al., 2012).

Extended Writing to Boost Understanding

Just as students become better readers by reading, students become better writers by writing. Reading followed by independent reflective writing supports student engagement and comprehension. When meaningful writing extension follows the reading, it allows yet another opportunity for the students to comprehend the text better. By engaging in extended writing based on text reading and followed by shared discussion, students will have three opportunities for deeper comprehension. Unfortunately, the writing typically follows the reading discussion, which negates finding out what each student actually knew and understood versus what the whole group understood (Lemov, 2017).

As an alternative to the reading, extended writing, and discussion sequence, teachers may opt to begin with a writing extension. Lemov (2017) suggests that teachers "identify specific teaching methods to help students build their background knowledge and to access knowledge-building nonfiction texts" (p. 16). One particular writing strategy, a Quick Write, is easy to facilitate and is competed at the beginning of a lesson as a way for students to "activate and summarize their knowledge and anticipate what they will read about" (Fountas & Pinnell, 2001, p. 453). Using a variety of strategies and active engagement in all areas, students will develop better listening, speaking, reading and writing skills.

Putting Together the Three-Way Plan to Deepen Comprehension

The discussion of effective teaching strategies now needs to shift to how to integrate the strategies in a three-way plan that works to broaden comprehension for all students. Each step brings together the aforementioned strategies and best practices in a comprehensive action plan that teachers can use as well as teach to students in order to produce positive outcomes.

Step 1: Teach the Reciprocal Strategies Before, During, and After Reading

The teacher begins by selecting a one to two-page nonfiction passage to model the Reciprocal Teaching Strategies throughout the text. Modeling the four specific Reciprocal Strategies using an interactive think aloud is critical to building student understanding of how the process works (Oczkus, 2010; Oczkus, 2009). It is important to stop and pause throughout the reading to demonstrate how the student will predict, clarify, question, and summarize the text. After modeling with a variety of text sections, articles, or picture books, the teacher reviews the strategies once more and has the students bring their thinking alive to explain how they will incorporate the strategies in their reading (Oczkus, 2009).

Once the students are confident in using the four strategies, the teacher will begin to facilitate the Reciprocal Teaching Model in small reciprocal circles, similar to a guided reading group (Oczkus, 2010). The difference here is that the students share responsibility for the use of all four strategies. Eventually, one of the students will take over the group facilitation. Prior to all lessons, including student-led lessons, a review of the four strategies must occur. Teachers may have anchor charts posted around the room for students to use as a reference, such as question stems ranging from the most literal to evaluative samples, or a summary chart detailing the rules of summarizing (Brown et al., 1981). This particular anchor chart would support students in understanding how to condense their knowledge into a three to five sentence summary. Bookmarks with the strategies printed on different colored laminated cards are another way to make available for students. The small group reciprocal circles can work collaboratively posing individual questions about the text, and then collectively deciding which question is best to answer as a small group. There are many different ways to facilitate deeper learning within the model itself (Oczkus, 2010).

Learning how to facilitate and integrate the strategies using multiple texts will take several modeled lessons by the teacher, and once mastery has been made, students will take turns modeling the lesson (Oczkus, 2010; Oczkus, 2009). Modeling can also be done in a chunked fashion. The teacher may opt to have a student lead any one of the strategies before, during, and after the reading; although it may be time-consuming, it is time well spent. In order to implement the strategies correctly, they must be modeled daily and integrated across content areas such as science and social studies.

Step 2: Facilitate Use of Graphic Organizers

Once the strategies have been taught and facilitated in an ongoing manner, the next step is to take the text reading and create an appropriate graphic organizer (McKnight, 2018). The graphic organizer may be selected based on the text structure of the reading; for example, if the class or small group was reading about various features of animals, a semantic feature analysis chart could be created. This particular graphic organizer is created to engage students in using what they know about key vocabulary words and new concepts (McKnight, 2018). The teacher, using large chart paper, whiteboard, or interactive board, will model why a certain graphic organizer has been selected to create a visual for the group. Student participation is highly encouraged to keep their engagement at a high level. The graphic organizer is instrumental in preparing students to write a clearly designed summary (McKnight, 2018). The teacher will release gradual responsibility to the students to create their own graphic organizers once the model is implemented in full.

Step 3: Writing the Summary Using the Graphic Organizer

The last step in this three-way plan to improve comprehension is writing the summary by actively using the information plotted on the graphic organizer (McKnight, 2018). The teacher first models how to best summarize and articulate - in writing - the patterns that are shown as a result of developing the graphic organizer. A simple five to six sentence paragraph is developed by analyzing and synthesizing the information on the graphic organizer (McKnight, 2018). This can be a difficult task for students and may need extended modeling and additional collaborative summary writing exercises for some individuals. It may be easier to start small; therefore, a time sequence organizer may be taught first with an article or text section that best represents a timeline (McKnight, 2018). Eventually, when students work on the organizer independently or in a small group, the collaborative nature of sharing why they decided on a certain organizer becomes a formative assessment in itself.

Teachers who follow this three-step plan of integrating specific strategic methods including the Reciprocal Teaching Model, the use of graphic organizers, and summary writing across a section text, will find that their students will become deeper thinkers whose comprehension skills increase and their abilities and confidence soar.

Final Thoughts

Response to Intervention is the first line of defense in providing struggling students with personalized learning that leads to an improvement (National Center for Learning Disabilities, n.d.). This three-tier intervention system begins with the classroom teacher who is tasked with providing differentiated instruction that is data-driven, student-specific, and monitored for progress (National Center for Learning Disabilities, n.d.). Educators who know the many strategies for students to use, can mix and match them in order to find the proper combination that leads to positive student outcomes.

The three-way plan works well for all students, but especially for those students who are struggling with comprehension. Although there are myriad reasons why a student may have gaps including, but not limited to, problems with decoding and or comprehension or a combination of both, incomplete instruction in the process of learning to read may escalate to the point of paralysis in learning and ineffective instruction. The use of data is especially important so that progress, or lack thereof, can be tracked and decisions made to help the student best.

Graphic organizers create visual supports for students who learn visually as well as those who benefit from active participation in the learning process (McKnight, 2018). Students who plan out their work in advance with a graphic organizer, benefit from a second dose of comprehension. Instead of merely reading a passage, article, or chapter, the student has an opportunity to demonstrate further understanding by plotting information in a systematic manner as a visual picture, chart, or model (McKnight, 2018).

When teachers follow the reading and the creation of the graphic organizers with meaningful writing extensions, such as summary writing, students have yet a third dose of comprehension work to benefit from. Often, students may read something once and be expected to understand the content. One reading, and a "cold reading" at best does not allow for deeper comprehension nor does it promote deeper understanding and learning. Teachers must be cognizant to offer multiple opportunities to develop deeper comprehension and critical thinkers. Using the close reading technique provides just such a model for students and educators need to ensure this happens at all times.

Points Remember

- *Response to Intervention (RTI) is mandated by the federal government and is a three-tier model for helping struggling students; however, it begins with tier I, which are essentially good teaching practices, in-class interventions, differentiated instruction, and specific strategies. Students are monitored for progress and reviewed every 6-8 weeks to decide if the intervention is working or if something else should be tried.*

- *Modeling the four Reciprocal Teaching strategies using an interactive think-aloud provides a visual and auditory simulation of the critical thinking activities students need to engage in once they understand the task to be completed.*

- *Graphic Organizers help students who struggle with putting thoughts together. A plethora of organizers exists dependent on the task at hand, the more commonly used include, timelines, webs, and Venn diagrams.*

- *Summary writing extensions give students a third chance to analyze and synthesize the information they read and transferred to the graphic organizer.*

- *The three-way plan deepens reading comprehension through the use of reciprocal teaching, graphic organizers, and summary writing extensions. In totality, this plan engages students in active reading, thinking, and writing – the necessary ingredients to becoming a successful student.*

References

Allington, R.L. (2012). *What really matters for struggling readers: Designing Research-Based Programs* (3rd ed.). Boston, MA: Pearson Education, Inc.

Beers, S. Z. (2011). *Teaching 21st century skills: An ASCD action tool.* Alexandria, VA:ASCD

Beers, K. & Probst. (2016). *Reading nonfiction: Notice and note: Stances, signposts, and strategies.* Portsmouth, NH: Heinemann.

Buffum, A., Mattos, M., & Malone, J. (2018). *Taking action: A handbook for RTI at work.* Bloomington, IN: Solution Tree.

Burke, B. (n.d.). *A close look at close reading: Scaffolding students with complex texts.* Retrieved from
https://nieonline.com/tbtimes/downloads/CCSS_reading.pdf

Ciercierski, L. M. (2017). What common core state standards do not tell you about connecting texts. *The Reading Teacher, 71*(3), pp. 285-293. DOI: 10.1002/trtr.1616/pdf

Common Core State Standards Initiative. (2018). *English language arts standards: Standard 10: Range, quality & complexity: Measuring text complexity: three factors.* Retrieved from
http://www.corestandards.org/ELA-Literacy/standard-10-range-quality-complexity/measuring-text-complexity-three-factors/

Dean, Hubbell, Pitler, & Stone. (2012). *Classroom instruction that works* (2nd ed.) Alexandra, VA: ASCD.

Fountas, I. & Pinnell, G. S. (2001). *Guiding readers and writers: Teaching comprehension genre, and content literacy.* Portsmouth, NH: Heinemann.

Goodwin, B. (2011). *Simply better: Doing what matters most to change the odds for student success.* Alexandria, VA: ASCD.

LAZEL. (2018). *About Reading A-Z.* Retrieved from
https://www.readinga-z.com/about-readinga-z/

Lehman, C. & Roberts, K. (2014). *Falling in love with close reading: Lessons for Analyzing texts – and life.* Portsmouth, NH: Heinemann.

Leithwood, K., Louis, K.S., Anderson, S., & Wahlstrom. K. (2004). How leadership influences student learning. *The Wallace Foundation.* Retrieved from http://www.wallacefoundation.org/knowledge-center/Documents/How-Leadership-Influences-Student-Learning.pdf

Lemov, D. (2017). How knowledge powers reading. *Educational Leadership,* 74(5). Retrieved from http://www.ascd.org/publications/educational-leadership/feb17/vol74/num05/How-Knowledge-Powers-Reading.aspx

Long, C. (2014). *The high-stakes testing culture: How we got here, how we get out.* Retrieved from http://neatoday.org/2014/06/17/the-high-stakes-testing-culture-how-we-got-here-how-we-get-out/

Marzano, R. J., Pickering, D. J., & Pollock, J. E. (2001). Classroom instruction that works: Research-based strategies for increasing student achievement. Alexandria, VA: Association for Supervision and Curriculum Development.

McCarthy, A.M. & Christ, T.J. (2010). *Test Review.* DOI: 10.1177/1534508410363127

McKnight, K. (2018). *Use graphic organizers for effective learning.* Retrieved from http://www.teachhub.com/teaching-graphic-organizers

Merriam-Webster. (2018). *Effective.* Retrieved from https://www.merriam-webster.com/dictionary/effective

National Behavior Support Service. (n.d.). *Reciprocal teaching: Reading and learning strategy.* Retrieved from https://www.nbss.ie/sites/default/files/publications/reiciprocal_teaching_strategy_handout__copy_2_0.pdf

National Center for Learning Disabilities. (n.d.) *What is RTI?* Retrieved from http://www.rtinetwork.org/learn/what/whatisrti

Oczkus, L.D. (2009). *Interactive think-aloud lessons: 25 surefire ways to engage students and improve comprehension.* New York, NY: Scholastic.

Oczkus, L.D. (2010). *Reciprocal Teaching at work: Powerful strategies* (2nd ed). Newark, DE: International Reading Association.

Palincsar, A. & Brown, A. (1986). Interactive Teaching to Promote Independent Learning from Text. *The Reading Teacher,* 39(8), 771-777. DOI: 10.1177/074193258800900110

Pearson. (2014). *Say hello to aimsweb.* Retrieved from https://www.aimsweb.com/about

Rosen, P. (2018). *Accelerated reader: What you need to know.* Retrieved from https://www.understood.org/en/school-learning/partnering-with-childs-school/tests-standards/accelerated-reader-what-you-need-to-know

Rothstein, D. & Santana, L. (2012). *Make just one change: Teach students to ask their own questions.* Cambridge, Massachusetts: Harvard Education Press.

Stronge, J.H. & Hindman, J.L. (2003). Hiring the best teachers. *Educational Leadership,* 60(8), 48-52. Retrieved from http://www.ascd.org/publications/educational-leadership/may03/vol60/num08/Hiring-the-Best-Teachers.aspx

Terrill, J. (2017). Intervention strategies evolve: New approaches address social-emotional learning and anxiety as well as academic instruction. *District
Administration.* Retrieved from
https://www.districtadministration.com/article/intervention-strategies-
evolve-K12

Tovani, C., (2015). Let's switch questioning around. Educational Leadership,
73(1), 30-35. Retrieved from
http://www.ascd.org/publications/educational-
leadership/sept15/vol73/num01/Let's-Switch-Questioning-Around.aspx

Whitten, E., Esteves, K. J., & Woodrow, A. (2009). *RTI success: Proven tools and
strategies for schools and classrooms.* Minneapolis, MN: Free Spirit Publishing Inc.

Chapter 5

Classroom Management: Strategies for All Teachers

Angela C. Fain, PhD,
University of West Georgia
and
Ellen L. Duchaine, PhD,
Texas State University

Educators are tasked with teaching a diverse group of students, providing a safe and structured learning environment, and ensuring academic success. When teachers build a safe and engaging classroom, they provide students with structured learning that encourages cooperative learning and fosters critical thinking (Garwood, Harris, & Tomick, 2017). Thoughtful planning allows all children to feel that their needs are being met in the classroom. Effective classroom management includes designing and preparing the initial classroom for instruction, planning for effective instruction by establishing clear learning goals, developing expectations, procedures, and classroom rules, and creating a classroom environment that is student friendly and promotes tolerance and acceptance (Garwood et al., 2017).

Today's classrooms look very different than they did a decade ago. Classrooms are more culturally diverse than ever (Lynch, 2014). Students with disabilities are being served in the general education classroom more often with their non-disabled peers (ASCD, 2001). Teachers face the challenge of providing instruction for students who span a wide range of learning abilities, needs, and interests.

Classroom Management

Management is one of the most important jobs, yet one of the biggest concerns, of the classroom teacher (Demirdag, 2015; O'Niell & Stephenson, 2012). Once a classroom management system is established, teachers must be consistent and implement it as planned (De Fazio, Fain, & Duchaine, 2011). General education teachers have greater responsibility to implement evidence-based behavioral interventions to ensure students' academic successes

(Chaffee, Briesch, Johnson, & Volpe, 2017). As teachers are required to achieve desired learning outcomes, meet district, state, and national standards, and manage a variety of student behaviors, effective classroom management is essential to the successful facilitation of teaching and learning (Lester, Allanson, & Notar, 2017). In fact, researchers have consistently shown that classroom management directly affects student achievement (Wang, Haertel, & Walberg, 1997; Korpershoek, Harms, de Boer, van Kuijk, & Doolaard, 2016).

Effective classroom management will increase the likelihood that students will be engaged in class activities, exhibit desirable behavior, and have positive academic outcomes (Reinke, Herman, & Stormont, 2013). This is a very important concept that cannot be stressed enough. When students are engaged in learning and attending to academic tasks, they cannot be engaged in off-task behaviors that are disruptive; therefore, they are more likely to have successful academic outcomes (Sutherland, Alder, & Gunter, 2003).

Excessive referrals for special education are exacerbated when teachers are unable to effectively manage the disruptive behaviors of students at risk and/or those of low socioeconomic status (Donovan & Cross, 2002; Harrell, Leavell, van Tassel, & McKee, 2004). In addition, students viewed as causing problems in the classrooms are often removed from the class for periods of time, negatively reinforcing the behavior of the student and the teacher. Removal from class not only negatively reinforces poor behavior; it continues to perpetuate low academic achievement performance (Maag, 2018; Oliver, Wehby, & Reschly, 2011).

Develop a Teaching Philosophy

It is helpful to develop a personal teaching philosophy, to identify an individual's beliefs, goals, and desires for the classroom. The statement should be written as the foundation of commitment to teaching and classroom management. A sample statement of teacher philosophy might include Benjamin Franklin's famous quote "Tell me and I forget. Teach me and I remember. Involve me and I learn."

It is within a collaborative environment where communication provides the fundamental basis for educational growth. Student-centered approaches to teaching that emphasize active participation from both students and teachers help to engage the students more in their own process of learning, provide opportunities for students to develop concepts of understanding, allow students to construct personal learning styles, and focus on applying the knowledge to real-life situations. Franklin's quote epitomizes the meaning of having a true understanding of a concept and it should be the goal of each teacher to provide that kind of meaningful experience in every lesson taught.

Ultimately, teachers should inspire, engage, and enlighten students when they attend and participate in class. They should leave feeling personally challenged by the content and the conversations that arise, inspired to be more passionate about the subject matter than they were before they entered the classroom. Educators should engage students through oral, written and group participation activities throughout the class to keep their minds active, alert and attentive.

Plan for Success

First and foremost, teachers must plan for and provide instruction that is engaging for all students. When students are engaged and actively learning, they are not engaged in disruptive behavior (Sutherland & Oswald, 2005). Plan academic instruction with high levels of student engagement, make efficient use of time, and have a well-paced class, and actively supervise learning activities (Haydon & Kroeger, 2016). Have high expectations for all students to help build self-esteem and encourage success (Marzano, 2010). Students are more likely to work harder when they know their teacher believes in them and has confidence that they can meet their expectations. Check in with students at the start of every class; ask questions, show photos, play video clips, provide a brainteaser, or anything else that will encourage students to want to learn more. Using these 'hooks' engages students and builds curiosity about a topic or lesson. Provide students with a variety of models, samples, hints, and examples/non-examples whenever possible (Haydon & Kroeger, 2016). Give explicit and clear written and verbal directions to help students stay on task and frequently check for understanding. Educators should set goals with their students and teach them a variety of ways to self-monitor in order to keep track of their completed tasks and evaluate their own success.

Structure the Classroom

Structure is the physical environment of the classroom. First, the classroom needs to be decontaminated by ensuring that wires and sharp objects are removed and out of the way. After making sure the room is safe, develop a seating arrangement to maximize learning (Garwood et al., 2017). When arranging the seats, teachers should make certain students will not be sitting with their backs to the teacher or the board. Student seating should be arranged for flexibility and ease of forming pairs and small groups for cooperative learning groups. There should be enough space around seats to provide easy access to all students, ensuring teacher proximity (Garwood et al., 2017). Then, consider high traffic areas such as trash cans, pencil sharpeners, teacher's desk, and doors. Minimize congestion in these areas. Finally, designate where items such as backpacks and personal items, textbooks, lesson materials, homework, and computers will be located.

To help prevent problem situations from occurring and to increase the time for academic instruction, it is essential to know and understand who your students will be. Review accompanying student records such as Response to Intervention (RTI) data, Academic Improvement Plans (AIPs), 504 Plans, Individualized Education Plans (IEPs), and Behavioral Intervention Plans (BIPs) for important information. These documents contain a variety of information including student strengths and needs, assessment scores, accommodations, behavioral and academic goals, and strategies shown to be effective for the individual. This information can help guide in planning seating charts as students with disabilities often need a wide range of accommodations to help them be successful in the general education classroom Garwood et al., 2017). Some of these accommodations can be met through seat placement. For example, a student with attention deficit hyperactivity disorder (ADHD) might be more successful seated in the back of the classroom so they can stand up as needed without disrupting others. A student with a learning disability (LD) may benefit being seated in the front of the classroom, close to the teacher's desk or next to a specific peer to access support easily. Placing students strategically in the classroom will minimize problems and increase academic learning.

Establish Procedures & Rules

Establish procedures. Procedures communicate expectations for behavior that apply to a specific activity or task (Lester et al., 2017). Establishing procedures that facilitate learning and help ensure the classroom will run smoothly should include student procedures such as how students will enter the classroom, form cooperative learning groups, distribute papers, turn in assignments, go to the bathroom, participate in discussions, and dismiss class. Collecting assignments, sharpening your pencil, and fire drills are other policies to consider. The following are some examples of common classroom procedures:

- Entering the room. Enter quietly and politely; begin working on the opening assignment on the board.

- Distributing papers. If you are at the beginning of a row, pass the assignments back to the person behind you.

- Turning in assignments. Put your name on your paper; place your paper in the "assignments" basket for your class period.

- Going to bathroom. Politely raise your hand and let me know you need to use the restroom; take a hall pass and sign out as you leave the classroom; return to class promptly; sign back in.

- Participating in group discussions. Listen carefully for new information; be patient and raise your hand to speak; respect others when they are speaking.

As students often forget, these procedures need to be taught, reviewed, and reinforced daily using teacher designed assignments that are specific to the task (Lodato, 2016).

Establish rules

In addition to procedures, it is essential that teachers establish three to five classroom rules to help communicate expectations for appropriate behaviors that are clearly displayed in the classroom (Myers, Freeman, Simonsen, & Sugai, 2017). Classroom rules should be positively stated and easy to remember. Good rules are fair, enforceable, age-appropriate, reasonable, and applied equally (Kronowitz, 2012). Students should understand the rules, be able to monitor their own behavior, and if they break a rule, they should be able to identify which rule they have broken. The following are examples of some classroom rules:

- Treat others the way you want to be treated.

- Be on time and prepared for class.

- Use inside voices inside the classroom.

- Raise your hand and wait to be called upon before speaking during class.

It is important to have a rationale for classroom rules as well. When a teacher has a rationale for a rule and believes in it, it will come across to the students and have a more positive impact. Rules are the basis for the climate of the classroom (Emmer & Evertson, 2017). The following is an example of the rationale that dovetails with the aforementioned rules:

- Treat others the way you would want to be treated: It is important for students to have empathy for one another and to learn how they want to be treated, in turn, learning how to treat others. This rule will help build respect in the classroom and facilitate classroom discussions that will help build character.

- Be on time and prepared for class: When students show up prepared for class and on time, it increases the amount of academic learning time. It also helps to instill a sense of respect for everyone in the class and the importance of being timely.

- Use inside voices inside the classroom: It is important for students to learn how to control the volume of their voice, especially when they are excited, frustrated, or upset. Students will learn how to communicate their feelings at an appropriate volume effectively.

- Raise your hand and wait to be called upon before speaking during class. To demonstrate respect to all, to learn from others, and give everyone an opportunity to respond and share when having discussions in class, students should raise their hands and wait for recognition to speak. Students need to be patient when raising their hands and respectfully wait until they are called on.

Once procedures and rules have been established, students need to be explicitly taught how to respond academically and behaviorally. Students need to be given frequent opportunities to practice the routines until they are established routines (Myers et al., 2017). They should be introduced to the procedures, routines, and rules on the first day of school, from the moment they walk into the classroom (Watson & DiCarlo, 2015). Putting procedures into place at the beginning of the year will help to maximize instructional time and maintain a well-paced class. It is important to allow enough time for students to practice and learn the procedures frequently and to check for understanding of the routines (Kronowitz, 2012). Throughout the year, procedures may need to be adjusted or changed, then retaught. Noting when a plan is not working is part of effective teaching.

Monitor Behavior

Teachers should consider the types of effective behavior supports they will be implementing in their classroom to encourage students to remain on task, achieve academic gains, and display desired classroom behaviors. Class-wide interventions (games that focus on good behavior, interdependent contingencies, token economies, peer tutoring) that are behaviorally oriented have been found to lead to improved outcomes for all students when implemented in the general education classroom (Chaffe et al., 2017; Mitchell et al., 2015). Disruptive behaviors such as being off task, talking out, and being out of seat can result in reduced instructional time, so it is important for teachers to be proactive and address these behaviors when they first occur (Emmer & Evertson, 2017).

Provide behavior specific praise statements to let students know exactly what they are doing correctly. Recognizing effort helps students develop self-efficacy by connecting effort and achievement. Educators should find ways to highlight the successes of all students in the class and communicate acceptance of imperfect initial performance when students struggle to master new content (Emmer & Evertson, 2017).

Preventing disruptive behaviors. Anticipating student behaviors that have the potential to disrupt the classroom and academic instructional time is just as important as recognizing good behaviors. Plan thoughtfully and carefully to keep students engaged and avoid downtime during class. Demonstrate to students a general awareness of classroom activities and make prompt decisions to identify and correct disruptive behaviors (Emmer & Evertson, 2017). Maintain active participation of all students by keeping the attention of the whole group while individuals are responding. Encouraging accountability and engaging all students in activities when they are not directly attending to the teacher will eliminate many of the behaviors.

Manage disruptive behaviors. Disruptive behaviors interfere with teaching and learning. There are numerous effective strategies for managing disruptive behaviors that are adaptations of the original classroom plan in the general education classroom depending on the severity of the behavior. For minor behaviors, teachers can make minor adaptations to the basic procedures and teaching methods to reduce problems (Trussell, Lewis, & Raynor, 2016). Some adaptations and descriptions of each include:

- Pre-correction: Tell the class, or small group, what exactly they need to do, before the activity changes. This reminds students of the expected behavior immediately before they need to use it, avoiding problems (for example: "We are about to line up. When your name/group is called, push in your chair, walk to the end of the line, stand directly behind the person in front of you, mouths are silent, hands are by your sides.").

- Planned Ignoring: Purposely ignoring a specific minor behavior in the hopes it will stop. However, it is important to determine the purpose of the behavior being ignored and to recognize an appropriate behavior the student is engaged in as soon as possible.

- Behavior Specific Praise Statements: Providing positive acknowledgment for the exact behavior immediately following the student's action (for example: "Juanita, that is excellent thinking! Nice job raising your hand and waiting to share your ideas!").

- Proximity Control: Circulate among the students when teaching. Move toward any students that begin to get distracted or off task. Generally, no words need to be said. Being close to the student(s) typically draws them back into the current lesson.

- Nonverbal Cues: Nonverbal cues such as making eye contact or giving a finger or hand signal to a disruptive student can be effective in redirecting the student.

- Modeling: Purposefully demonstrate behavior needed to achieve a task. Showing a partial/complete product, and thinking aloud the steps taken to accomplish the task. Step-by-step reducing confusion, increasing completion.

- Signaling: An action to redirect the student(s) to the task at hand, without calling attention to any one person, and without stopping the teacher talk. Point to the board, book, or assignment to refocus attention; raise a hand to signal students to raise a hand to contribute; and cup a hand around an ear to signal students should listen.

- Provide Choices: Give the student a choice to change their behavior or receive a consequence.

- Redirection: A statement of what is currently expected. Use redirection to remind students of appropriate behaviors and expectations. This statement uses planned ignoring, in that attention is not given to the undesirable behavior, but students are reminded what they are expected to be doing at the moment.

- Social Skills Instruction: Social skills can be taught at this level by teaching the classroom and school rules, embedding skills into the curriculum, and using books to introduce topics of various behaviors as a means to open discussion.

Manage challenging behaviors. For more challenging behaviors, change the approach to academic instruction, provide remedial academic intervention, add out of class tutoring, use temporary positive reinforcement such as behavior contingency plans, implement a classroom token economy, and develop individual behavior contracts to effectively address the cause or function of the problematic behaviors (Maag, 2018). Self-monitoring strategies, daily student evaluations/behavior report cards, functional behavioral assessments (FBAs), behavior intervention plans (BIPs), goal setting and monitoring, and anger management techniques are effective intensive individualized supports (Maag, 2018).

For chronic behaviors, an individual behavioral contract that identifies the disruptive behavior, appropriate solutions, and specific changes the student will make may be necessary. Include consequences for the student if they fail to follow through as well as incentives to encourage positive behaviors. Take time to model and teach social skills using effective instructional strategies by emphasizing social skills such as taking turns, listening, and waiting patiently.

Use role-playing as a way to have students provide feedback to each other, hold classroom meetings to build a sense of community and practice social skills, and use both good and bad examples of social skills as learning opportunities (Zirpoli, 2016). Most importantly, teachers should always be sure to follow the IEP/504 for any student with a disability or with accommodations/modifications when addressing academic and behavioral issues. Some websites specific to academic and behavioral interventions include www.pbis.org and http://www.interventioncentral.org/home.

Provide consequences. Consequences are any action that follows a behavior and either increases the likelihood of the behavior or decreases the likelihood of the behavior. Teachers want to increase desirable behaviors and decrease undesirable behaviors consistently.

Increase desirable behaviors. While it is important to build intrinsic motivation and promote the idea that a "job well done" is reward enough, building extrinsic reinforcement into the curriculum is often important to reinforce positive behavior and productivity (Akin-Little, Eckert, Lovett, & Little, 2004). It may be necessary during times when students' academic and behavioral efforts have proven to be extraordinarily challenging to provide positive reinforcement for approximations of the desirable behaviors shaping student actions until they are successful. Extrinsic reinforcement for academic and behavioral outcomes has been successfully employed in schools for decades (Slavin, 1997). When planning on the type of reinforcers to use, consider the specific behavior, not the student(s). Include the student in the process when choosing reinforcers to ensure they are rewarding to the student. This can easily be done by giving students a survey, requesting preferences for incentives. Provide reinforcers that can quickly be delivered and embedded into activities. The following is a progression or list of options easily implemented, and often valued by students across grade levels:

- Provide Positive Behavior Statements Frequently: Recognizing students works best at the rate of four positives for every one redirection. Good news is that when giving praise to one student, it positively affects the other students, resulting in more students exhibiting the desirable behavior.

- Build a short-term Token Economy: Accompany positive praise with a ticket, token, or sticker. Student(s) earn a preset number to earn the desired activity, lunch with the teacher, reduced homework, a privilege, or a tangible item.

- Develop Class Contingency Plans: Choose replacement behaviors to teach the class that will alleviate the problem behaviors. Have all students work together to earn an interactive learning activity, demonstrating how more fun can be had when everyone learns co-operatively.

- Create Individual Behavior Contracts: Behavior contracts are written agreements that define a goal, stating specifically what is expected of the student, how the teacher will support the student to achieve the goal, what the student will get when the goal has been met, and finally what consequence happens if the goal is not met.

- Implement a Check-in/Check-out (CICO) Process: Check-in/Check-out is a positive, supportive systematic process using a daily report card that lists behaviors the student needs to exhibit (i.e., follow directions immediately; complete assignments; ask for help). Teachers review the rules on the sheet each class session and assign points (i.e., 2 = met expectations; 1 = met expectations part of the class; 0 = did not meet expectations). The teacher discusses these with the student throughout the day, encouraging the student to adjust the behavior the next part of the day. Generally, the student and teacher set a point goal weekly. When the goal is met, a prearranged privilege, reward, or activity is provided.

Decrease undesirable behaviors. Interventions need to be considered and carefully planned for students who may need more support. The following is an example of a general plan of progressive consequences for students, in steps from a warning to an office discipline referral (ODR):

- Step 1-Verbal Warning: First, students receive a verbal warning that the behavior he/she is demonstrating is inappropriate.

- Step 2- Disciplinary Action Plan: If the behavior persists, a Disciplinary Action Plan will be completed. In the Plan, the inappropriate behavior the student is demonstrating will be clearly described, and a plan for how to correct the problem in the future will be described. The teacher will discuss the plan with the student. The student and parent will be asked to sign the Plan and return it within forty-eight hours.

- Step 3- Phone Call Home: If the behavior persists or the student does not return a signed copy of the Disciplinary Plan, the parents will be contacted to discuss the behavior.

- Step 4-Morning Detention: If the behavior continues, the student will receive detention. During detention, the student must complete teacher-provided academic tasks related to the class (e.g., make-up work, assignment corrections, enrichment, etc.). Students who fail to show up will have double the detention time. Parents will be contacted via phone and/or email to inform them of the progression of events.

- Step 5- Referral: If the behavior persists, students will receive an ODR. The student's parents will be contacted, and the student will have the referral placed in his or her district file. In addition, the student will have to adhere to the school-wide disciplinary process if applicable.

- Step 6- Tier 2 & 3 Interventions: The general education teacher should consider implementing more intensive interventions at the Tier 2 and Tier 3 levels of Positive Behavior Interventions and Supports (PBIS) for students who demonstrate chronic behavior such as an individual behavior contract, a behavior contingency plan, a positive behavior intervention plan, or check-in/check-out. For more information on PBIS visit https://www.pbis.org/

Final Thoughts

Classroom management is one of the main concerns of teachers (Cerit & Yüksel, 2015) and the number two cause for teacher burnout yet, it is one of the most important jobs of the teacher (Hultell, & Gustavsson, 2013). The general education classroom is filled with students from diverse backgrounds with a variety of academic, social, and emotional needs (Lynch, 2014). Classrooms can become chaotic and disruptive if teachers do not implement evidence-based strategies and interventions to manage the class effectively. Teachers need to provide instruction that engages all learners, promotes a positive learning environment, and establish procedures and rules that provide students with the tools they need to be successful in the classroom. When educators take the necessary time to prepare for the school year and begin using all procedures and policies on the first day of school, success is almost guaranteed to occur. Students appreciate order and knowing the expectations in advance so that they can be professional students who are able to learn in a climate that values them and their contributions.

Points to Remember

- *Classroom management directly affects student achievement. Ensuring policies and procedures are in place contributes to successful learning.*

- *Provide instruction that engages all students using a variety of teaching techniques as well as behavioral controls such as token economies and positive rewards.*

- *Establish procedures and rules on the first day, teach them to students immediately, and review them often. Students thrive when there is order in the classroom.*

- *Maintain high expectations for all students and make sure they know what those expectations are using meeting time and anchor charts to remind them.*

- *Implement behavior supports to encourage appropriate classroom behaviors. There are a variety of supports available from a simple ticket system to more complex and involved systems. Teachers who know their students well can provide differentiated supports based on personal need.*

- *Be proactive and anticipate problem behaviors to avoid classroom disruptions. When planning activities and lessons, it is just as important to account for what might go wrong as what might go well. Doing so ensures that those students who need additional support, both academic and behavioral, are noticed in advance of a total blow-up or melt-down.*

References

ASCD. (2001). *Classroom Leadership*. Retrieved from
http://blogs.edweek.org/edweek/education_futures/2014/11/6_ways_teachers_can_foster_cultural_awareness_in_the_classroom.html

Akin-Little, K. A., Eckert, T. L., Lovett, B. J., & Little, S. G. (2004). Extrinsic reinforcement in the classroom: Bribery or best practice. *School Psychology Review*, 33(3), 344-362.

Retrieved from
http://www.misd.net/mtss/consequences/extrinsic_rewards.pdf

Cerit, Y. & Yüksel, S. (2015). Teachers' perceptions of classroom management orientations in Turkish and Latvia contexts: A comparative study. *Journal of Educational & Instructional Studies in the World*, 5(3). Retrieved from
http://www.wjeis.org/FileUpload/ds217232/File/01a.yusuf_cerit.pdf

Chaffe, R. K., Briesch, A. M., Johnson, A. H., & Volpe, R. J. (2017). A meta-analysis of class-wide interventions for supporting student behavior. *School Psychology Review*, 46(2), 149-164. DOI: 10.17105/SPR-2017-0015.

De Fazio, C. M., Fain, A. C., & Duchaine, E. L. (2011). Using treatment integrity in the classroom to bring research and practice together. *Beyond Behavior*, 20, 45-49. Retrieved from
https://www.aea1.k12.ia.us/documents/filelibrary/special_education_services/behavior_resource_team/Treatment_Integrity_Article_382F2457E806C.pdf

Demirdag, S. (2015). Classroom management and students' self-esteem: Creating positive classrooms. *Educational Research and Reviews*, 10 (2), 191-197. DOI:10.5897/ERR2014.2000

Donovan, M. S. & Cross, C. T. (2002). *Minority students in special and gifted education.* Washington, DC: National Academy Press.

Emmer, E. T. & Evertson, C. M. (2017). *Classroom management for middle and high school teachers* (10th ed.). Upper Saddle River, NJ: Pearson.

Garwood, J.K., Harris, J.D., & Tomick, J.K. (2017). *Starting at the beginning: An intuitive choice for classroom management.* Retrieved from https://www.researchgate.net/publication/316982528_Starting_at_the_Beginning_An_Intuitive_Choice_for_Classroom_Management

Harrell, P., Leavell, A., van Tassell, F., & McKee, K. (2004). No teacher left behind: Results of a five-year study of teacher attrition. *Action in Teacher Education,* 26, 47-59. DOI:10.1080/01626620.2004.10463323

Haydon, T. & Kroeger, S. D., (2016). Active supervision, precorrection, and explicit timing: A high school case study on classroom behavior. *Preventing School Failure,* 60(1), 70–78. Retrieved from https://eric.ed.gov/?id=EJ1082690

Hultell, D., Melin, B., & Gustavsson, J. P. (2013). Getting personal with teacher burnout: A longitudinal study on the development of burnout using a person-based approach. *Teaching and Teacher Education,* 32, 75-86. DOI: 10.1060/j.tate.2013.01.007

Korpershoek, H., Harms, T., de Boer, H., van Kuijk, M., & Doolaard, S. (2016). A meta-analysis of the effects of classroom management strategies and classroom management programs on students' academic, behavioral, emotional, and motivational outcomes. *Review of Educational Research,* 86(3), 643-680. DOI: 10.3102/0034654315626799

Kronowitz, E. L. (2012). *The teacher's guide to success* (2nd ed.). Boston, MA: Pearson.

Lester, R. R., Allanson, P. B., & Notar, C. E. (2017). Routines are the foundation of classroom management. Retrieved from https://eric.ed.gov/?id=EJ1144313

Lodato W. G. (2016). Revisiting classroom routines. *Educational Leadership,* 73(4), 50-55. Retrieved from http://www.ascd.org/publications/educational-leadership/dec15/vol73/num04/Revisiting-Classroom-Routines.aspx

Lynch, M. (2014). *6 ways teachers can foster cutlrual awareness in the classroom.* Retrieved from http://blogs.edweek.org/edweek/education_futures/2014/11/6_ways_teachers_can_foster_cultural_awareness_in_the_classroom.html

Maag, J.W. (2018). *Behavior Management from Theoretical Implications to Practical Applications* (3rd ed). Belmont, CA: Thomson/Wadsworth

Marzano, R. (2010). High expectations for all. *Educational Leadership,* 68(1), 82–4. Retrieved from https://stoyleissuesintechnology.wikispaces.com/file/view/Marzano+High+Expectations+for+all.pdf

Mitchell, R. R., Tingstrom, D. H., Dufrene, B. A., Ford, W. B., Sterling, H. E., & van der Heyden, A. (2015). The effects of the Good Behavior Game with general education high school students. *School Psychology Review,* 44(2), 191-207. DOI: 10.17105/spr-14-0063.1

Myers, D., Freeman, J., Simonsen, B., & Sugai, G., (2017). Classroom management with exceptional learners. *Teaching Exceptional Children*, 49(4), 223-
230. DOI: 10.1177/0040059916685064

Oliver, R., Wehby, J., & Daniel, J. (2011). Teacher classroom management practices: Effects on disruptive or aggressive student behavior. *Campbell Systematic Reviews*, 4. DOI:10.4073/csr.2011.4

O'Niell, S., & Stephenson, J. (2012). Does classroom management coursework
influence preservice teachers' perceived preparedness or confidence?
Teaching and Teacher Education, 28, 1131-1143. DOI:
10.1016/j.tate.2012.06.008

Reinke, W.M., Stormont, M., Herman, K.C., Puri, R., & Goel, N. (2011). Supporting children's mental health in schools: Teacher perceptions of needs,
roles, and barriers. School *Psychology Quarterly*, 26(1), 1-13. doi:
10.1037/a0022714

Slavin, R. E. (1997). *Educational psychology* (5th ed.). Needham Heights, MA:
Allyn & Bacon.

Sutherland, K. S., Alder, N., & Gunter, P. L. (2003). The effect of varying rates of
opportunities to respond to academic requests on the behavior of students
with EBD. *Journal of Emotional and Behavioral Disorders*, 11, 239-248. DOI:
10.1177/10634266030110040501

Sutherland, K. S. & Oswald, D. P. (2005). The relationship between teacher and
student behavior in classrooms for students with emotional and behavioral
disorders: Transactional processes. *Journal of Child and Family Studies*, 14,
1-14. DOI:10.1007/s10826-005-1106-z

Trussell R. P. Lewis, T. J., & Raynor, C. (2016). The impact of universal teacher
practices and function-based behavior interventions on the rates of problem behaviors among at-risk students. *Education and Treatment of Children*, 39 (3), 261-282. Retrieved from
https://eric.ed.gov/?id=EJ1111488

Wang, M. C., Haertel, G. D., & Walberg, H. J. (1997). *What helps students learn?
Spotlight on student success.* Retrieved from
https://eric.ed.gov/?id=ED461694

Watson, K. J., & DiCarlo, C. F. (2015). Increasing completion of classroom routines through the use of picture activity schedules. *Early Childhood Education Journal*, 1-8. DOI 10.1007/sl0643-015-0697-2

Zirpoli, T. J. (2016). *Behavior management: Positive applications for teachers*
(7th ed.). Boston, MA: Pearson.

Chapter 6

Daily Classroom Instruction: Embedding Social-Emotional Skills for Optimal Learning

Micheline Susan Malow, PhD,
Manhattanville College

One well-respected educational theorist contends that all learning is social and that "…all higher mental functions are internalized social relationships" (Vygotsky, quoted in Wells, 2000, p. 54). Social relationships are implicated in learning; thus, changes in social contexts and interactions can positively or negatively affect student learning. Social-emotional learning (SEL) is not a new concept; however, the idea that it should be incorporated into schools and taught in classrooms in the same manner that academic skills are taught is still a work in progress (Malow, 2015).

In 1994, the Collaborative for Academic, Social, and Emotional Learning (CASEL) began working to change the status quo of SEL instruction through the pursuit of the organization's mission "…to help make evidenced-based social-emotional learning (SEL) an integral part of education from pre-school through high school" (CASEL, 2018a). The volunteer group of CASEL educators and researchers that came to form the leadership team of CASEL was a collection of individuals who saw that the isolated SEL initiatives being thrust into schools in the early 1990s was not an effective means of social-emotional skill development and implementation (CASEL, 2018b). Over the last 23 years, CASEL collaborators and other professionals have worked tirelessly to promote the beneficial effects of regular implementation of SEL in schools (CASEL, 2018b).

As a result of CASEL's efforts, SEL has been acknowledged as an essential component in the healthy development and well-being of all children (CASEL, 2018c). The release of a national survey of 600 teachers confirmed that teachers across America agree with the need to integrate SEL in the classroom setting, while recognizing that many teachers have already been engaging in some form of this practice, with or without the support and guidance from school administration (Bridgeland, Bruce, & Hariharan, 2013). Furthermore, a meta-analysis conducted in 2011 (Durlak, Weissberg, Dymnicki, & Schellinger, 2011) demonstrated that students enrolled in SEL enhanced curriculums performed better overall than a comparison group of students not engaged in SEL programming; supporting both the push for the inclusion of SEL instruction in classrooms by CASEL, as well as teachers' opinions that SEL skills need to be infused into school settings (CASEL, 2018c).

Social and Emotional Learning Defined

Even though every person utilizes social and emotional skills every day, what SEL skills are, how they develop, and how to control these learned abilities are not well understood (Malow, 2015). Generally speaking, SEL focuses on developing student ability to recognize emotions, while providing them the skills necessary to regulate and communicate this emotional understanding (CASEL, 2018a). CASEL has defined SEL as "the process through which children and adults acquire and effectively apply the knowledge, attitudes, and skills necessary to understand and manage emotions, set and achieve positive goals, feel and show empathy for others, establish and maintain positive relationships, and make responsible decisions" (CASEL, 2018d). This definition of SEL has been operationalized by CASEL through a Framework for Systemic Social and Emotional Learning (CASEL, 2018d).

The framework emphasizes that SEL transcends environmental settings and elaborates on the competencies deemed essential in the development of core knowledge in the expression of intrapersonal, interpersonal, and cognitive understanding (CASEL, 2018e). Teachers, administrators, and parents are encouraged to explicitly teach and reinforce the competencies during daily instruction and/or interactions with students. The five areas of proficiency focus on the defined capacities of: 1) self-awareness, 2) self-management, 3) social-awareness, 4) relationship skills, and 5) responsible decision-making (CASEL, 2018e). The SEL competencies inspire knowledge of self and others, support the ability to manage impulses in order to engage in respectful behaviors toward and communication with others, as well as encourage an appreciation of diversity in all forms in order to empower ethical choices and decision-making by all individuals (CASEL, 2018e).

Educational Applications

One established framework for infusing consistent reinforcement of desired behavioral outcomes throughout educational settings is the multi-tiered system of support (MTSS); a service delivery model that targets all children in a school setting with the universal goal of problem prevention (Cook, Frye,

Slemrod, Lyon, Renshaw, & Zhang, 2015). When employing an MTSS approach, schools utilize evidence-based practices that were chosen for implementation because of a desired goal; following the instruction, decisions are data-driven (Cook et al., 2015). This common educational practice, known as progress monitoring, indicates that curriculum implementation and change are based on the outcomes of ongoing assessment of the progress students make in the curriculum (Cook et al., 2015).

Response to Intervention (RTI) is a well-known academic MTSS while Positive Behavioral Interventions and Supports (PBIS) is one social-emotional/behavioral correlate of a tiered support system (National Center for Learning Disabilities, n.d.; Positive Behavioral Interventions and Supports, 2018). PBIS has been described by the pioneers in the field as a systems framework for establishing a safe and effective learning environment for all students, implemented through a change in the social culture of the school and maintained through individualized behavior supports as needed (Sugai & Horner, 2009). A survey of PBIS practitioners, revealed that whereas most teachers agreed that PBIS initiatives fostered positive improvement in school climate, many did not find the application of PBIS methods to be practical; although the more consistently a program is implemented, the more viable it is perceived by its stakeholders (Miramontes, Marchant, Allen Heath, & Fischer, 2011).

Schools often employ the PBIS framework through the implementation of stand-alone programs, focused on addressing a specific need or goal identified as important by the school community (Sugai & Horner 2009). Examples of this type of MTSS include substance use prevention programs and/or bullying prevention programs. Although employing a specific program to address a school need may work in the short-term, the problem with this approach is that it does not comprehensively teach the SEL skills that are missing in the student population, to begin with; the very same skill deficits that may have contributed to the growth of the problem. Students in schools that have employed a PBIS program for bullying, for example, may learn throughout the school year how to identify, manage, and prevent bullying in their school, yet they may not have learned how to identify what they are feeling, how to self-regulate those emotions, and problem-solving techniques to make a better decision than to engage in the bullying of a fellow student who may have aroused feelings of anger.

To address this gap, Cook and colleagues (2015) investigated an integrated approach to universal MTSS prevention; specifically, the researchers sought to examine the efficacy of two widely adopted evidence-based practices in combination by incorporating both PBIS and SEL in the classroom. Results from the classroom-based randomized control conditions demonstrated that although students in individual PBIS and SEL conditions outperformed students receiving no social-emotional skill instruction at all, providing instruction and reinforcement in both PBIS and SEL concurrently, the combination condition, obtained the best results (Cook et al., 2015). Of note, students who received regular instruction utilizing both a PBIS model and SEL skill development had the most significant improvement in measured overall mental health improvement and in externalizing behavior reduction (Cook et al., 2015).

Teachers as SEL Instructors

Integrating SEL curriculums into daily educational programming is one way to foster the development of resiliency, enabling students to hold an attitude of optimism and trust during times of uncertainty. Explicitly embedding SEL goals into schools addresses the teaching of interpersonal skills such as emotional self-awareness, and self-management, as well as provides students beneficial self-regulatory tools when engaging with others in the school and community (Reinke, Stormont, Herman, Puri & Goel, 2011). Teachers are the obvious choice for implementing SEL into classroom settings as they are the individuals who are most likely to impact student behavior due to their daily interactions throughout the school day. Teachers, as the instructional experts of all schools, are often the ones asked to implement school-based universal models of behavioral support; despite this, many teachers do not feel adequately prepared to do so (Reinke et al., 2011). A survey of approximately 300 early childhood and elementary school teachers found that school psychologists were identified as the individuals best suited to implement SEL in classrooms (Reinke et al., 2011). Although teachers feel prepared to teach academics, and results of the survey indicated that teachers felt responsible for implementing behavioral interventions in the classroom, most teachers did not feel adequately prepared to teach SEL (Reinke et al., 2011). Despite feeling unprepared to provide instruction on SEL concepts, teachers were well aware of the need for SEL in order to address mental health concerns revealed in the classroom. In the same survey (Reinke et al., 2011), teachers identified five major social-emotional concerns in the classroom to include 1) disruptive, defiant, and aggressive behavior problems, 2) hyperactivity and attentional difficulties, 3) students with significant family stressors, 4) social skills deficits, and 5) depression. These are areas of concern that would be targeted when implementing social-emotional skills instruction on a regular basis.

When using SEL language and embedding competencies into daily instruction, teachers reinforce the importance of SEL, similar to that of other academic learning, as well as provide examples and reinforcement for these skills (Malow, 2015). Teachers are the school personnel communicating regularly with parents; clearly letting parents know what SEL skills are being worked on in class, using and teaching parents the language of SEL and the competencies, and asking for support and help in the reinforcement of these competencies in the home setting is one way to infuse SEL skills across multiple environments (CASEL, 2018f). Within the school setting, teachers can request professional development opportunities from their administration in how to embed SEL competencies into their daily curriculums; this lets the administration know that teachers believe this is an important area to both understand and cultivate in students (Yoder, 2014). Furthermore, administrators can be encouraged by teachers to infuse SEL into school and district-wide goals, cementing the importance of this area of learning (Yoder, 2014).

Communication among the proximal influences in a student's life is key when seeking to develop SEL skills. Like academic skills, SEL skills develop most effectively when they are not a stand-alone program once a week, or twice a month for 30 minutes. Instead, the language and concepts of SEL skills need to be infused into the student's daily life, highlighting the need for parents to understand not only the mathematics and language arts curriculum the child will be exposed to throughout the year, but also the developmentally appropriate SEL skills that the class will be working to master (Center on Great Teachers & Leaders at American Institutes for Research, 2014).

As with all good instruction, teachers become the conduit through which the unknown becomes known. Furthermore, as with all heterogeneous groupings of students, teachers need to be prepared to provide scaffolding to students as they acquire the targeted knowledge and skills. Some students will come to class with the foundations of SEL skills in place, while for others the understanding of SEL concepts may not be part of the core language that they bring with them from home (Raimundo, Marques-Pinto, & Lima 2013). When teachers are prepared to accept each student's level of development as a starting point from which to improve greater knowledge of SEL skills, the assumption that students should come to school armed with these skills will fall away. Research on universal, classroom-wide SEL programs has documented notable behavioral improvements for the students involved in those programs (Raimundo et al., 2013).

Many instructional practices already in a teacher's toolbox are utilized in the development of SEL knowledge and skills. For example, the common classroom practice of collaborative learning places students together in work groups to achieve a common goal. Collaborative learning can be used to promote the five competencies noted above as the foundational concepts of SEL: self-awareness, self-management, social awareness, relationship skills, and responsible decision making, in addition to providing an opportunity to embed these competencies into the academic curriculum being taught (CASEL,

2018e). Another common educational practice that lends itself as a natural way to enrich SEL instruction is the morning meeting. When a classroom comes together as a community and takes time to recognize the members of that community by engaging in open, respectful communication, a platform for discussion and understanding is opened. Ultimately when utilizing collaborative learning and morning meeting strategies, teachers are provided an opportunity to model and coach skills such as reflective listening, group decision-making, perspective taking, problem-solving, and empathy (Center on Great Teachers & Leaders at American Institutes for Research, 2014).

When seeking to embed SEL approaches into a school setting, CASEL (2018g) suggests that successful implementation will often embody four elements captured by the acronym SAFE (CASEL, 2018g). The SAFE approach supports the development of SEL skills by directing teachers' best practice implementation:

- Sequence. Teachers plan and coordinate activities within and across the curriculum in order to promote SEL skills.

- Active. Teachers ensure that the activities selected engage students in active forms of learning; students discover connections as they employ the newly learned skills.

- Focus. Teachers emphasize and reinforce the developing acquisition of the targeted SEL skill to promote mastery.

- Explicit. Specific SEL skills are taught through direct instructional practices; students understand the goal of the activities from the outset

Fostering SEL Through MTSS Educational Practices

There are many ways in which teachers can infuse SEL approaches into the classroom settings so that students and, through ongoing teacher-parent communication, parents can begin to understand the language and the concepts of SEL. One framework previously mentioned, MTSS, provides a common point from which teachers can start to build their SEL curriculums. Some MTSS that are specifically geared to employing social-emotional learning include the Teaching Pyramid and the Social Support Model (Fox, Dunlap, Hammeter, Joseph and Strain, 2003; Meadan & Monda-Amaya, 2008).

The Teaching Pyramid

There are numerous ways for teachers to manage the development of SEL in students; however, many teachers feel at a loss when forced to choose what intervention to implement. In an effort to inform the process, a developmental progression has been identified to standardize teachers' actions. A framework developed by Fox et al. (2003), known as The Teaching Pyramid, aimed to guide educators in how to address the social-emotional development of students. Although researchers have adopted and adapted the Teaching Pyramid model to suit a variety of needs (Kostelnik, Gregory, Soderman, & Whiren, 2012), the leveled approach to the social-emotional education of all students remains a "best practice" model.

Like the MTSS and PBIS approaches, the Teaching Pyramid represents a hierarchical structure that directs teachers through four successive levels of strategies (Fox et al., 2003). Educators work their way through the first three levels of the Teaching Pyramid to provide all students in a classroom a universal approach to build the skills necessary for the development of social-emotional competence (Fox et al., 2003). When a student experiences a higher level of behavioral difficulty, the individualized approach of the fourth level provides the appropriate guidance. The steps in the Teaching Pyramid include 1) Positive relationships, 2) Supportive environments, 3) Social-emotional strategies, and 4) Individualized interventions (Fox et al., 2003).

Positive relationships form the base on which all classroom interactions are built. The first step in promoting SEL is to create positive relationships between teachers and children, teachers and families, and between teachers and the other professionals in the school. Positive relationships allow children to feel safe and secure. Throughout the regular learning process, students will make mistakes and experience setbacks; knowing that the teacher accepts all student effort allows for the engagement in the process of learning. In an educational setting, feeling secure allows students of all abilities to open up to new experiences. Suggestions for strategies that build positive relationships include: (Fox et al., 2003):

- Greet students at the door by name
- Have informal conversations when breaks in the instructional flow occur
- Offer praise and encouragement
- Send positive notes home
- Have families complete interest surveys about the students
- Encourage students to share what is important to them

Supportive environments are the second level of the Teaching Pyramid, encouraging teachers to create environments for students that are both physically and verbally supportive (Fox et al., 2003). In the production of a supportive physical environment, teachers account for "…environmental elements such as color, light, materials, room arrangement, sounds and routines" (Kostelnik et al., 2012, p.24). Teachers are well aware that classroom design supports the development of, and engagement with, appropriate behavior. Furthermore, the manner in which the various adults in the room speak, listen and interact with students enhances the environment (Fox et al., 2003). Verbal and non-verbal interactions between teacher and student foster self-awareness, providing the messages from others that signal to students how they should feel about themselves; for example, when Ms. Smith, the teacher, catches a student appropriately engaging in academic work and smiles, the student may think, "Ms. Smith likes the way I am doing my work." This brief interaction strengthens the already established relationship between the pair, making it more likely that the student will repeat the behavior in the future.

Teaching social-emotional strategies is the third level and final universal phase provided routinely to all the students in the classroom setting as part of the Teaching Pyramid framework (Fox et al., 2003). Teachers engage in the explicit instruction of social skills, emotional understanding and behavioral controls that all children need to learn in order to be competent in SEL by providing continuous support to students through "…discussing, modeling, instructing on the spot, redirecting, reminding, reinforcing, implementing consequences, and following through" (Kostelnik, et al., 2012, p.24). Teaching social-emotional strategies requires planning, individualization, opportunities for students to engage in active learning, and careful attention paid to students as they engage in socially competent behavior. When a teacher reminds a student, "It's Johnny's turn to use the classroom computer, you must wait to take a turn when he finishes" the teacher is directly instructing the student about turn-taking, impulse control, and behavioral expectations.

When the three levels of the Teaching Pyramid are consistently presented in a classroom, and school setting, the majority of students achieve adequate levels of social-emotional instruction and reinforcement. A small percentage of children will continue to demonstrate challenging behaviors; these students benefit from the fourth tier, an individualized intervention (Fox et al., 2003). These students may have learning or emotional disabilities that require a more intensive approach to instruction and may benefit from a Behavior Intervention Plan (BIP) (PBIS World, 2018). A BIP employs a team approach drawing on the cumulative expertise of teachers, parents, school psychologists and other school-based professionals in an effort to identify the specific area(s) of difficulty experienced by the student (PBIS World, 2018). A functional assessment of behavior starts the BIP process and is compiled utilizing student observations, interviews of relevant individuals, a review of the student's records, and an analysis of the purpose the behavior serves for the particular child (von Ravensberg & Blakely, 2015). Once the behavioral analysis is complete, the team implements the selected intervention and monitors behavioral progress throughout the intervention's implementation.

Social Support Model

Another MTSS that represents a three-tiered model from which to infuse SEL is the Social Support Model (Meadan & Monda-Amaya, 2008). Assuming that children come into a classroom with all the social skills that they will need to achieve in that setting is a false assumption. Teachers can enhance their classroom environment by acknowledging that all students need instruction and support for both academic and social skills. Through collaboration and by embedding the three levels of the Social Skill Model into the classroom instruction provided throughout the day, teachers can provide students with a foundation of tools for school and life success (Meadan & Monad-Amaya, 2008).

In level one of this model, the teacher seeks to structure the many unique individuals that make up the student classroom population into a classroom community (Meadan & Monad-Amaya, 2008). Within this entry level, there are three classroom priorities that address both the physical environment as well as the effective environment of the classroom. Each priority has suggested activities that support each priority.

- Create an accepting classroom environment
    - Post positive class rules
    - Make expectations clearly known
    - Discuss differences and acceptance of all
- Value students by enabling their role and voice
    - Post classroom jobs and responsibilities
    - Recognize individual talents and interests
- Provide opportunities for social interaction
    - Use cooperative learning and peer tutoring
    - Encourage collaboration
    - Structure out-of-class activities such as in gym and recess

The second tier in the Social Support Model is aimed at incorporating strategies and curriculum that embed SEL instruction into daily classroom activities (Meadan & Monad-Amaya, 2008). At this level, teachers can utilize direct instructional practices aimed at the entire class to promote vocabulary and behavioral expectations for all. A standardized social skills program could be incorporated if the teacher prefers a manualized approach, or various prob-

lem solving, conflict resolution, role-playing, reinforcement, and generalization strategies can be used. Some suggested skills to be taught at this level are:

- Interpret environmental cues
- Identify feelings in self and others
- Set guidelines for conflict resolution during cooperative activities
- Use social stories, scenarios, and books for problem-solving models

The top tier, level three, recognizes that because all students do not learn or
process information in the same way, nor do they have the same opportunities for reinforcement, not all strategies are effective for all students (Meadan
& Monad-Amaya, 2008). Recognizing the strengths and weaknesses of each
individual allows the teacher to identify specific social skills needs in order to
provide targeted individual interventions. The most effective response to
instruction is produced when specific social skills strategies are used that
match the specific social skills deficits observed in the student (Gresham,
Sugai, & Horner, 2001). There are four types of social skills deficits, and each
calls for a different intervention (Gresham et al., 2001).

- Acquisition Deficit — Provide direct instruction of missing skills
- Performance Deficit — Deliver instruction about when and how to
  use the skills
- Fluency Deficit — Create opportunities for practice and generalization of skills
- Competing Behavior — Teach and provide motivation for utilizing
  appropriate social skills

In addition to targeting interventions to combat deficits at this level, teachers can provide instruction to students about his/her unique set of strengths
and weaknesses Gresham et al., 2001). Once the student's behavior has been
demystified, he/she can learn to monitor, reinforce, value and advocate for
him or herself, thus empowering them to be their own advocate (Levine,
2002).

Classroom Approaches to SEL

The acquisition of self-disciplined, socially and emotionally aware behavior in
students occurs gradually (Kostelnik et al., 2012). The progression toward
internal regulation takes time and a responsive, supportive environment;
these elements are essential as the student develops, allowing the acquisition
of skill and understanding as the child progresses through a series of changes.

The progression begins with students who display no self-regulation and then move to a position of external regulation where the teacher is in control. As understanding increases, a state of shared regulation unfolds in which both the teacher and the student understand what needs to take place, and finally the student arrives at a sense of internal regulation where the management of his/her own emotions and behaviors takes over (Kostelnik et al., 2012). One way to foster this movement toward SEL in the classroom is to implement a consistent approach to structuring and managing classroom activities. Once the students adjust to the strategies and techniques that the teacher utilizes, they will internalize those techniques and classroom interactions will be expected to occur in this manner consistently.

Responsive Classroom Approach

One classroom approach that embodies many of the aspects of the MTSS programs and the elements of SEL is the Responsive Classroom Approach (Responsive Classroom, 2018). Here, the goal is to integrate social and academic learning in ways that help all children in any given class. The Responsive Classroom accomplishes this goal by implementing seven principles to guide the thinking and actions of teachers (Responsive Classroom, 2018). Following these principles helps to meet students' social-emotional needs, reduce discipline problems, and enhance academic, as well as social, competencies and as a consequence, students can focus on learning. The seven principles of the Responsive Classroom are:

- Treat social and academic curriculums as equally important.
- Remember that how children learn is as important as what they learn.
- Remember that cognitive growth occurs through social interaction.
- Remember that the social skills of cooperation, assertion, responsibility, empathy, and self-control are essential for learning.
- Know your children individually, culturally, and developmentally.
- Know the families of your children and invite them to participate in your classroom.
- Establish good working relationships with all adults in your school.

To assist teachers in making these principles work, specific Responsive Classroom practices have been established. These practices emphasize social-emotional and self-regulatory skills as the first step toward academic achievement. The established practices include 1) the daily greeting, 2) classroom rules and logical consequences, 3) the language of encouragement, 4) the morning meeting, and 5) academic choices to facilitate discovery (Responsive Classroom, 2018). In their classrooms, teachers would consistently incorporate these five practices in their day-to-day work and interactions with students.

- The daily greeting. As the students enter the classroom, teachers routinely greet them individually. The teachers' language reflects knowledge of the child, the child's family and the positive relationship they're developing with each child. This brief exchange lets students know that the teachers care about them and are aware of what's going on in their lives.

- Classroom rules and logical consequences. Because classroom rules would have been established at the beginning of the year, students know what to do as they enter the classroom. If a rule is broken, the logical consequence follows. These consequences reflect the student's individual circumstances, including developmental level, and reflect the positive relationship between teachers and students. Consequences are never harsh, unfair, or retaliatory.

- The language of encouragement. If students get sidetracked on handling their responsibilities, teachers use words of encouragement to guide them. Teachers make descriptive comments on students' work products, which shifts emphasis away from praising students' products to encouraging them to engage in learning actively.

- The morning meeting. When students have settled in, teachers conduct a morning meeting. During this daily meeting, students participate in sharing, games, and playful intellectual activity. The meeting's purpose is to establish and maintain a cohesive classroom community. By holding morning meetings, teachers convey the importance of getting to know and respect all the members of the classroom community.

- Academic choices to facilitate discovery. Finally, as the day progresses, each teacher presents the curriculum. Within each content area, new material is presented to keep interest and motivation high. In addition, the students are guided to discover new information or ways of learning. Trial and error are encouraged. Whenever possible, students are given choices in activities and assignments. These choices allow for creativity and help students to develop a sense of control, which encourages them to practice self-regulation skills, which in turn, fosters academic achievement.

Mindfulness

Students who engage in self-regulation skills have developed the ability to voluntarily control their behavior (Calkins & Williford, 2009). Teachers may refer to the processes involved in self-regulation as socialization and the student's emerging abilities as self-discipline (Flook, Goldberg, Pinger, & Davidson, 2015). Researchers in the area of child development understand that no matter what this ability is called, all adults working with children impart these essential skills in an effort to foster the inner controls a child needs to carry out successful social interactions, resist negative impulses and delay gratification (Thompson & Twibell, 2009). Adults teach pro-social behavior and children learn societal rules through observation, direct instruction, and positive and negative consequences; thus, the developmental emergence of self-regulation requires appropriate environmental structure and the opportunity to apply the learned skills (Thompson & Twibell, 2009). These practices result in the internalization of the rules of acceptable and unacceptable behavior as demonstrated in the environment.

One tool that can help students apply emerging skills of self-regulation is mindfulness. Mindfulness is designed to direct thoughts through the self-regulation of awareness, directing internal and external attention, and increasing metacognition (Mindful Schools, 2018). A meta-analysis of mindfulness research concluded that mindfulness activities lead to positive psychological feelings, improved functioning, and less psychological distress (Mindful Schools, 2018; Hart, Ivtzan, & Hart, 2013). Individual studies have found that mindfulness activities convey benefits to children evidencing difficulties with social competence (Flook et al., 2015). Support for mindfulness activities in school settings by Zenner, Herrnleben-Kurz, and Walach (2014) reported beneficial results in academic improvement, increased attendance rates, decreased suspensions, and in increased feelings of wellbeing. Individual teachers with a little practice can implement mindfulness techniques, as well as any other SEL strategy into daily classroom instructional time.

The Personal Message

Remembering that self-discipline is a developmental process that is grounded in warm, caring relationships and respectful teaching will guide teachers' interactions with students when they do not display appropriate self-regulation. Students of all ages and ability levels benefit when the adults in their lives use personal messages to guide and shape their behavior. An effective strategy for communicating expectations and rules to students is the personal message (Kaiser & Rasminsky, 2007). This three-part strategy is an effective method to convey to a student that his/her point of view is understood while communicating feelings about his/her behavior and if needed, providing an acceptable alternative of behavior to the student. When used effectively, personal messages provide students with information, understanding, and guidance about their behavior, enabling this knowledge to be stored for self-regulation behaviors in the future. The three-part personal message strategy is summarized as follows (Kaiser & Rasminsky, 2007):

- Reflection. Think about what the student is trying to accomplish with his/her behavior; each student has his/her own perspective and goals. This shows the students that you respect them and are trying to understand his/her personal point of view. The teacher communicates that respect through a statement such as "I can see that you are very angry right now."

- React and provide a reason. Tell the student how you feel in response to the behavior he/she displayed. "I am upset that you ripped up your paper." Then tell him/her why you feel that way. "Now I will not be able to hang your paper on the wall with the rest of the class's papers."

- State a rule or redirection. Tell the students what to do; this provides them with explicit behavioral expectations. Do not fall into the trap of telling the student what not to do. When a student is told what not to do, he/she may not know what the appropriate behavior is. "Take a new paper to complete at home tonight. Bring the paper in tomorrow morning so that I can hang it on the wall."

Final Thoughts

There are system-wide, developmentally sequenced, programs that are supported by empirical evidence and can be implemented in a school setting to promote SEL. In the absence of a formal, structured and developmentally sequenced program in a teacher's school setting, there are still many things educators can implement in their own classrooms as a means to promote optimal social and emotional development.

- Help students by accepting instead of banishing emotions. This can be accomplished through active listening and reflecting back of students' feelings when they are distressed and demonstrates empathy with the student's plight that can often be helpful in defusing a stressful situation.

- Help students by sharing relevant information that might provide a context for a student's distress; for example, a teacher can indicate to a student that the test was a difficult one and the highest grade in the class was low.

- Help students by providing important direction and coaching throughout stressful situations. An example of this would be to direct the student to take a break from a classroom assignment by going to get a drink of water, or by prompting students to use a specific strategy that was discussed previously when dealing with this particular problem.

- Practice impulse control through role-playing. When rules are established in the classroom, the teacher should first model how the rule should be implemented and then have the entire class practice it. Afterwards, the teacher can reinforce the rule and give corrective feedback through the use of role-playing that involves student practice; for example, if the rule taught is to refrain from criticizing other people's ideas, the teacher can discuss how inappropriate criticism or name calling has a negative impact on others and ask students to take the perspective of the students who are ridiculed.

- Teachers can instruct, demonstrate and provide feedback to students when employing self-talk as a means of directing their own behavior during stressful situations. Students can be guided to create a list of proactive self-statements to address negative emotional responses. This will help them to get back on the right track along with reinforcing adaptive emotional responses when engaging in self-talk that promotes a positive outcome.

- Promote an impulse control strategy called the "turtle technique." This technique teaches students to become more aware of their physiological responses to anger, such as clenching their fists and feeling warm in the face. The technique asks that the student 1) Stop what they are doing and think 2) Retract into their shell by taking several deep breaths, and thinking about things that can calm them down, and 3) Leave the shell when calm and able to problem solve the issue.

Points to Remember

- *Students can to be taught SEL skills through explicit instruction, modeling, and coaching to recognize how they feel or how someone else might be feeling.*

- *Teachers should prompt students on the use of a taught SEL skill, such as acceptance of diversity or a conflict-resolution skill. Understanding and mastery are developmental processes and students will not all learn SEL skills at the same rate.*

- *Teachers and more knowledgeable peers can use SEL language and effective communication skills to guide students through appropriate steps as an effective approach to helping students apply the newly learned skills in different situations.*

- *Through class meetings students can practice group decision-making, set classroom rules, and work to develop respect for all by building a classroom community.*

- *Students can learn cooperation and teamwork through participation in collaborative learning groups and games embedded throughout the academic curricula.*

- *Teachers can help students deepen their understanding of a SEL skill by pairing it with the analysis of an academic content task; analyzing the academic content through a set of questions based on a problem-solving model.*

- *Cross-age mentoring, in which a younger student is paired with an older one, can be effective in building academic and personal self-confidence, a sense of belonging, and enhancing academic skills.*

- *Active engagement in practicing the SEL skills taught in the classroom is an essential step on the road to mastery and generalization. Engage in role-playing or have one member of a pair describe a situation to his/her partner while having the partner repeat what he or she heard is an effective tool in teaching reflective listening, empathy, and active communication skills.*

References

Bridgeland, J., Bruce, M., & Hariharan, (2013). *The missing piece: A national teacher survey on how social and emotional learning can empower children and transform schools.*

Collaborative for Academic, Social, and Emotional Learning. Chicago, IL: Author.

Calkins, S.D., & Williford, A.P. (2009). Training the terrible twos: Self-regulation and school readiness. In O.A. Barbarian & B.H. Wasik, *Handbook of child development and early education: Research to practice.* (pp.172-198). New York, NY: The Guilford Press.

CASEL. (2018a). *Our work. Retrieved from https://casel.org/our-work/*

CASEL. (2018b). *History.* Retrieved from https://casel.org/history/

CASEL. (2018c). *SEL research.* Retrieved from https://casel.org/research/

CASEL. (2018d). *What is SEL?* Retrieved from https://casel.org/what-is-sel/

CASEL. (2018e). *SEL Core competencies.* Retrieved from https://casel.org/core-competencies/

CASEL. (2018f). *SEL in the home.* Retrieved from https://casel.org/in-the-home/

CASEL. (2018g). *Approaches.* Retrieved from https://casel.org/what-is-sel/approaches/

Center on Great Teachers & Leaders at American Institutes for Research. (2014). *The SEL school: Connecting social and emotional learning to effective teaching.* Retrieved from https://www.gtlcenter.org/sel-school

Cook, C., Frye, M, Slemrod, T., Lyon, A., Renshaw, T., & Zhang, Y. (2015). An integrated approach to universal prevention: Independent and combined effects of PBIS and SEL on youths' mental health. *School Psychology Quarterly,* 30(2), 166-183. doi:10.1037/spq0000102

Durlak, J., Weissberg, R., Dymnicki, A., & Schellinger, K. (2011). The impact of enhancing students' social and emotional learning: A meta-analysis of school-based universal interventions. *Child Development,* 82(1), 405-432. doi: 10.1111/j.1467-8624.2010.01564.x

Flook, L., Goldberg, S.B., Pinger, L., & Davidson, R.J. (2015). Promoting prosocial behavior and self-regulatory skills in preschool children through a mindfulness-based kindness curriculum. *Developmental Psychology,* 51(1), 44-51. doi: 10.1037/a0038256

Fox, L., Dunlap, G., Hemmeter, M.L., Joseph, G.E., & Strain, P.S. (2003, July). The teaching pyramid. *Young Children.* Retrieved from http://www.challengingbehavior.org/do/resources/documents/yc_article_7_2003.pdf

Gresham, F. M., Sugai, G., & Horner, R.H. (2001). Interpreting outcomes of social skills training for students with high-incidence disabilities. *Exceptional Children,* 67, 331-344. DOI: 10.1177/001440290106700303

Hart, R., Ivtzan, I., Hart D. (2013). Mind the gap in mindfulness research: A comparative account of the leading schools of thought. *Review of General Psychology,* 17(4), 453-466. doi:10.1037/a0035212

Kaiser, B., & Rasminsky, J.S. (2007). *Challenging behavior in young children: Understanding, preventing, and responding effectively.* Boston, MA: Pearson.

Kostelnik, M.J., Gregory, K.M., Soderman, A.K., & Whiren, A.P. (2012). *Guiding children's social development and learning* (7th ed.). Belmont, CA: Wadsworth, Cengage Learning.

Levine, M. (2002). *A Mind at a Time.* New York, NY: Simon & Schuster.

Malow, M. (2015, September). *Embedding social emotional learning in the schools. Strategies for Successful Learning.* Retrieved from https://www.ldworldwide.org/single-post/2015/09/01/V9-1-Social-Emotional-Development---Embedding-Social-Emotional-Learning-in-the-Schools

Meadan, H. & Monda-Amaya, L. (2008). Collaboration to promote social competence for students with mild disabilities in the general classroom: A structure for providing social support. *Intervention in School and Clinic,* 43, 158-167. DOI:10.1177/1053451207311617

Mindful Schools. (2018). *Research on mindfulness.* Retrieved from https://www.mindfulschools.org/about-mindfulness/research/

Miramontes, N. Y., Marchant, M., Heath, M. A., & Fischer, L. (2011). Social validity of a positive behavior interventions and support model. *Education and Treatment of Children, 34*(4), 445-468. DOI: 10.1177/1098300712459356

National Center for Learning Disabilities. (n.d.). *What is RTI?* Retrieved from http://www.rtinetwork.org/learn/what/whatisrti

PBIS World. (2018). *Behavior Intervention Plan (BIP).* Retrieved from http://www.pbisworld.com/tier-2/behavior-intervention-plan-bip/

Positive Behavioral Interventions and Supports. (2018). *What is school-wide PBIS?* Retrieved from http://www.pbis.org/school

Raimundo, R., Marques-Pinto, A. & Lima, M.L. (2013). The effects of a social-emotional learning program on elementary school children: The role of pupils' characteristics. *Psychology in the Schools. 50*(2), 165-180. DOI: 10.1002/pits.21667

Reinke, W.M., Stormont, M., Herman, K.C., Puri, R., & Goel, N. (2011). Supporting children's mental health in schools: Teacher perceptions of needs, roles, and barriers. School *Psychology Quarterly, 26*(1), 1-13. doi: 10.1037/a0022714

Responsive Classroom. (2018). *Principles & practices.* Retrieved from https://www.responsiveclassroom.org/about/principles-practices/

Sugai, G. & Horner, R. H. (2009). Defining and describing schoolwide positive behavior support. In W. Sailor, G. Dunlap, G. Sugai, & R. Horner (Eds.), *Handbook of Positive Behavior Support* (pp. 307-326). New York, NY: Springer.

Thompson, J.E., & Twibell, K.K. (2009). Teaching hearts and minds in early childhood classrooms: Curriculum for social and emotional development. In O.A. Barbarian & B.H.

von Ravensberg, H. & Blakely, A. (2015). *When to use a functional behavioral assessment? A state-by-state analysis of the law.* Retrieved from https://www.pbis.org/Common/Cms/files/pbisresources/EvalBrief_Oct2015.pdf

Wasik (Eds.), *Handbook of child development and early education: Research to practice* (pp.199-222). New York, NY: The Guilford Press.

Wells, G. (2000). Dialogic inquiry in education. Building on the legacy of Vygotsky. In C. Lee & P. Smagorinsky (Eds.), *Vygotskian Perspectives on literacy research: Constructing meaning through collaborative inquiry* (pp. 51-85). Boston, MA: Cambridge University Press.

Yoder, N. (2014). *Teaching the whole child: Instructional practices that support social-emotional learning in three teacher evaluation frameworks.* Retrieved from https://gtlcenter.org/sites/default/files/TeachingtheWholeChild.pdf

Zenner, C., Herrnleben-Kurz, S., & Walach, H. (2014). Mindfulness-based interventions in schools – A systematic review and meta-analysis. *Frontiers in Psychology*, 5. doi:10.3389/fpsyg.2014.00603

Chapter 7

Penciling in Parents:
Making Time for Partnerships that Count

Nicholas D. Young, PhD, EdD,
American International College
and
Elizabeth Jean, EdD,
Endicott College

Positive family-school partnerships are the backbone of a student's successful educational experience. Family connections matter and research suggests that the more educators and parents share pertinent information regarding their shared student, the better equipped both will be to help that student achieve (Castro, Exposito-Casas, Lopez-Martin, Lizasoain, Navarro-Asencio, & Gaviria, 2015; Povey, Campbell, Willis, Haynes, Western, Bennett, Antrobus, & Pedde, 2016). Offered as more evidence to the necessity of partnerships between families and educators, research shows that in schools with a high level of parent engagement, teacher effectiveness and student achievement is high (Flamboyan Foundation, 2011; Henderson & Mapp, 2002; Castro et al., 2015). For these reasons, relationship-building should be a necessary component of every educator's repertoire.

Strong associations have been found between parental and educator expectations, open communication between stakeholders, and the development of good reading habits (Castro et al., 2015). As such, it is no surprise that family engagement is, "rapidly shifting from a low-priority recommendation to an integral part of education reform efforts" (Mapp & Kuttner, 2013). Parents are interested in what is happening in the classroom, and specifically with their child, while it is of value to educators to understand the dynamics at home; thus, transparent, two-way communication needs to be a priority.

Parents need the support of schools and educators to help them understand the dynamics and inner workings of the school system (McQuiggan & Megra, 2017). Technology, unique classroom environments, diverse classmates, and social-emotional dynamics all come into play as a member of a school community. At times, any and all of those factors may produce stress and anxiety for parents as well as the students themselves. For these reasons and many more, educators must invest time and energy into creating opportunities for families to understand the school, classroom, and learning that takes place (McQuiggan & Megra, 2017).

Educators are not only responsible for the education of their students but also must provide families with the information necessary to increase academic support in the home. Families that have trust in their child's teacher are more likely to be involved in the learning process (Adams & Christenson, 2000). Leveraging the family voice in order to facilitate conversations surrounding the educational process requires all stakeholders to work together so that the student is the beneficiary (Department of Education, n.d.). Schools and educators must understand the various models of partnerships, as well as the tools that can assist them in creating a bond with families (Epstein, 2011; Mapp & Kuttner, 2014; Grant & Ray, 2016; Mapp, Carver, & Lander, 2017).

A Historical Perspective of Family Engagement

A path has been cleared to ensure families are engaged in the educational opportunities of students with the help of the United States Department of Education. With the creation and passing of the Elementary and Secondary Education Act of 1965 and its subsequent iterations, as well as the Individuals with Disabilities Act of 1975, schools have been tasked by the federal government to include families in many student-centered aspects of the school day, and in all processes related to special education (Lipkin & Okamoto, 2015; VCA, 2017). It is surprising then, that even with the federal mandates many families remain uninvolved and that educators often put this important step last on their to-do list.

Elementary and Secondary Education Act of 1965

In 1965, the United States Department of Education wrote and ratified the Elementary and Secondary Education Act (ESEA); it was meant to provide quality and equality in education and was part of President Johnson's "war on poverty" (VCU, 2017, n.p.). The legislation had four primary components, three of which required allocating funds to support educational programming, professional development for educators, and educational materials (VCU, 2017). The fourth component ensured the "promotion of parental involvement" (VCU, 2017, n.p.). The ESEA was reauthorized every five years as mandated in the original act, allowing each president to weigh in, offering modifications that represented changes in the educational climate.

The 2001 reauthorization, known as the No Child Left Behind Act (NCLB), included increased accountability from districts, schools, and teachers through standardized testing and annual report cards (VCA, 2017; U.S. Department of Education, n.d. a). Fifteen years and three iterations later, the 2015 reauthorization, the Every Student Succeeds Act (ESSA), including college and career readiness standards and a teacher/principal evaluation system (VCA, 2017; U.S. Department of Education, n.d. b). Both NCLB and ESSA also included provisions for parent engagement and acknowledged the importance of supporting and strengthening family-school partnerships to close the achievement gap (Grant & Ray, 2016).

The provision for family engagement under ESSA, Title 1, requires districts who receive federal funds to ensure outreach efforts to all families, implement programs and provide activities that directly involve families, and consult in meaningful ways with families on a variety of topics related to school and students (Henderson, 2015). This latest iteration of the ESEA clearly shows the efforts being made to include and engage families in the educational outcomes of their students.

Individuals with Disabilities Act of 1975

The long-held public belief in educating students with disabilities became a reality when, in 1975, Congress passed the Individuals with Disabilities Act (IDEA) (Lipkin & Okamoto, 2015). IDEA included six main points:

- free and appropriate education to all students between the ages of 3 and 21;

- states are responsible for finding, evaluating and determining eligibility, a process known as child find;

- children whose disability prevented them from accessing the general education curriculum were given either an Individualized Family Service Plan (IFSP), for children under three years of age, or an Individualized Education Plan (IEP) for children 3-21;

- teaching children in the least restrictive environment (LRE) possible;

- offering process and procedural safeguards to families such as mediation and due process;

- Collaboration between families, students, and schools in shared decision making and communication.

    (Lipkin & Okamoto, 2015)

It is the partnership piece that teachers and schools need to focus on as families whose children have disabilities often benefit from assistance in finding outside help and understanding classroom supports. With an understanding of the federal laws surrounding parental engagement, it is important to look at the evolution of family-school partnership models.

The History of Family-School Partnership Models

Although the federal government recognized the need for including families in the educational process, ESEA and the Title I provision did not include any language that referred to the inclusion of, or partnership with, families (Mapp, 2012). Finally, in 1967, federal leaders included wording that required "local school officials to create appropriate activities and services in which parents could be involved" (Mapp, 2012). With each updating of the ESEA, the wording and requirements for family engagement strengthened. Some twenty years later, one of the first family-school models was created based on the assumption that when families, schools, and communities share the responsibility for student growth, they learn more (Epstein, 1987).

Family School Partnership Framework

Epstein (2010) believed that if students heard the collective message from educators and families that "the importance of school, of working hard, of thinking creatively, of helping one another, and of staying in school" (p. 82) it was more powerful and had more influence. The Family School Partnership Framework used a visual that included overlapping spheres, one external (including the child in the middle with family, school, and community surrounding it) and one internal (again with the child in the middle and family and institution on either side), each was flexible enough to overlap more or less, depending on the fluidity of collaboration or, equally important, the distance sometimes created when a lack of understanding exists or a partnership is in flux (Epstein, 2011).

This led to a group of "Keys to Successful Partnerships: Six Types of Involvement" (Grant & Ray, 2016, p. 53). Each key represents a necessary component for family involvement: (1) parenting, (2) communicating, (3) volunteering, (4) learning at home, (5) decision making, and (6) collaborating with the community (Epstein, 2011). Epstein's model led to several others, each taking what is believed to be the best parts and adding to what each researcher thought was missing.

Dual Capacity-Building Framework for Family-School Partnerships

Perhaps the most up-to-date and most utilized framework is Dual Capacity by Mapp and Kuttner (2013). Based on research that supported family-school partnership strategies, leadership development and adult learning and motivation, four tenets were developed (Mapp & Kuttner, 2013). The four components move an organization from ineffective to effective partnerships and include (1) identifying the challenge, (2) understanding the challenges – both process and organizational, (3) creating policy and program goals based on skills and knowledge (Capabilities), networks (Connections), beliefs and values (Cognition), and self-efficacy (Confidence), and (4) family and staff capacity outcomes (Mapp & Kuttner, 2013).

A variety of states are currently aligning their partnership strategies with the Dual Capacity Building Framework as a way to encourage both educators and families to partner and be "authentically engaged" (Wood, n.d, n.p.) as they move to a more equitable system of education. With an understanding of frameworks developed, it is important to consider a variety of tools and strategies educators can use to increase parent partnerships, which, in turn, will increase student achievement.

Tools and Strategies to Increase Home School Partnerships

The benefits of engaging with families is clear; students are less likely to be retained, they score higher on tests and get better grades, they attend school more regularly, have better social skills and fewer discipline reports, and they tend to attend and graduate from post-secondary institutions (Grant & Ray, 2016; Henderson & Mapp, 2002). Families also benefit from these partnerships as they tend to have a better understanding of the school and classroom, as well as procedures and policies, they are more positive in terms of school satisfaction and are more likely to take on leadership roles at school, and are better able to help their student with work and the stresses associated with school (Henderson & Mapp, 2002; Grant & Ray 2016).

There are barriers to engagement, however, both for the educator and the parent. Despite best efforts by school districts, some educators do not believe that families have anything to offer and that it is easier if they do not include the family (Grant & Ray, 2016). Additionally, educators may not trust a particular person, or family, based on past experiences or personal biases. Interestingly, this may also be the case for families who may show distrust for the educator or the school without really getting to know either (Grant & Ray, 2016). For both educators and families, a language barrier can either be a detriment or a benefit depending on how each perceives the difference.

An examination of core beliefs may help guide the educator to a better understanding of what it means to partner with families. According to Mapp, Carver, and Lander (2017), the four beliefs are (1) knowing that every family wants what is best for their child and "all families have dreams for their children" (p. 20), (2) all families are able to support learning in some form, (3) a true partnership is equal parts parent and educator, and (4) school leaders bear the brunt of "cultivating and sustaining" (Mapp, Carver, and Lander, 2017, p. 20) positive partnerships. Once the educator believes these, it is quite easy to see how engaging with families is possible as everyone wants the same thing – sometimes, however, the caregiver needs assistance to join in. For these reasons and more, it is vital that educators use every tool and strategy to partner with families.

Foundational strategies

Strategies that take place before school begins or soon after the school year has started are referred to as foundational strategies. The first phone call home, a home visit, and back to school night all set the tone for the year, pull families into the partnership and open the door for exemplary two-way communication (Mapp, Carver, & Lander, 2017). Although at times these tasks can be difficult, it is well worth the time and effort.

First call home. Often, the first call home is negative, happening only after the student has misbehaved or had an issue. Instead, it is important to call in advance of an issue, either prior to the first day or within the first few days. During the call the educator should introduce herself, speak a bit about the class, and ask for information about the student; these are all helpful in creating a bridge (Aguilar, 2015). A positive call "sets a powerful and lasting welcoming tone" (Mapp, Carver, & Lander, 2017, 52).

Home visit. In most cases, educators expect the family to come to school, either for an event or a conference; however, going to the home is a powerful way to learn about the student as well as make the family feel more comfortable (Mapp, Carver, & Lander, 2017). The Parent Teacher Home Visit model connects "the expertise of the family on their child with the classroom expertise of the teacher" (Parent Teacher Home Visits, 2016). It is a mutually agreed upon visit that is exclusively relationship-building in nature. There are two visits, one at each end of the school year, with ongoing, two-way communication in between (Parent Teacher Home Visits, 2016).

Open house/back to school night. Traditionally, the open house has been a time when families come in and listen to the teacher explain the rules and rituals of the classroom as well as the expectations for homework and behavior. Instead, teachers should consider making this an interactive event where there is a brief discussion, and then families can investigate the room, see student work, meet other parents (Mapp, Carver, & Lander, 2017). At a maximum, educators should offer an overview of the instruction for the year, share a strategy or two that might help with homework or a difficult topic, and explain the importance of two-way communication (Watson, 2017). Families can complete an exit ticket prior to leaving that asks three quick questions

such as "share at least one important thing you learned tonight that will benefit your child," "What activities did you enjoy the most/the least," and "Do
you have suggestions for upcoming family events?" (Grant & Ray, 2016, p.
424).

Creating Positive Meetings

Family conferences and Individualized Education Plan (IEP) meetings are two
very stressful times that call for educators to be informative yet listen carefully
to the questions and thoughts of the family involved. Often, they have insights that are important to the child's progress in school, behavior issues
that need assistance, and there are times that families may need assistance
(Mapp, Carver, & Lander, 2017). Regardless of the meeting, coming to the
table with an open mind increases the chances for success and partnership.

Another aspect of creating positive meetings is planning ahead, specifically,
for a translator, if necessary. While it is always preferred to have a translator in
the building, especially someone the family already knows, it is sometimes
necessary to use an on the phone translation services such as TheBigWord
(2017). Parents will appreciate the forethought in having someone available
who speaks their language. A word of caution, though, ensure that the translator is familiar with educational terms and even the specific school where the
child is enrolled as it is sometimes difficult to translate and understand unfamiliar terms.

Family conference. Traditionally called Parent/Teacher Conferences, Mapp,
Carver, and Lander (2017) suggest this change in terminology creates a more
open space where all stakeholders can participate in meaningful conversations to support the student. Bringing the family together can include anyone
who is important to the child's upbringing – parent, grandparent, friend of
the family, caregiver. The student is also part of the meeting and is an active
participant. These meetings are primarily a time to collaborate for the benefit
of the student.

Educators should collect student work in advance and prepare a goal-
setting conference form that will be completed during the family conference.
The form has sections for teacher, family, and student comments, concerns,
areas of strength and areas of weakness as well as a goal-setting section and
signature section (Mapp, Carver, & Lander, 2017). The form guides the meeting along with a well-defined beginning, middle, and end.

The beginning should be interactive, with each family member taking a turn
to discuss how the year is going and any questions they have. It is important
to let the family speak first as it shows them the educator is honestly interested in them and the student (Mapp, Carver, & Lander, 2017). The middle of the

meeting is the time to look together at student work and let the student have a voice. The educator will share both academic and behavioral successes and concerns during this time as well (Pruslin, 2017). The end of the family conference is the time for the group to set goals and discuss how each member can help the student reach them (Pruslin, 2017).

While not ideal, it is sometimes necessary to conduct a conference via the phone. During these family conferences, educators should try to obtain as much information as possible and complete the form, sending it home to the parent, while retaining a copy prior to sending it home. Let the family know you are taking notes and will share them to ensure everyone is in agreement.

Individualized Education Plan (IEP) meeting. While most school districts have a dedicated team leader to run the IEP meeting, it is important for the educator to have a positive mindset and open communication with the family (Mapp, Carver, & Lander, 2017). These two over-arching ideas should guide every meeting and, beyond that, educators should be prepared with student work, current grades, anecdotal stories, and suggestions for future progress (Johnson, 2017). Using a one-page "cheat-sheet" can help focus the conversation. The educator would complete this in advance and bring it to the meeting. The questions include:

- 4 things the student can do independently
- 3 things the student is beginning to do
- 2 things the student can do with support
- During the school year, we will focus on (2-4 skills)
- Key accommodations to use in class (2-4 essential to that student)

  (Mapp, Carver, & Lander, 2017; Johnson, 2017)

The best IEP meeting is one in which the team, collectively, takes into consideration student abilities and weaknesses and creates a plan that is positive and helps the student strive for success; as such, this document supports the process. During the meeting, it would be in the best interest of the student to hold it similar to the family conference for added collaboration.

Partnerships Throughout the School Year

All of the ideas previously discussed set the groundwork for a successful partnership between the family and the educator, yet there is so much more that can be done to engage families. Maintaining strong ties requires both parties to be "equal partners rather than observers" (Mapp, Carver, and Lander, 2017, p. 104). Teachers can provide families with engagement activities and meetings that best meet the needs of all involved. Educators should consider the five guiding principles when seeking to "transform traditional approaches" (Mapp, Carver, and Lander, 2017, p. 104). As such, educators should:

- Link developmental goals to student need;

- Develop relationships between parents and between themselves and parents;

- Create environments that involve all stakeholders and are collaborative by nature;

- Honor differences and experiences in people;

- Strive to be more interactive.

    (Mapp, Carver, Lander, 2017)

Using the principles above, schools and educators can create a whole school or single classroom opportunities such as math and literacy nights, field day, end-of-year celebrations, and publishing parties (Grant & Ray, 2016; Mapp, Carver, Lander, 2017). Anything is possible, limited only by the imagination and determination of the educator.

Additional Tools for Successful Partnerships

Other, simple, yet powerful tools can assist the educator who wishes to increase family engagement. These range from simple letters home to phone calls and text messages, as well as asking for volunteers and creative homework assignments that get the whole family involved.

"You Can" letters. Sending home a letter with information about what students have been learning in class helps families understand the work and the expectations. Including concrete suggestions to help posed in "You Can" statements provide clarity for the family (Mapp, Carver, Lander, 2017).

Phone script. For new teachers or those who want to change up their routine, creating a script for calling home increases the chance they won't forget the important stuff! Including open-ended questions such as "can you tell me about your child?", asking for the best contact number and time to call, as well as other pertinent information starts the year off on the right foot (Mapp, Carver, Lander, 2017).

Letter of introduction. Educators can start the year off with a letter of introduction that describes the goals for the class, a bit about the teacher and any other information families may need to know for a successful year. Educators can invite families to respond in kind for a deeper connection (Mapp, Carver, Lander, 2017).

Asking for volunteers. Educators can increase participation in the classroom and on field trips by asking for volunteers. This group of helpers is capable of working with small groups of students, reading or listening to others read, gathering or preparing materials for the teacher, working one-on-one with struggling students and many more tasks (Bantuveris, 2013; Grant & Ray, 2016).

Interactive home-learning activities. Not the average homework copy page, these are based on real-life experiences and "designed so families and children will have interactions related to what they are learning" (Grant & Ray, 2016, p. 297). The characteristics of this activity include: individualized assignments at ability level, culturally relevant linking home to school, participation of family members, clear directions and materials must be supplied, a building of self-esteem for the student, and flexibility in activity and completion time frame (Barbour, 2010).

Communicating with technology. ClassDojo (Class Twist, 2017) is a technology-based communication tool that parents can access on their cell phone or laptop. Teachers can share pictures, information, homework assignments and, likewise, parents can comment, ask questions, and offer information that may help make the day go smoothly for the student (Class Twist, 2017). An additional benefit is that ClassDojo can be translated so that all students and families can participate (Class Twist, 2017). ClassDojo is just one way to increase communication; however, it is perhaps the easiest and often preferable to a paper journal that the student must remember to take back and forth each day.

Final Thoughts

The research is clear that family-school partnerships are one of the most important pieces of a student's academic career. (Povey et al., 2016; Flamboyan Foundation, 2011; Henderson & Mapp, 2002; Castro et al., 2015; Mapp & Kuttner, 2013; McGuiggan & Megra, 2015). High levels of family involvement are associated with increased school attendance and lower discipline reports, higher reading scores, and fewer academic gaps, as well as students who are more likely to go on to post-secondary institutions (Grant & Ray, 2016; Henderson & Mapp, 2002).

Federal mandates dating back to 1965 show the importance of family involvement, and while legislators did not include it in the original version of the Elementary and Secondary Education Act (ESEA), it was quickly amended (VCA, 2017). The Individuals with Disabilities Education Act (IDEA) of 1975 further delineated the inclusion of families when working with children who have disabilities (Lipkin & Okamoto, 2015). With the most recent revisions to the Elementary and Secondary Education Act, those of the No Child Left Behind Act of 1994 and the Every Student Succeeds Act of 2015, family-school partnerships continue to play a prominent role; each iteration bringing more clarity and substance to the topic (Grant & Ray, 2016; VCU, 2017).

One of the first to offer a framework for engagement, Epstein (1987), offered a complex model with six keys for involvement by families that included parenting, communicating, volunteering, learning at home, decision-making, and collaborating with the community. Several researchers expanded this model, and eventually, Mapp & Kuttner (2013) debuted the Dual Capacity Building Framework. The model begins with an ineffective partnership and, moving through four stages – those of identifying challenges, understanding the challenges, creating policies and programs, and determining family outcomes – converts into a high functioning partnership. Dual Capacity Building Framework has become the gold standard for the family-school engagement and, in fact, several states, including Connecticut, are currently implementing its tenets (Wood, n.d.; Mapp & Kuttner, 2013).

A wide range of strategies exists to encourage and support family-school partnerships. Educators are wise to begin the year with a positive phone call home, and an interactive open house (Mapp, Carver, & Lander, 2017). During the course of the year, providing meaningful and open dialogue during family conferences engenders families and educators alike, and creates a bond between the stakeholders that has the potential to increase student outcomes (Mapp, Carver, & Lander, 2017). Many other strategies can be used to bring families and educators together including requesting volunteers, offering interactive homework, and communicating through technology (Class Twist, 2017; Grant & Ray, 2016). Family-school partnerships have the potential to create a winning combination for students and their families when the educators that support them put engagement strategies at the top of their to-do list.

Points to Remember

- *The Elementary and Secondary Education Act of 1965 was created as a war on poverty that sought to create equity among diverse students.*

- *The Individuals with Disabilities Act of 1975 required all school districts to include families in the decision-making process for students who had disabilities that prevented them from accessing the curriculum.*

- *The most recent federal mandate, the Every Student Succeeds Act of 2015, included directives to increase family-school engagement activities.*

- *The Dual Capacity Building Framework is a four-step model that increases engagement by identifying the challenges, understanding the challenges, creating policies and programs to mitigate the challenges, finally to improve student and family outcomes.*

- *A plethora of tools are available to help educators engage with and meet the needs of families, and ultimately their deserving children.*

References

Adams, K.S. & Christenson, S.L. (2000). Trust and the family-school relationship: Examination of parent-teacher differences in elementary and secondary grades. *Journal of School Psychology, 38*(5), 477-497. Retrieved from https://eric.ed.gov/?id=EJ617586

Aguilar, E. (2015). *The power of the positive phone call home.* Retrieved from https://www.edutopia.org/blog/power-positive-phone-call-home-elena-aguilar

Bantuveris, K. (2013). *5 tips for engaging parent volunteers in the classroom.* Retrieved from https://www.edutopia.org/blog/strategies-for-engaging-parent-volunteers-karen-bantuveris

Castro, M., Exposito-Casas, E., Lopez-Martin, E., Lizasoain, L., Navarro-Asencio, E., &   Gaviria, J.L. (2015). *Parental involvement on student academic achievement: A meta-analysis.* Retrieved from https://www.sciencedirect.com/science/article/pii/S1747938X15000032

Class Twist. (2017). *ClassDojo.* Retrieved from https://www.classdojo.com/resources/

Epstein, J. L. (1987*). Toward a theory of family-school connections: Teacher practices and parent involvement across the school years.* In K. Hurrelmann, F. Kaufmann, and F. Losel (Eds.), *Social Intervention: Potential and constraints*, 121-136. New York: de Gruyter.

Epstein, J. L. (2010). School/family/community partnerships: Caring for the children we share. *Phi Delta Kappan,* 81-96. Retrieved from http://www.kappanmagazine.org

Epstein, J. L. (2011). *School, family, and community partnerships: Preparing educators and improving schools* (2nd ed.). Boulder, CO: Westview Press.

Flamboyan Foundation. (2011). *Setting the stage: The family engagement field.* Retrieved from http://flamboyanfoundation.org/wp/wp-content/uploads/2011/06/Setting-the-stage-4-28-11.pdf

Grant, K. B., & Ray, J. A. (2016). *Home, school, and community collaboration: Culturally responsive family engagement* (3rd ed.). Thousand Oaks, CA: Sage Publications, Inc.

Henderson, A. & Mapp, K.L. (2002). *A new wave of evidence: The impact of school, family, and community connections on student achievement.* Austin, TX: National Center for Family and Community Connections with Schools. Retrieved from https://www.sedl.org/connections/resources/evidence.pdf

Johnson, B. (2017). *How to make IEP meetings more effective.* Retrieved from https://www.edutopia.org/blog/how-make-iep-meetings-more-effective-ben-johnson

Lipkin, P.H. & Okamoto, J. (2015). *The individuals with disabilities act (IDEA) for children with special educational needs.* Retrieved from http://pediatrics.aappublications.org/content/136/6/e1650

Mapp, K.L. (2012). *Tightening up Title I: Title I and parent involvement: Lessons from the past, recommendations for the future.* Retrieved from https://edsource.org/wp-content/uploads/old/-title-i-and-parental-involvement_091556561921.pdf

Mapp, K.L., Carver, I, & Lander, J. (2017). *Powerful partnerships: A teacher's guide to engaging families for student success.* New York: NY: Scholastic

Mapp, K. L. & Kuttner, P. J. (2013). *Partners in education: A dual capacity-building framework for family-school partnerships.* Retrieved from http://www.sedl.org/pubs/framework/FE-Cap-Building.pdf

McQuiggan, M. & Megra, M. (2017). *Parent and family Involvement in Education: Results from the national household education surveys program of 2016.* Retrieved from https://nces.ed.gov/pubs2017/2017102.pdf

Parent Teacher Home Visits. (2016). *PTHV Model.* Retrieved from http://www.pthvp.org/what-we-do/pthv-model/

Povey, J., Campbell, A.C., Willis, L.D., Haynes, M., Western, M., Bennett, S., Antrobus, E., & Pedde, C. (2016). *Engaging parents in schools and building parent-school partnerships: The role of school and parent organization leadership.* DOI: 10.1016/j.ijer.2016.07.005

Pruslin, S. (2017). *Meeting the parents: Making the most of parent-teacher conferences.* Retrieved from http://www.educationworld.com/a_curr/curr291.shtml

TheBigWord. (2017). *OnDemand translations.* Retrieved from https://en-us.thebigword.com/solutions/translation

U.S. Department of Education. (n.d.a). *No child left behind.* Retrieved from https://www2.ed.gov/nclb/landing.jhtml

U.S. Department of Education. (n.d.b). *Every Student Succeeds Act.* Retrieved from https://www.ed.gov/essa?src=rn

VCU. (2017). *Elementary and Secondary Education Act of 1965.* Retrieved from https://socialwelfare.library.vcu.edu/programs/education/elementary-and-secondary-education-act-of-1965/

Watson, A. (2017). *Tips for open house and back to school night.* Retrieved from https://thecornerstoneforteachers.com/open-house/

Wood, L. (n.d.). *Promoting equity through family-school partnerships.* Retrieved from https://www.ed.gov/family-and-community-engagement/bulletin-board/promoting-equity-through-family-school-partnerships

Chapter 8

Administrative Factors:

Supporting Teachers and Contributing to

the Success of All Students

Nicholas D. Young, PhD, EdD,
American International College
and
Kristen Bonanno-Sotiropoulos, MS,
Bay Path University

According to the U.S. Department of Education (n.d.), top performing teachers can make dramatic improvements in student achievement. Great teachers are not just made, but rather they are supported and nurtured throughout their careers (Stein, 2016). An excellent teacher can make the difference between having high achieving students and those that fall through the cracks (Toor, 2011; U.S. Department of Education, n.d.). For teachers to develop and gain the highly effective qualities they need, superior teacher preparation programs are only just the beginning. Career-long assistance from school administration is imperative as well (Stein, 2016). School leaders can help mold teachers to achieve better student outcomes by creating positive school cultures, embracing relationships of mutual respect, employing collaborative efforts, and providing ongoing support and recognition (Bettini Crockett, Brownell, & Merrill, 2016; Lynch, 2015).

Under federal regulations, teachers must be identified as highly-qualified for the license in which they hold (U.S. Department of Education, n.d.). Highly-qualified teachers work to close the achievement gap by consistently engaging in research-based instructional practices (Lynch, 2015). Teacher preparation programs, state licensure exams, subject-matter knowledge expertise, and school districts are responsible for ensuring that all teachers become and stay highly-qualified.

According to Stein (2016), there is a body of knowledge pertaining to beneficial administrative factors for developing, nurturing, and supporting highly-effective teachers. Leadership factors and working conditions rank as the two overarching factors that contribute to the effectiveness of teaching and learning, as well as teacher retention rates (Hightower, Delgado, Lloyd, Wittenstein, Sellers, & Swanson, 2011). A review of the literature on working conditions that support effective teaching and teacher retention revealed six promising components: (1) nurturing collaborative relationships between administration, teachers, and teacher unions; (2) providing academic and instructional supports such as coaches and specialists; (3) housing central office staff within school buildings; (4) providing financial incentives so that teachers feel that schools are vested in them; (5) restructuring school time to include longer prep-periods and smaller class sizes; and (6) increasing common planning time to support increased collaboration (Hightower et al., 2011; Methner, 2013).

School leaders need to be effective enough to nurture environments that truly support teaching and learning through adequate training and continuous support (Lynch, 2015; Stein, 2016). Administrative preparation programs must encompass the struggles and hardships that face American public schools today. In addition, after completing an approved preparation program, new administrators should experience a mentoring phase alongside a highly-effective administrator (Hightower et al., 2011).

Effective Leadership Initiatives that Support Highly Effective Teachers

The Role of an Effective School Leader

Over the past several years, the role of the school principal has evolved into more than a managerial identity and school leaders now engage in supportive practices of empowering and inspiring their teachers to excel in the profession (Stein, 2016). Principals can accomplish some of this using managerial skills; however, most of the time the ability to create and maintain a positive culture of support, relationships, and collaboration between all parties yields beneficial results (Stein, 2016; Toor, 2011).

The research is clear on the positive correlation between school leadership and student achievement, school culture, teacher satisfaction, and teacher retention (Stein, 2016). With regard to teacher satisfaction, that there are certain skills that school leaders should develop in order to ensure educator fulfillment (Stein, 2016). Being transparent and openly communicating the school's mission as well as the reasons why it is important is only the beginning (Stein, 2016). The school leader must also clarify how the stakeholders will accomplish meeting the school's mission and what they can expect for support.

Supporting a community where shared decision-making is the norm allows teachers to feel that they have a voice and are empowered to share their ideas and take an active role in the facilitation of change (Lynch, 2015; Stein, 2016). Finally, the school leader should be visible within the school, including in classrooms, the hallways, team meetings, etc. By being visible, the principal has opportunities to model the school's mission, gain awareness of the day to day happenings, and engage in critical communication with all individuals including students. (Stein, 2016).

Administrator & Teacher Relationships

Building administrators are charged with the task of recruiting, hiring, and retaining high-quality teachers (Lynch, 2015). School leadership is the largest school-based variable that directly impacts student achievement (U.S. Department of Education, n.d.). In order to strengthen the values of the school and increase teacher retention, principals must embrace a culture of high expectations and secure quality instructional staff through meaningful relationships and on-going support including professional development opportunities (Lynch, 2015). It is imperative to stress that school leader support is the leading factor for teacher retention found in the literature (Bettini et al., 2016; Stein, 2016).

According to Methner (2013), the most significant factor in student success is the administrator and teacher relationship. This partnership sets the cultural tone for the school and provides a model for respectful and nurturing connections. There are certain qualities and behaviors most beneficial for developing positive principal and teacher relationships, including having a shared vision of responsibilities, fostering teacher development with a focus on student achievement, and increasing positive faculty energy through shared and individualized learning goals (Methner, 2013; Stein, 2016).

Principals or other school leaders can support and empower teachers in several ways. Shared decision-making inspires teachers to take more ownership in school initiatives, student learning, and increase their effectiveness as a teacher (Kraft & Papay, 2014). Principals can encourage teacher improvement through the recognition of accomplishments and effort. Supporting teacher leaders within the school culture is a positive way to motivate and encourage educators to take on more leadership roles within their school communities (Bettini et al., 2016; Kraft & Papay, 2014; Methner, 2013).

Further examination reveals the importance of building professional learning communities as a way of strengthening the principal and teacher relationship. Professional learning communities should be facilitated by either the principal or a teacher leader (Kraft & Papay, 2014; Methner, 2013). The focus of these collaborative groups supports collegiality, professional growth, and student achievement goals. In order to engage the highest number of teachers in professional learning communities, administrators should provide incentives for participation in addition to recognizing and celebrating collaborative efforts (Bettini et al., 2016; Methner, 2013).

Using Teacher Evaluations to Support Teacher Quality

The goal of teacher evaluations should be on increasing the effectiveness of the individual's impact on student learning (Archer, Cantrell, Holtzman, Joe, Tocci, & Wood, 2016; Van Soelen, 2016). Through the use of constructive evaluation strategies, school leaders have opportunities to intervene and support the growth and development of their teachers, which in return will increase student achievement (Archer et al., 2016). First and foremost, teacher evaluations need to be aligned to clear performance standards and include multiple rating options for the evaluators (Van Soelen, 2016).

Throughout the evaluation process, frequent and consistent feedback, and monitoring are crucial at producing results. Similar to formative assessment in the classroom, school administrators need to provide actionable and supportive feedback with options for change for teachers (Archer et al., 2016). In conjunction with opportunities to engage in meaningful and relevant professional development, providing teachers with the support and resources needed to achieve the intended professional and student goals are critical to ensuring this occurs (Van Soelen, 2016).

Factors that Contribute to Creating Highly Effective Schools

Much research suggests that there are two overarching factors that determine whether or not a school is successful or not (Lynch, 2015; Stein, 2016). The first idea examines student achievement scores. If schools produce high scores on standardized tests across most of their student populations, then that school would be labeled as effective by some groups of researchers (Stein, 2016). On the other hand, the second idea simply looks at the social characteristics and personal growth outcomes for students to determine the effectiveness of the school (Lynch, 2015).

Five common themes emerged in the literature as significant in contributing to school effectiveness (Bettini et al., 2016; Lynch, 2015). The first, quality leadership, includes leaders who are visible, transparent, efficiently model the mission of the school, and continually engage in and support collaborative activities alongside their teachers (Zepeda, 2013). The second, setting high expectations, not only applies to students but teachers as well. Schools can support the high expectation initiative through ongoing and meaningful professional development opportunities (Bettini et al., 2016; Lynch, 2015).

Engagement in on-going screening and monitoring of student performance make up the third element (Lynch, 2015). Using student data wisely to make informed instructional decisions has been proven highly effective time and time again (Lynch, 2015). Creating and providing directionality to identified goals is the fourth component necessary to support an effective school. Administrators usually identify the goals of the school; however, effective communication and guidance in relation to achieving goals to all stakeholders is critical in achieving them (Bettini et al., 2016; Lynch, 2015).

The fifth and final piece of the giant puzzle of school effectiveness is security and organization. Creating safe learning environments for all students and staff is a fundamental component for maximum learning to occur (Bettini et al., 2016). One critical aspect of a safe learning environment is showing respect for all individuals and property within the school community (Lynch, 2015). When students and staff feel safe and comfortable within their environments, they are more likely to take educational risks and succeed.

Additional research identified several other aspects that contribute to an effective school culture including smaller school and class sizes (Darling-Hammond, Wei, Andree, Richardson, Orphanos, 2009). When class sizes are smaller or actual schools are smaller, students feel a stronger sense of connection to their peers and teachers. Another highly researched aspect is participation in a preschool experience (Sanchez, 2017; Scherman, 2014). Studies have proven that children who attend preschool have higher levels of academic and social success than those students with no preschool experiences when starting the early grades (Sanchez, 2017). This success continues throughout consecutive grades.

The last two commonly identified aspects of effective schools and teachers include extended time on learning and professional development opportunities (Farbman, 2015; Mizell, 2010). Extended time on learning should include quality instruction as well as trusting and respectful relationships between school and families. Finally, professional development should always be relevant, frequent, and of high quality to support the instructional practices occurring in the classrooms and the population of students being served (Darling-Hammond, Hyler, & Gardner, 2017).

Working Conditions that Support Highly Effective Teachers and Increase Teacher Retention

According to Bettini et al. (2016), working conditions include such things as the physical features; the organizational structure of a school and/or district; the sociological, political, psychological features of the school environment; and the educational features. The working conditions that teachers face daily, directly affect school effectiveness and instructional practices (Bettini et al., 2016).

Research has identified six working conditions that contribute to the success of instructional quality and student achievement (Kraft & Papay, 2014). The six elements include: the culture of the school and/or district, having an instructionally focused administration and collegial support, the quality of the instructional materials and resources, the make-up of the instructional groupings, extended time for instruction, and ample time for planning (Bettini et al., 2016; Kraft & Papay, 2014).

School culture is essential to the retention and attrition of teachers. Cultures that embrace academic press, collaboration and collective responsibility have the highest rates of teacher retention (Bettini et al., 2016; Kraft & Papay, 2014). When teachers stay in their positions and students have consistency, student achievement increases. In addition to academic performance, teacher consistency contributes to maintaining safe and secure learning environments, thus increasing students' social development.

Teacher effectiveness improves greatly when schools engage in frequent collaborative efforts and activities. Instructionally focused administration, and collegial support are two of the best predictors of teacher efficiency and, therefore, higher student performance (Venables, 2017). The curriculum is an important component of instructional quality and is critical to supporting student achievement, as are the quality and availability of instructional materials and resources (Venables, 2017). Instructional materials define the scope of instruction, the methods for introducing new content, and the evaluation of learning. Quality instructional materials can shape pedagogical practices (Venables, 2017).

Extensive research suggests that instruction is most effective when classes and student groupings are small and similar abilities are combined (Wanzek, Vaughn, Scammacca, Metz, Murray, Roberts, & Danielson, 2013). When students are placed in smaller classrooms or groups and surrounded by peers with similar ability levels, they feel more connected and receive more frequent and quality instruction (Bettini et al., 2016; Wanzek et al., 2013).

The final two components, time for instruction and planning, provide some of the best opportunities for increased student achievement. Extended time on instruction is highly guarded as the best possible outcome for student performance (Farbman, 2015). Planning time provides teachers with time to think through and improve their instructional practices (Skowron & Danielson, 2015). This is an important step in student outcomes as the best planning is a blueprint for learning and produces lessons where the educator facilitates deep thinking and skills acquisition (Skowron & Danielson, 2015).

Final Thoughts

Highly effective teachers are not just made, they must be supported, nurtured, and recognized for their hard work and devotion to the profession (Lynch, 2015; Stein, 2016). Research continually supports the notion that highly qualified teachers have the potential to increase student achievement (Lynch, 2015) substantially. In order for teachers to be effective and continue to be successful, certain elements must be present. School leaders, through the creation of well-structured instructional teams and collaboration opportunities, can facilitate the positive growth of highly-qualified teachers (Venables, 2017; Bettini et al., 2016).

Research has identified many components to ensuring effective schools and teachers are secured. Elements such as quality teacher and administrator relationships, setting high expectations for teachers in addition to students, creating and supporting collaborative activities such as professional learning communities, visible and transparent administrators, frequent monitoring and feedback, and ensuring safe learning environments all ensure effective schools (Lynch, 2015; Methner, 2013; Stein, 2016).

The new role of the school principal embraces the qualities of both a manager and an instructional leader (Zepeda, 2013). In addition to having good managerial skills, today's principals need to inspire and support their teachers and staff to strive for individual and student growth. Principals can ensure they are championing their teachers and staff through effective communication skills, transparency, and shared decision-making efforts (Zepeda, 2013). In addition to encouraging and supporting their teachers, the relationships between administrators and teachers is a critically important factor to setting the cultural tone of the school community and student success (Kraft & Papay, 2014; Lynch, 2015). School leaders can help to strengthen these important relationships through engagement in professional learning communities and supporting teacher leaders through shared decision-making and instructional leadership teams (Venables, 2017; Methner, 2013).

Further research identified several critical factors that contribute to the overall effectiveness of a school (Stein, 2016). Leaders who are highly visible and embrace a transparent point of view for running and supporting the mission of the school are highly sought after for increasing the success of schools (Lynch, 2015).

Schools that openly embrace and practice a culture of collaborative efforts, both with teachers and students, are most efficient (Stein, 2016). Collaboration and cooperative learning through meaningful professional development is crucial to improve teaching, develop collegial partnerships, and ultimately increase student outcomes (Darling-Hammond et al., 2017).

Creating safe learning environments provides all individuals, teachers, staff, and students, with the security they need to thrive and honor mutual respect, acceptance, creativity, risk-taking, and empathy for all individuals (Lynch, 2015). The ability to create and maintain quality relationships enables people to feel connected and develop a sense of belonging within the school community, which ultimately leads to productivity, commitment, and increased performance (Darling-Hammond, 2009).

When thinking about teacher retention and providing instructional consistency for students, working conditions play a huge role in supporting these efforts (Betini et al., 2016). This same research has identified certain factors that contribute to maintaining exceptional work environments and therefore support teacher retention. Instructionally focused administration is at the top of the list (Bettini et al., 2016).

Focusing on instruction first and foremost, ensure that student achievement is at the forefront of all decisions and change efforts (Skowron & Danielson, 2015). When an instruction is the main focus, the availability and access of appropriate resources and materials is another critical piece of the puzzle (Skowron & Danielson, 2015). Equally important, extended time on learning, additional time for planning, and collaborative efforts are highlighted in the literature as essential for retaining teachers and increasing teaching and learning efforts (Farbman, 2015; Venerables, 2017). In addition, smaller class sizes and instructional groupings are key to supporting student achievement, social engagement, and lessen undesirable behaviors (Kraft & Papay, 2014).

Points to Remember

- *For teachers to develop and gain the highly effective qualities they need, effective teacher preparation programs are only the beginning, schools need to continue from there. School administrators need to ensure certain elements are in place to support the continued growth of our teachers.*

- *Six promising elements found in the literature for supporting effective teachers include: nurturing collaborative relationships with all stakeholders; providing on-going academic and instructional supports; placing a few central office staff within school buildings; incorporating incentives for teachers to show a belief in them; restructuring school time to include longer prep periods and smaller class sizes; and increasing common planning time, which will support increased collaboration.*

- *Five themes exposed in the research for creating high-quality schools include quality leadership, setting high expectations, using frequent*

> *student data to make informed decisions; providing directionality per-*
> *taining to school goals, and ensuring security and organization within*
> *the school community.*

- *Six critical components to ensure positive working conditions for*
  teachers include an encouraging school and/or district culture; an in-
  structionally focused administration; high-quality instructional ma-
  terials; student groupings; extended time on learning; and increased
  time for planning.

References

Archer, J., Cantrell, S., Holtzman, S.L., Joe, J.M., Tocci, C.M., & Wood, J. (2016). *Better feedback for better teaching: A practical guide to improving classroom observations.* San Francisco, CA: Jossey Bass

Bettini E., Crockett, J., Brownell, M., & Merrill, K. (2016). Relationships between working conditions and special educators' instruction. *The Journal of Special Education.* 50(3). 178-190. doi: 10.1177/0022466916644425

Darling-Hammond, L., Hyler, M.E., & Gardner, M. (2017). *Effective teacher professional development.* Retrieved from https://learningpolicyinstitute.org/product/effective-teacher-professional-development-report

Darling-Hammond, L., Wei, R., Andree, A., Richardson, N., & Orphanos, S. (2009). Professional learning in the learning profession: A status report on teacher development in the United States and abroad. *National Staff Development Council and the School Design Network.* Retrieved from https://learningforward.org/docs/pdf/nsdcstudytechnicalreport2009.pdf?sfvrsn=0

Farbman, D.A. (2015). The case for improving and expanding time in school: A review of research and practice. *National Center on Time & Learning.* Retrieved from www.timeandlearning.org/sites/default/files/resources/caseformorelearningtime.pdf

Hightower, A., Delgado, R., Lloyd, S., Wittenstein, R., Sellers, K., & Swanson, C. (2011). Improving student learning by supporting quality teaching: Key issues, effective strategies. *Editorial Projects I Education, Inc.* Retrieved from https://www.edweek.org/media/eperc_qualityteaching_12.11.pdf

Kraft, M., & Papay, J. (2014). Can professional environments in schools promote teacher development? Explaining heterogeneity in returns to the teaching experience. *Educational and Policy Analysis.* 36. 476-500. DOI: 10.3102/0162373713519496

Lynch, M. (2015). What factors make an effective school? *The Edvocate.* Retrieved from http://www.theedadvocate.org/what-factors-make-a-school-effective/

Methner. G.V. (2013). *Perceptions of administrative support and follower readiness in middle school teachers.* Retrieved from https://etd.ohiolink.edu/rws_etd/document/get/bgsu1383582751/inline

Mizell, H. (2010). *Why professional development matters.* Retrieved from
https://learningforward.org/docs/pdf/why_pd_matters_web.pdf

Sanchez, C. (2017). *Pre-K: Decades worth of studies, one strong message.* Retrieved from https://www.npr.org/sections/ed/2017/05/03/524907739/pre-k-decades-worth-of-studies-one-strong-message

Scherman, J.M. (2014). *Why is preschool important? Debunking the myths.*
Retrieved from

http://www.rasmussen.edu/degrees/education/blog/why-preschool-important-myths/

Skowron, J. & Danielson, C. (2015). *Powerful lesson planning: Every teacher's guide to effective instruction.* New York, NY: Skyhorse Publishing.

Stein, L. (2016). Schools need leaders not managers: It's time for a paradigm shift. *Journal of Leadership Education.* 15(2). 21-30. doi: 10.12806/v15/12/13

Toor, S. (2011). Differentiating leadership from management: An empirical investigation of leaders and managers. *Leadership & Management in Engineering.* 11(4). 310-320.DOI:10.1061/%28ASCE%29LM.1943-5630.0000138

U.S. Department of Education (n.d.). Great teachers and great leaders. Retrieved from

https://www2.ed.gov/policy/elsec/leg/blueprint/great-teachers-great-leaders.pdf

Van Soelen, T.M. (2016). *Crafting the feedback teachers need and deserve: A guide for leaders.* New York, NY: Routledge.

Venables, D. (2017). *Facilitating teacher teams and authentic PLCs: The human side of leading people, protocols, and practices.* Alexandria, VA: ASCD.

Wanzek, J., Vaugh, S., Scammacca, N., Metz, K., Murray, C., Roberts, G., & Danielson, L. (2013). Extensive reading interventions for students with reading difficulties after grade 3. *Review of Educational Research.* 83. 163-195. DOI: 10.3102/0034654313477212

Zepeda, S.J. (2013). The principal as instructional leader: A practical handbook (3rd ed). New York, NY: Routledge.

Chapter 9

Stemming Teacher Shortages:
A Community Apprenticeship Model

Dr. Tracey Benson, EDLD,
University of North Carolina at Charlotte
and
Justin MacDonald, MA,
Digital Arts and Technology Academy

High teacher turnover rates have created teacher shortages that affect all schools, especially those in hard-to-staff urban settings (Ronfeldt, Loeb, & Wyckoff, 2013). Alternative teacher certification programs have helped fill some of the voids, yet shortages and high levels of attrition persist. With nearly all fifty states requiring a four-year degree as a prerequisite to applying for teacher certification, large pools of potential teachers are excluded as they lack the required educational background; however, research shows that teaching ability and aptitude, more than content knowledge, is a strong predictor of student achievement (Constantine et al., 2009). A community-based apprentice model of alternative teacher certification, if implemented with fidelity, may provide the key to increasing student achievement through stemming persistent teacher shortages.

Transitioning away from a paradigm that requires a 4-year degree as a prerequisite to become a full-time teacher toward a model that builds upon research that identifies teaching ability, rather than teaching credentials, a community-based apprentice model of alternative teacher certification significantly widens the teacher pipeline through recruiting individuals with at least a high school degree who would like to teach in local schools (Alvarez, 2017). This paradigm proposes employing best practice in coaching through providing daily, side-by-side coaching for new teachers throughout the duration of the program. Other programs aimed at recruiting and training teachers who do not already possess a 4-year college degree, such as paraprofessional-to-teachers, fail to produce significant numbers of full-time classroom teachers (NYC Teaching Fellows, 2018). This new paradigm aims not only to produce a significant number of qualified teachers but may also halt teacher turnover through employing best practices in teacher growth, development, and support.

Teacher Experience and Student Achievement

Teacher attrition and shortages impact both student achievement and school and district economic sustainability. In a study that included 850,000 observations of fourth and fifth graders in New York elementary schools for eight years, Ronfeldt, Loeb, & Wyckoff (2013) examined the effect of teacher turnover on student achievement, as well as the effects of teacher turnover in different kinds of schools. High teacher turnover was found to lead to lower student achievement in both math and ELA scores (Ronfeldt et al., 2013). Specifically, students who were taught by new teachers resulted in scores that were 8.2% to 10.2% of a standard deviation below more experienced teachers (Ronfeldt et al., 2013).

Research has shown that teacher effectiveness is correlated with a number of years of classroom experience, and that teachers generally undergo a steep learning curve during their first three years (Kini & Podolsky, 2016). Studies reveal that students taught by well-trained, experienced teachers achieve at considerably higher levels compared to students taught by inexperienced teachers (Kini & Podolsky, 2016). While seemingly intuitive, research has consistently shown that more experienced teachers, on average, produce higher rates of student achievement (Kini & Podolsky, 2016).

Teacher turnover is particularly harmful to the achievement of students in schools with large populations of students from disadvantaged backgrounds (Ronfeldt et al., 2013). Current analysis stipulates that high-poverty urban and rural districts require more than 700,000 new teachers annually (Garcia & Huseman 2009; Rice 2010). Legislation aimed at reducing class size has increased the demand for teachers, particularly in schools that serve disadvantaged students; however, corresponding regulations or incentives to support hard-to-staff schools in retaining teachers has yet to be addressed in any substantive fashion (Chingos & Whitehurst, 2011).

Teacher Attrition

In 2008 in Nebraska, it was found that six percent of teachers leave the profession each year, one-fifth of new hires quit teaching within three years, and in urban areas, 50 percent of educators quit after five years (Garcia & Huseman, 2009). Nationally, high poverty schools tend to experience considerably higher teacher turnover, and instead of focusing on student learning and narrowing the achievement gap, these schools spend valuable time and scarce human and financial resources rebuilding their staff (Sutcher, Darling-

Hammond, & Carver-Thomas, 2016; Carver-Thomas & Darling-Hammond, 2017; Aragon, 2016).

New teachers tend to leave before ascending their learning curve for several reasons. First, many new teachers feel overwhelmed by the tasks they are expected to master, including lesson planning, time management, and establishing positive connections with parents; this feeling may be exacerbated by the fact that beginning teachers are more likely to be assigned lower-performing students (Podolsky, Kini, Bishop, & Darling-Hammond, 2016; Aragon, 2016). In addition, as they are usually the only adult in the room for much of the day, many novice teachers feel isolated and unsupported (Aragon, 2016). One in four of all teachers who depart the teaching profession report leaving the classroom to pursue another career, or aspirations to improve career opportunities in or out of education (Podolsky et al., 2016; Papay & Kraft, 2017). Dissatisfaction underlying attrition is most often listed as being due to low salaries, lack of support from the school administration, student discipline problems, and lack of teacher influence over decision-making (Podolsky et al., 2016; Aragon, 2016).

Teacher Attrition in Urban Settings

Since 2000, teacher attrition has been on the rise across the United States (Strauss, 2017). Chicago, New York City, and Los Angeles have all experienced high rates of teacher attrition (Barnum, 2016). All three cities host alternative teacher certification programs; however, regardless of the numerous traditional and alternative routes to teacher certification, each of these three cities continues to struggle with teacher recruitment and retention.

- From 2005 to 2007, Chicago Public Schools reported that 46% of all K – 12 schools experienced 20% or more teacher turnover annually, with the vast majority in chronically low stability schools serving a student body comprised of majority African-American, low income, and low achieving students (Allensworth, Ponisciak, & Mazzeo, 2009). Even more broadly across the state of Illinois, it was found that "36 percent of new teachers remain in the highest achieving schools through their first five years compared to only 22 percent of new teachers in the lowest performing schools" (DeAngelis & Presley, 2007). The significant difference in teacher turnover rates between low-income and non-low-income schools may be one of the many contributors to the persistent achievement gaps in large cities like Chicago.

- Teachers hired by the New York City Department of Education during the school year 2009 – 2010 left their school placements after two years at a rate of 37% (NYU: Steinhardt, 2015). Numerically, of the 2,595 teachers hired during this time, only 1,635 teachers remained in their assigned classroom after two years on the job. This same study reports that since 2006, of teachers who left their teaching jobs at their first assigned school, those who served in high-poverty schools left, on average, at a rate 14% higher than those who served in low-poverty schools (NYU: Steinhardt, 2015). Therefore, if the estimated 2-year teacher attrition rate in New York City is nearly 40% and teachers in high-poverty schools were shown to leave at a rate 14% higher than the average, this means that on average, students who attend low-income schools can reasonably expect nearly half of the teaching core to be new to their school every year.

- Mayer (2016) estimates that, in Los Angeles, "on any given school site, that if…a child…starts kindergarten in 2016, and another [child] start[s] in 2021, approximately *half* of the staff will be new by the time [the] second child enters a classroom" (p. 1). Between school years 2002 – 2003 and 2008 – 2009, of the 13,255 first year teachers hired during this span of time, nearly 40%, approximately 5,300 teachers, left their placement after one year (Mayer, 2016). From the east coast to the midwest, all the way to the west coast, teacher turnover rates have been at a staggeringly high rate for quite some time.

These examples illustrate that the traditional national model for teacher preparation continues to fail to stem teacher attrition and shortages. Despite numerous traditional and alternative teacher certification programs operating in these three cities, and the United States as a whole, teacher attrition, and shortages continue to significantly plague the educational program (Strauss, 2017; American Teachers Federation, 2017). This coast-to-coast analysis highlights the urgent need for another paradigm. As an education sector, a different model of teacher preparation is sorely needed, and it must be specifically designed to attract and train teachers who will *remain* in the classroom and overcome the learning curve to become master teachers, especially in high-needs, low-income urban schools (Podolsky, et al., 2016; Papay & Kraft, 2017).

Barriers to Teacher Certification

In a time of teacher shortages, districts feel the strain of trying to enforce the certification criteria while facing the reality that every classroom of children requires an adult, certified to teach (Corcillo, 2016). Sass (2014) argues that within traditional and alternative certification programs, minimum educational requirements could actually reduce quality by differentially raising the cost of licensure thereby dissuading talented potential teachers from entering the profession. Moreover, because the intent of teacher certification is to ensure that teaching candidates have taken a prescribed set of coursework, certification often serves as a barrier to anyone who has not done so (Sass, 2014). This means that while districts may experience the hardships of teacher shortages, often leading schools to fill vacant teaching spots with long-term uncertified or retired substitute teachers, these same districts are constrained by restrictive certification policies that will not allow them to explore creative options for stemming shortages (Ben-Shahar, 2017). To address this ongoing issue of barriers to entry, the community-based teacher apprenticeship model proposes creating a pathway for individuals who would like to teach but do not meet the entry requirements for contemporary traditional or alternative teacher preparation programs.

Teacher Effectiveness and Entry Requirements

Research conducted by Kane, Rockoff, & Staiger (2008) suggests that the emphasis on certification status may be misplaced because little difference is found between the average academic achievement that certified, uncertified, and alternatively certified teachers have on students. Constantine et al. (2009) conducted a study that included comparisons of teachers who chose alternative certification routes to certification to teachers who chose traditional routes. The findings from the experimental analyses indicate that there was no statistically significant difference in student achievement from placing an alternatively certified teacher in the classroom compared to a traditionally certified teacher. In this study, it is particularly telling that average differences in reading and math achievement were not statistically significant either. Similarly, a 2001 study by the National Center for Education Evaluation also found no statistical difference between the academic achievements of students taught by alternatively certified teachers and those taught by traditionally certified teachers (Garcia & Huseman, 2009).

In another study, it was found that teachers with master's degrees were not significantly more effective than those without, unless the teacher was at the secondary level and possessed a master's degree in the academic discipline being taught (Greenwald, Hedges, & Laine, 1996). Moreover, Constantine et al. (2009) found that there was no evidence of a statistically positive relationship between majoring in education and student achievement. While certification status and educational attainment do not show statistically significant differences in classroom effectiveness of teachers, Darling-Hammond (2000) found that knowledge about teaching and learning (pedagogy) showed a strong relationship to teaching effectiveness.

The absence of statistically significant differences in student achievement between certification routes or level of education, coupled with evidence that "pedagogical knowledge" shows a strong relationship with student achievement suggests teaching ability may be the dominant factor in determining the effectiveness of a classroom teacher (Guerriero, n.d.). Said another way, it is how well a teacher teaches, not what degree a teacher possesses that is the dominant indicator of a whether a teacher is effective or not.

Traditional Teacher Preparations: What's not working?

Traditional teacher preparation programs have changed little in the last twenty years, and that lack of change has further enabled high teacher attrition rates, teacher shortages, and lack of teacher effectiveness (Freeman, Simonson, Briere, MacSuga-Gage, 2014). These programs focus on ways to theoretically prepare teachers to enter the classroom by teaching them in traditional college courses and providing short, often un-mentored or unstructured, practicums at school sites. These practicums provide real-life experiences that are sometimes counter to the teachers' theoretical training, and they often feel unprepared or disenfranchised, particularly in dealing with student behavior. Freeman et al. (2013) found that many programs do not effectively train teachers in classroom management and some don't have any requirements to implement the teaching of these skills. As well, these programs also offer a limited follow-up on graduate persistence or effectiveness in the field as teachers are rarely contacted after they finish their degree and practicum (Freeman et al., 2013).

These types of programs can be onerous and time-consuming endeavors that create unnecessary barriers to teacher recruitment and retention. There are three main difficulties that traditional programs have in creating a consistent pool of qualified teachers: 1) much of the learning is disconnected from the context in which it will be utilized, and the coursework is often onerous, theoretical, and rigid, 2) they take numerous years and require numerous weekly hours in which there is most often no compensation and often cost the pre-service teacher money, 3) particularly in urban schools, the pool of pre-service educators is often not from the communities in which they will be teaching, and little to no recruitment takes place within these programs (Stronge, 2007).

Knowledge should not be primarily taught in a disconnected teacher preparation program but should be taught within the classroom in which it will be used (Scott, Gentry & Phillips, 2014). This is particularly important in teaching, as the knowledge of pedagogy, classroom management, curricular design, and assessment, are only as good as a teacher's ability to effectively utilize that knowledge in the classroom (Scott et al., 2014). Furthermore, the flexibility and adaptability of knowledge is highly increased when it is used within its context, as one must adapt to variable situations (Scott et al., 2014). This creates a much more robust and applicable knowledge than the often rigid understanding of concepts taught outside of the classroom environment.

The practical skills needed in teaching, such as coaching, building relationships, classroom management, and delivery of instruction, are becoming more relevant in the classroom due to high stakes testing and increased teacher accountability, and yet the existing priorities of teacher preparation programs are more aligned with critical thinking and improving academic knowledge (Arnett, 2013). Teaching is not only an academic endeavor, but it is also a practical skill that should be treated as such.

The cost of traditional teacher preparation programs is often quite high as it includes tuition costs for undergraduate or graduate degrees or for online courses. According to one website, the cost of a teaching certificate program is typically between $10,000-$30,000, and the cost of a bachelor's or master's degree program is typically between $12,000 - $100,000+ (CostHelper, 2018). Given current teacher salaries, there is little incentive for individuals to invest such large sums of money for what may be little return on their investment in the short term. Much of this money goes to institutes of higher learning, who are often not directly impacted by the quality of teachers in the community in which they serve.

Lastly, traditional teacher preparation programs do not actively recruit individuals, and therefore don't target individuals from areas with teacher shortages. This can mean that teachers are even less prepared to teach in the classroom as they are not familiar with the culture or area in which they will teach (Mader, 2016). If traditional preparation programs were to recruit and support individuals from high needs areas, the cultural expertise of these individuals would be a great advantage in overcoming classroom challenges around discipline and student relationships. Furthermore, these community-based teachers would know the resources both needed and available, in the area to make a larger impact on the school as a whole (Alvarez, 2017).

Contemporary Alternative Certification and Teacher Attrition

While an overwhelming majority of alternative certification programs across the United States require a four-year college degree to enroll, several states have developed alternative certification routes for paraprofessionals who do not hold a formal four-year degree (Woods, 2016). Other alternative certification programs, like Teach for America, target college graduates without degrees in the field of education (Teach for America, 2017). The federal government has incentivized individuals to pursue teacher certification via these alternative routes by offering loan repayment under the Federal Stafford Program anytime within the life of the borrower's loan, eligibility for 100% cancellation of Federal Perkins Loans, and access to federal grants to fund master's degrees while teaching (U.S. Department of Education Office of Postsecondary Education, 2014). As a result of the expanded efforts to recruit teachers to the profession, every year, thousands of new teachers pass through hundreds of different preparation programs and are hired by our nation's schools, and one in five new hires are from alternative certification programs (Kamentz, 2014).

Leap to Teacher (New York State), and Paraprofessional Teacher Preparation Grant Program (Massachusetts), are examples of programs that work with paraprofessionals who do not have a four-year degree to pursue higher education and advance their careers (Massachusetts Department of Higher Education, 2018). In a study conducted on graduation rates from the Leap to Teacher program at Queens College in New York it was found that, from 1996 to 2009, 43% of the 706 part-time students successfully graduated from the program, with only 60% of the sampled graduates remaining in New York City Schools for more than six years (Abramovitz, D'Amico, Mason, & DeLutro, 2011). Mathematically, given graduation rates and speculating on the sample rate of 60% being representative of the larger graduate population, the Queens College Leap to Teacher program produced a little under 200 teachers over 14 years (an average of 13 teachers per year) who chose to serve more than six years in the local public school system (Abramovitz et al., 2011). The Massachusetts program offers grant money to paraprofessionals who wish to become teachers. The monies awarded are not need-based but rather are meant to reduce the overall monetary burden, and one of the few requirements is that recipients must file with Free Application for Federal Student Aid (FAFSA) (Massachusetts Department of Higher Education, 2018).

Other contemporary alternative teacher certification programs, like Teach for America (TFA), have sought to recruit and train college graduates to teach in high needs, urban schools (Teach for America, 2017). TFA employs many of the same entry requirements as other alternative teacher preparation programs. In particular, it combines fast-track training with an emphasis on recruiting high achieving college graduates; many from colleges and universities outside of the urban communities in which they will be placed (Teach for America, 2017). While TFA focuses on the effectiveness of new to the classroom teachers, this model overlooks the importance of teacher retention; upwards of 80% or more leave the field by the fourth year of teaching (Heilig & Jez, 2010). TFA places corps members in areas of the most need, as opposed to communities they are familiar with, and this reality compounds the difficulties TFA teachers face when working in both a new field and in a new culture (Heilig & Jez, 2010). While TFA has been in existence since the early 1990's and provides a viable route for certification, the urban school districts in which they serve have continued to struggle with teacher retention.

New York Teaching Fellows are college graduates who are trained by the district to become forward thinking educators (NYC Teaching Fellows, 2018). They have very similar retention rates to regular certified teachers, with Teaching Fellows having slightly higher retention rates in the first two years, yet by their fifth year in teaching, after four years of consistent service, only 50% of both groups are still with the district (Kane et al., 2008). While uncertified teachers have somewhat lower retention rates (approximately 45%), both groups leave the classroom at high rates (Kane et al., 2008).

Charter schools have become more widespread in recent years with efforts to provide accessible, high-quality educational opportunities for students; however, they have consistently been found to have higher rates of teacher attrition than traditional public schools (Goldring, Taie, & Riddles, (2014). In the 2012-13 school year, public school attrition rate was 15.7 percent nationally, while the turnover rate of teachers in charter schools was slightly higher at a rate of 18.4 percent (Goldring et al., 2014). While research has shown wide variation in student academic outcomes from school-to-school and year-to-year, a consistent thread of low teacher retention in charter schools has sustained over time (Goldring et al., 2014).

In 1994, the Department of Defense established *Troops to Teachers* to help improve public school education by recruiting, preparing, and supporting former members of the U.S. military services to be teachers in high-poverty schools (U.S. Army, 2018). The program has been in existence since 1994 and placed more than 11,000 former troops in public schools nationwide (U.S. Army, 2018). Troops to Teachers program completers receive highly positive reviews for their classroom effectiveness, yet the low number of teachers produced will make little impact on the estimated 2 million teacher vacancies occurring over the next decade (Nunnery, Kaplan, Owings, Pribesh, 2010).

These early iterations of alternative teacher preparation programs have provided a much-needed human resource pipeline. As the phenomenon of high teacher turnover continues to plague hard-to-staff, urban schools, independent non-profit organizations, colleges, and universities respond through developing innovative programming to churn out higher numbers of certified teachers (Aragon, 2016). The models, while moderately successful in providing pathways for individuals with four-year degrees to access a route to certification, have done little to stem persistent problems with teacher attrition. Community-based models should at the very least be considered as a necessary next evolution of alternative teacher preparation. Persistent teacher turnover within our current models is evidence that our public school system is in dire need of a new paradigm that is specifically designed to reduce barriers to entry, increase retention, and lower attrition (Alvarez, 2017).

Changing the Paradigm: Community-based Teacher Apprenticeships

Given the evidence that high teacher attrition negatively affects student achievement, produces negative financial impacts on schools and school districts, and current alternative certification routes struggle to retain teachers, more attention is needed to exploring other human resource models to address this nationwide phenomenon. Research from Sass (2014) finds that that certification programs with low entry requirements can produce teachers that are as productive, or even more productive, than traditionally prepared teachers. Using this understanding, districts and states should consider exceptions to the 4-year college degree required to enter the teaching profession. Without this requirement, community-based apprenticeship programs can function to make teaching a viable option for those who would like to teach, but cannot due to the lack of the currently mandated prerequisite educational requirements (Alvarez, 2017).

A New Paradigm: Community-based Apprentice Alternative Certification Programs

New teachers often leave the profession because they are given little professional support, feedback, or demonstration of what it takes to help their students succeed (Podolsky et al., 2016). New teacher turnover rates can be cut considerably through comprehensive induction—a combination of high-quality mentoring, professional development and support, scheduled interactions with other teachers in the school and in the larger community, and formal assessments for new teachers during at least their first two years of teaching (Loschert, 2015). The community-based certification model is specifically designed to 1) dramatically expand the pool of prospective teachers through targeting individuals with at least a high school degree who would like to teach, but currently do not have a viable route to pursue certification, 2) decrease teacher attrition within high-poverty, high-minority schools by selecting individuals who exhibit high interest in teaching in their local school, and 3) increase new teacher efficacy by providing high-quality, on-the-job professional development (Alvarez, 2017).

A community-based model should seek to break down barriers to entering the teaching profession by implementing eligibility requirements such as: 1) successful completion of high school, 2) a passing score on the basic knowledge and skills test for teacher certification (differs by state), and 3) a successful work history that indicates the ability to sustain stable employment (NYC Teaching Fellows, 2018). The community-based model mirrors many of the current alternative teacher certification programs such as aggressive recruiting of high-quality candidates, summer induction, and hands-on training; however, this model includes enhancements, such as daily professional development delivered under a master teacher at a 3-to-1 ratio of master teacher-to-apprentice and facilitated access to the appropriate course of study to obtain full teacher licensure through partnerships with local colleges and universities. Through implementing best practice by significantly increasing the teacher pipeline, providing intensive professional development, decreasing social and proximal distance of teachers to the school site, and stemming teacher attrition, this model seeks to increase the quality of classroom instruction in hard-to-staff schools significantly.

These types of programs would be shorter in length than traditional programs. Being focused primarily on the practical activities of teaching and the applicable knowledge within the context. Theoretical knowledge and pedagogical practices can be learned throughout the teacher's work while being applied in the workplace. The teachers in these programs will receive most of their training and mentorship within the contextual environment. This is done so that teachers learn how theories and practices are employed in dynamic real-life environments. As discussed previously, research shows that learning within the context that that knowledge is applied makes for better retention, understanding, and elasticity in practice of that knowledge. Furthermore, teachers can take part in the professional learning communities and professional development at their work site, further providing learning opportunities.

As teachers in this program, they are working for schools throughout the mentorship and training components; thus, they will be paid by the district for their work. A formal mentoring process for the teacher's first two years teaching is suggested. The community-based mentorship programs are based in and should seek out candidates from, the community in which the teaching is needed. This creates a more consistent pool of potential teachers who are familiar with the needs and resources of the community in which they hope to teach. Not only does this benefit the district, school, and the students within them, but it also benefits the teachers to be familiar with the students and community in which they will teach.

Costs and Benefits

This model has the potential to substantially increase teacher pipelines by tapping into currently ineligible high school graduates as potential teachers. In 2015, 88 percent, or 9 out of 10 adults, held at least a high school diploma or GED and of those only 50% are eligible to teach because of four-year degree requirements (Ryan & Bauman, 2016). This fact contrasts sharply with the large number of urban school districts now facing double-digit teacher attrition rates. If community-based teacher preparation programs were an option for adults who would like to teach, but who do not currently have a viable route, the pipeline for potential teachers would be significantly larger (Alvarez, 2017).

Hiring teachers from the local community may decrease attrition due to factors associated with long commutes to work. One such study found that employee retention could be reasonably predicted based on the miles they commuted to work (Sullivan, 2015). It was found that distances from work over 12 miles increase an employee's likelihood of quitting by 18 percent, and commutes between 30 – 45 minutes increase the probability of quitting to more than 92 percent (Sullivan, 2015). Therefore, cutting the commute of teachers to their place of work, in hard-to-staff-schools, may likely lead to a natural decrease in teacher attrition.

Research consistently finds that social distance has a significant impact on teacher-student relationships, levels of interpersonal connection, and relational trust (Wark & Gallinher, 2007). "Social distance is generally understood as a uniquely sociological concept, irreducible to spatial or biological (genetic) distance" (Karakayali, 2009). Within the social distance framework, individuals who are in close contact with one another and share similar social characteristics tend to be less prejudiced, thereby increasing the probability of establishing more trusting and mutually supportive relationships (Wark & Gallinher, 2007). Employing the philosophy that decreasing the social distance between student and teacher through seeking to hire teachers from the local community, community-based models seek not only to improve school climate but also to decrease student disconnection from school and increase teacher investment in student success.

Final Thoughts

The community-based apprentice model provides a research-based roadmap to improve student achievement by specifically targeting teacher attrition (Alvarez, 2017). Understandably, there are practical district, state, and federal policy barriers to implementing such a model; however, the potential benefits to sustainable student achievement far outweigh the long road to realizing an innovative alternative teacher preparation model. The benefits of this new paradigm include not only the academic benefits for students, but also substantial economic and budgetary benefits for schools and school districts as a result of stabilizing the costly effects of high rates of teacher attrition. Over the years there have been attempts to provide alternative programs to solve teacher shortages with no sustained evidence of substantive progress. A new model is more pressing than ever. The community-based apprenticeship model has the potential to succeed where so many other programs continue to fail.

Points to Remember

- *High rates of teacher turnover are correlated with lower student achievement.*

- *Replacing public school teachers is very costly to schools and school districts.*

- *New teachers tend to leave due to feeling overwhelmed, isolated, and unsupported.*

- *Cost, accessibility, and college degree requirements render a significant number of potential teachers as ineligible, even when local school districts face double-digit teacher shortages.*

- *Popular, contemporary teacher preparation programs have done little to stem persistent problems with teacher attrition.*

- *A community-based teacher apprenticeship model creates a pathway for individuals who would like to teach but cannot because they do not meet the entry requirements for contemporary traditional or alternative teacher preparation programs.*

References

Abramovitz, M., D'Amico, D., Mason, J., & DeLutro, I. (2011). *Triple Pay Off: The Leap to Teacher Program.* Retrieved from http://silbermanssw.org/ssw/wpcontent/uploads/2014/07/triple_pay_off.pdf

Allensworth, E., Ponisciak, S., & Mazzeo, C. (2009). The schools teachers leave: Teacher mobility in Chicago Public Schools. *Consortium on Chicago School Research.* Retrieved from https://consortium.uchicago.edu/sites/default/files/publications/CCSR_Teacher_Mobility.pdf

Alvarez, B. (2017). *A growing recruitment strategy for a diverse teacher workforce.* Retrieved from http://neatoday.org/2017/05/24/grow-your-own-teacher-diversity/

American Federation of Teachers. (2017). *2017 educator quality of work life survey.* Retrieved from https://www.aft.org/sites/default/files/2017_eqwl_survey_web.pdf

Aragon, S. (2016). *Teacher shortages: What we know.* Retrieved from https://www.ecs.org/wp-content/uploads/Teacher-Shortages-What-We-Know.pdf

Arnett, T. (2013) Challenges to reforming Teacher Preparation. *The Clayton Christensen Institute.* Retrieved from https://www.christenseninstitute.org/blog/challenges-to-reforming-teacher-preparation/

Barnum, M. (2016). *Eleven things you might not know about teacher retention and teurnover – but should.* Retrieved from https://www.the74million.org/article/eleven-things-you-might-not-know-about-teacher-retention-and-turnover-but-should/

Ben-Shahar, O. (2017). *Teacher certification makes public education worse, not better.* Retrieved from https://www.forbes.com/sites/omribenshahar/2017/07/21/teacher-certification-makes-public-school-education-worse-not-better/#65a6db0730fe

Carver-Thomas, D. & Darling Hammond, L. (2017). Teacher turnover: Why it matters and what we can do about it. *Learning Policy Institute.* Retrieved from https://learningpolicyinstitute.org/product/teacher-turnover-report

Chingos, M.M. & Whitehurst, G.J. (2011). *Class size: What research says and what it means for state policy.* Retrieved from https://www.brookings.edu/research/class-size-what-research-says-and-what-it-means-for-state-policy/

Constantine, J., Player, D., Silva, T., Hallgren, K., Grinder, M., & Deke, J. (2009). An Evaluation of Teachers Trained Through Different Routes to Certification. *National Center for Education Evaluation and Regional Assistance. U.S. Department of Education.* Retrieved from http://ies.ed.gov/ncee/pubs/20094043/

CostHelper. (2018). *How much does college cost?* Retrieved from http://education.costhelper.com/college.html

Darling-Hammond, L. (2000). *Reforming Teacher Preparation and Licensing: Debating the Evidence.* Retrieved from www.teacherscollegerecord.org

DeAngelis, K. & Presley, J. (2007). Leaving Schools or Leaving the Profession: Setting Illinois' Record Straight on New Teacher Attrition. *Illinois Education Research Council.* Retrieved from http://ierc.siue.edu

Freeman, J., Simonson, B., Briere, D. E., & MacSuga-Gage, A.S. (2014). *Pre-Service Teacher Training in Classroom Management a Review of State Accreditation Policy and Teacher Preparation Programs.* 37, Issue 2. DOI: 10.1177/0888406413507002

Garcia, R. & Huseman, J. (2009). Alternative certification programs: meeting the demand for effective teachers. *Brief analysis No. 675, National Center for Policy Analysis (NCPA).* Retrieved from http://www.ncpa.org/pub/ba675

Goldring, R., Taie, S., & Riddles, M. (2014). *Teacher attrition and mobility: Results from the 2012-13 teacher follow-up survey.* Retrieved from https://nces.ed.gov/pubs2014/2014077.pdf

Greenwald, R., Hedges, L., & Laine, R. (1996). Interpreting research on school resources and student achievement: *Review of Educational Research,* 66(3), 361-396. DOI: 10.3102/00346543066003411

Guerriero, S. (n.d.). Teachers' pedagogical knowledge and the teaching profession: Background report and project objectives. *OECD.* Retrieved from http://www.oecd.org/edu/ceri/Background_document_to_Symposium_ITE L-FINAL.pdf

Heilig, J. & Jez, S. (2010). Teach For America: A Review of the Evidence. *The Great Lakes Center for Education Research & Practice.* Retrieved from http://www.greatlakescenter.org/docs/Policy_Briefs/Heilig_TeachForAmeri ca.pdf

Kamenetz, A. (2014). *For teachers, many paths into the classroom...some say to many.* Retrieved from https://www.npr.org/sections/ed/2014/09/12/347375798/for-teachers-many-paths-into-the-classroom-some-say-too-many

Kane, T., Rockoff, J., Staiger, D. (2008). What does certification tell us about teacher effectiveness? Evidence from New York City. *Economics of Education Review,* 27, 615–631. Retrieved from http://www.dartmouth.edu/~dstaiger/Papers/nyc%20fellows%20 march%2020 06.pdf

Karakayali, N. (2009). Social Distance and Affective Orientations. Sociological Forum, 24(3), 538-562. DOI: 10.1111/j.1573-7861.2009.01119.x

Kini, T. & Podolsky, A. (2016). Does teaching experience increase teacher effectiveness? A review of the research. *Learning Policy Institute.* Retrieved from https://learningpolicyinstitute.org/product/does-teaching-experience-increase-teacher-effectiveness-review-research

Loschert, K. (2015). *Here today, gone tomorrow?: New research tracks retention rates of teachers in teaching residency programs.* Retrieved from https://www.all4ed.org/articles/here-today-gone-tomorrow-new-research-tracks-retention-rates-of-novice-educators-in-teaching-residency-programs/

Mader, J. (2016). *To increase teacher diversity, ignore selectivity of teacher education programs?* Retrieved from http://hechingerreport.org/increase-teacher-diversity-ignore-selectivity-teacher-education-programs/

Massachusetts Department of Higher Education. (2018). *Massachusetts Teacher Preparation Grant Program.* Retrieved from http://www.mass.edu/osfa/programs/teacherprep.asp

Mayer, J. (2016). Commentary: The hidden crisis of teacher turnover in Los Angeles' public schools. *LA School Report.* Retrieved from from http://laschoolreport.com/ commentary-the-hidden-crisis-of-teacher-turnover-in-los-angeles-public-schools/

Nunnery, J., Kaplan, L., Owings, W., Pribesh, S. (2010). *The Effects of Troops to Teachers on Student Achievement: One State's Study.* DOI: 10.1177/0192636509359338

NYU: Steinhardt. (2015). *Keeping the Teachers: The Problem of High Turnover in Urban Schools.* Retrieved from http://teachereducation. stein-hardt.nyu.edu/high-teacher-turnover/

NYC Teaching Fellows. (2018). *Our Vision.* Retrieved from http://nycteachingfellows.org/our-vision

Papay, J.P. & Kraft, M.A. (2017). Developing workplaces where teachers stay, improve and succeed: Recent evidence on the importance of school climate for teacher success. In E.

Quintero (ed). *The social side of education reform,* (p.15-36). Cambridge, MA: Harvard Press.

Podolsky, A., Kini, T., Bishop, J, & Darling-Hammond, L. (2016). *Solving the teacher shortage: How to attract and retain excellent educators.* Palo Alto, CA: Learning Policy Institute.

Rice, J.K. (2010). *The impact of teacher experience: Examining the evidence and policy implications.* Retrieved from https://www.urban.org/sites/default/files/publication/33321/1001455-The-Impact-of-Teacher-Experience.PDF

Ronfeldt, M., Loeb, S., & Wyckoff, J. (2013). How teacher turnover harms student achievement. *American Educational Research Journal.* Retrieved from http://aer.sagepub.com/content/ 50/1/4

Ryan, C.L. & Bauman, K. (2016). *Educational attainment in the United States: 2015.* Retrieved from https://www.census.gov/content/dam/Census/library/publications/2016/demo/p20-578.pdf

Sass, T. (2014). *Licensure and worker quality: A Comparison of Alternative Routes to Teaching.* DOI: 10.1086/682904

Scott, L.A., Gentry, G., & Phillips, M. (2014). *Making preservice teachers better: Examining the impact of a practicum in a teacher preparation program.* DOI: 10.5897/ERR2014.1748

Strauss, V. (2017). *Where have all the teachers gone?* Retrieved from https://www.washingtonpost.com/news/answer-sheet/wp/2017/09/18/where-have-all-the-teachers-gone/?utm_term=.98362adbefe2

Stronge, J.H. (2007). *Qualities of effective teachers* (2nd ed). San Francisco, CA: ASCD

Sullivan, J. (2015). *How commute issues can dramatically impact employee retention.* Retrieved from https://www.tlnt.com/how-commute-issues-can-dramatically-impact-employee-retention/

Sutcher, L., Darling-Hammond, L., Carver-Thomas, D. (2016). *A coming crisis in teaching? Teacher supply, demand, and shortages in the U.S.* Palo Alto, CA: Learning Policy Institute.

Teach for America. (2017). *Our history.* Retrieved from https://www.teachforamerica.org/about-us/our-work/our-history

U.S. Department of Education Office of Postsecondary Education. (2014). *Teacher Shortage Areas Nationwide Listing.* Retrieved from http://www2.ed.gov/about/offices/list /ope/pol/tsa.pdf

U.S. Army National Guard. (2017). *Troops to teachers.* Retrieved from https://www.nationalguard.com/education-programs/troops-to-teachers

Wark, C., & Gallinher, J. (2007). Emory Bogardus and the Origins of the Social Distance Scale. *The American Sociologist. 38*(4), 383-395. DOI: 10.1007/s12108-007-9023-9

Woods, J.R. (2016). *Mitigating teacher shortages: Alternative teacher certification.* Retrieved from https://www.ecs.org/wp-content/uploads/Mitigating-Teacher-Shortages-Alternative-Certification.pdf

Chapter 10

"Physician, Heal Thyself:"
A Guide to Wellness as an Antidote to
Teacher Burnout

Vance L. Austin, PhD,
Manhattanville College

Students that present significant behavioral challenges, demanding and unsupportive principals, inadequate and inauthentic teacher preparation programs, the pressures of annual performance review, poor compensation, a lack of effective professional development programs, and a shortage of dedicated, competent peer mentors contribute to the exceedingly high attrition rate of new teachers (Westervelt & Lonsdorf, 2016; Riggs, 2013). In fact, approximately 35% of new teachers leave the profession within the first three years of employment and between 40 and 50 % of teachers will leave the classroom within their first five years of teaching (Ingersoll, Merrill, & Stuckey, 2014; Riggs, 2013).

The New Teacher Project reports that approximately 66% of the best teachers in the U.S. leave the teaching profession for careers in other professions (Chartock & Wiener, 2014). Despite these significant challenges and disheartening statistics, there are things nascent or more seasoned teachers can do to guard against "teacher burnout" and help sustain their love of the profession and desire to make a difference in the lives of students. It is important to understand the strategies that help teachers prioritize self-care, deflect negative thoughts and insecurities, and become "authentic" and "complete" teachers.

The *Real* Reasons Teachers Leave the Profession

According to Fernet, Guay, Senecal, and Austin (2012) the principal reasons that teachers leave the profession include: unruly students, a lack of control over the work environment, a sense of disempowerment, a dearth of administrative support that includes the provision of mentoring and quality as well as a lack of sustained professional development. Another cause of early teacher attrition is attributed to the mounting stress-inducing responsibilities assigned to new and inexperienced teachers (Fernet et al., 2012). One example of these stressful duties involves endlessly preparing students to take and pass an increasing number of obligatory high stakes tests. Factors that influence teacher burnout include, most notably, teacher self-efficacy. Brouwers and Tomic (2000) found a negative correlation between teacher self-efficacy and emotional exhaustion caused, in part, by stressful working conditions and a lack of support in the classroom.

In a recent study, Seidel (2014) reported that 15% or 500,000 U.S. teachers leave the profession every year. Sutcher, Darling-Hammond, and Carver-Thomas (2016) provide further information relative to the problem of teacher attrition and corresponding teacher shortages in the U.S., noting that the current attrition rate among U.S. teachers is approximately 8%, twice that of most other modern, industrialized countries to include Finland, Singapore, and Canada. The principal causes of teacher attrition include dissatisfaction with administrators and a perceived lack of support from them, a lack of control over teaching methods, the increase in testing and accountability pressures, unhappiness with the working conditions, as well as family factors to include minimal accommodation for parental leave (Sutcher et al., 2016). Consequently, enrollment in teacher preparation programs in the United States has fallen 35% or a reduction of 240,000 teacher education students since 2012, this at a time when, according to conservative estimates, 300,000 new teachers will be needed nationwide (Sutcher et al., 2016).

Teacher Burnout and the Case for Teacher Self-Care

When one looks up the term, "burnout" in the dictionary, it is paired with "teacher" (Merriam-Webster, 2015, p. 1) and is described as a condition caused by exhaustion due to a demanding job. According to Glasser (1992), teaching constitutes the hardest job one can do in our society. Teacher burnout is also not limited to the U.S. workforce, but negatively impacts teachers worldwide (Alkhateeb, Kraishan, & Salah, 2015; Shukla & Trivedi, 2008). Stanley (2014) notes that from 2012-2014, 74% of teachers in the U.K. experienced anxiety they reported as caused by an excessive teaching workload. Similar figures relative to stress and concomitant anxiety have been reported in the U.S.; for example, 73% of teachers surveyed by the American Federation of Teachers in 2015 stated that they are "often" under stress, with 48% reporting they regularly experienced great stress in conjunction with their duties (American Federation of Teachers, 2015). One hundred percent of the 30,000 teachers surveyed by the American Federation of Teachers (2015) stated that they felt enthusiastic about teaching during their first years in the profession; however, only 53% still shared that sentiment at the time they responded to the survey.

Adding to teachers' stress levels are the demands of a constantly evolving profession that prides itself on sweeping curricular changes, new 'best practice' techniques that border on faddism, and an ever-increasing list of duties and responsibilities (American Federation of Teachers, 2015). The requirement that teachers now "individualize" instruction through differentiation techniques seems commendable and appropriate in a western democracy until one considers the fact that most teachers are responsible for the education of 25-30 students in each of five classes taught daily. Which means that, hypothetically, a teacher is expected to individualize instruction for 150 students each school day, an untenable expectation.

How does "teacher burnout" impact students? First, as noted by Neufeldnov (2014), teachers are less able to provide quality instruction when they are stressed, overworked, and frustrated. The high teacher attrition rate costs the U.S. $2,200,000,000 every year, an unsustainable and unnecessary expense (Haynes, 2014). In addition, this high turnover rate is particularly detrimental to students in impoverished, minority neighborhoods, who truly benefit from and require consistency in teaching staff. Sadly, the attrition rate for high-poverty schools is 20%, significantly higher than the 8% in more affluent districts (Seidel, 2014).

Clearly, these dire statistics underscore the need for effective teacher self-care strategies to help prevent teacher burnout and promote recovery, many of which can and should be initiated by policymakers and school administrators. Some of these suggested reforms include: (a) prioritizing, consolidating, and better organizing teacher tasks and responsibilities so they are not overwhelmed, (b) facilitating the adoption of well-researched interventions and instructional technologies, (c) helping to improve the effectiveness and viability of teacher preparation programs by using data to inform educational decision-making (Grant Rankin, 2017).

Warning Signs of Teacher Burnout

As a rule, teachers do not do a good job of self-assessment, self-reflection, and, thus, exploring and engaging in self-care (Gladwell, 2008). This is concerning since it would seem reasonable that teachers, of all the professionals in the U.S., would know how to evaluate themselves for signs of stress. After all, they engage in the assessment of their students about 30-40% of their school day (Gladwell, 2008). One theoretical perspective, however, that has been used to explain this phenomenon comes from Hofstede's Dimension Scale (Hofstede, Hofstede & Minkov, 2010). In his investigative work as a social psychologist, Hofstede posited that Americans, in general, are a modest, self-sufficient people, who engage in "mitigating speech" and score at the highest level in "individualism," as compared with the other nations of the world. Furthermore, he observed, they are very tolerant of "ambiguity-uncertainty," and achieve a high score on the "low-power distance index" (Hofstede, Hofstede, & Minkov, 2010). Simply put, Americans tend to value individual initiative, are tolerant of conflicting beliefs, are not rigid in their thinking, and are not easily impressed or influenced by rank or celebrity. These tendencies make it more unlikely that the American teacher will acknowledge their vulnerability and search out the resources that mitigate stressors that lead to teacher burnout.

Despite the emphasis on greater teacher collaboration in schools, American teachers continue to be evaluated on their individual contribution to student progress as measured by their performance on a surfeit of standardized tests (Sawchuk, 2015). Those teachers that stay the course and aspire to achieve tenure are adjudicated solely as individuals, and succeed or fail based solely on individual merit, as determined by the prevailing APPR metric (Sawchuk, 2015). Consequently, many teachers develop an independent determination to succeed and, in the process, often underestimate the effects of a very stressful profession on their social-emotional well-being, frequently abjuring self-care resources (Gladwell, 2008). Like a responsible caregiver, the good teacher typically attends to the needs of others before her own, and even when she acknowledges the need for help, may not know where or how to obtain the necessary emotional support.

Given the stressful nature of the job, teachers often experience "compassionate fatigue" or "secondary traumatic stress," terms used by psychologists to formally classify "teacher burnout" (Kenardy, DeYoung, LeBrocque, & March 2011). Some of the symptomatic characteristics of this disorder include: (a) reduced capacity for concentration and attention, (b) increased petulance or distress with students, (c) problems in planning and preparing, lessons, and maintaining procedures, (d) feeling disconnected, (e) experiencing intense anxiety about specific students' academic progress or emotional welfare (Kenardy et al., 2011). These symptoms are persistent and will only intensify if not properly addressed (Kenardy at al., 2011).

In an investigation of teacher burnout, three dimensions were identified; namely, (a) emotional fatigue: feelings of being emotionally strained and exhausted, (b) depersonalization: a negative, uncaring, extremely disconnected response to people who are in one's care, and (c) reduced personal achievement: a person's negative self-assessment relative to the individual's job performance (Brouwers & Tomic, 2000). In another study involving 5,426 U.S. and Canadian teachers, 63% reported that discipline problems were the most stressful aspect of their teaching experience (Fernet, Guay, Senecal, & Austin, 2012). In a similar study, Bauer et al. (2006) found that in Germany, where the teacher burnout rate is as high as 25-35%, aside from large class size, destructive, aggressive pupil behavior was the primary stress factor reported by teachers.

Perceived self-efficacy is defined as, "...a belief in one's capability to organize and execute courses of action required to produce given attainments" (Bandura, 1999, p. 3). Likewise, teacher efficacy can be described as, "...the extent to which the teacher believes he or she has the capacity to affect student [academic] performance" (Bergman et al., 1977, p. 137), or as "...teachers' beliefs or conviction that they can influence how well students learn, even those who may be difficult or unmotivated" (Guskey & Passaro, 1994, p. 4). When teachers feel confident in themselves and their ability to affect positive change in their students and contribute substantively to their learning, they are less likely to experience burnout and thus more inclined to stay in the classroom. Understanding the previous studies is a necessary step in providing effective "self-care" strategies that will help teachers develop a greater sense of self-efficacy and avoid burnout.

The Road to Wellville: Teacher Self-Care as an Antidote to Teacher Burnout

A review of the literature on "teacher self-care" techniques reveals a surfeit of strategies, some hypothetical and other supported by extensive research that stands as "best practices" and has been thoroughly vetted.

Professional Development

To improve teacher self-efficacy, administrators are encouraged to introduce an on-going training or professional development program that affords teachers the necessary skills to cope effectively with disruptive student behavior (Hawkins, 2017). Experienced teachers, for example, can share their most successful techniques and video clips displaying teachers employing a successful management strategy (a vicarious experience) can be shown. Teachers can then practice these techniques in a laboratory classroom setting with feedback provided by experienced teacher mentors (referred to as 'verbal persuasion'). Once the teacher mentees have been persuaded of their competence in managing student behaviors, they should be able to manifest these new-found skills in their own classrooms (Brouwers & Tomic, 2000).

Self-care Strategies

Teachers need to develop a sense of "team" and acknowledge their innate need to belong to a social group, in this case, teacher colleagues (Ronfeldt, Farmer, McQueen, & Grissom, 2015; Baumeister & Leary, 1995). The teaching profession can seem like a solo enterprise at times, which increases a teacher's sense of isolation. Teachers need extensive opportunities to collaborate, which is supported in the popular inclusion movement (Ronfeldt, Farmer, McQueen, & Grissom, 2015; Austin, 2001). While teaching often seems paradoxical since teachers are, as noted earlier, evaluated as individuals based on their performances in the classroom; nonetheless, teachers, especially new ones, need a mentor and the support of more seasoned colleagues. Bonhoeffer (1954) captures this seeming paradox when he writes, "Let the person [teacher] who cannot be alone beware of community. Let the person [teacher] who is not in community beware of being alone" (p. 78).

Teachers, both novice and seasoned, need to develop a pedagogical foundation or framework (Austin & Sciarra, 2016), that can greatly enhance their sense of self-efficacy and help prevent teacher attrition. One such framework offered by Palmer (1998) involves the development of two key precepts: "identity" (as a teacher and a member of the human race) and "integrity," not in a religious or moral sense but as a "truth seeker," a teacher who embraces learning and truth and pursues both, despite the discomfort of the journey and its destination. Palmer (1998) asserts that "good teaching cannot be reduced to technique; good teaching comes from the identity and integrity of the teacher" (p. 10).

One way to avoid teacher burnout and engage in self-help is to take the time to reflect on who we are, where we come from, and what, in our lives, has helped to shape who we are. Teaching, like medicine, is an imprecise craft and both new and veteran teachers need to be reminded of the fact that not every lesson will be effective or well-received by students. Teaching is clearly a reciprocal enterprise that involves the sharing of knowledge, reflection on practice, critical analysis, listening and receiving feedback, and learning about and imparting new skills and concepts. Often allowing a five-minute break, taken with your students helps everyone refocus and reduce the stressors inherent in teaching and learning a rigorous curriculum.

Relationships. Strive to cultivate a rich and satisfying life outside of school and apart from teaching by developing affirming, prosocial relationships and pursuing enjoyable recreational activities and avocations. Take periodic mental health days and engage in activities that are unrelated to teaching but that you find enjoyable. Learn to accept the fact that not every day will be successful, and you cannot inspire every student you teach to develop a passion for learning nor can you "rescue" every student that has exceptional needs. Spend your teaching days wisely - focus your efforts strategically to benefit the many who can receive what you have to give. Lastly, develop mutually supportive relationships with individuals with whom you can share your challenges and successes, without fear of judgment or rejection (Cavin, 1998).

Three Tenets of an Effective Pedagogy

The three "pillars" of an effective teaching pedagogy are: (a) the establishment of genuine and caring teacher-student relationships, (b) a passion for and thorough knowledge of one's subject, and (c) the determination to truly "know" oneself and share that knowledge, courageously, with the world. These three tenets comprise what Palmer refers to as "integrity" (Palmer, 1998). Ideally, these precepts should be integral to the curricular objectives of all teacher preparation programs, but can be introduced to novice and veteran teachers' praxis through effective and sustained professional development. Their acquisition can help ensure a long and successful teaching career.

Behavior-Based Interventions

The effective instruction of meaningful content is the first line of defense in defusing disruptive behavior, the principal concern of most teachers. Teachers need to learn to employ explicit, direct instructional techniques to engage all their students in the learning process. One technique that has demonstrated success is TAPPLE: **T**each first, **A**sk a specific question, **P**ause, **P**air-Share, **P**ick a random non-volunteer, **L**isten to the response, provide **E**ffective feedback (Dataworks Educational Research, 2014). Another explicit, direct instructional strategy that involves every student in the class in the learning process is "Cold Call" whereby the teacher, after asking a question based on what was just taught, calls on one or two students to contribute responses (Lemov, 2015). A creative alternative is to place students' names on popsicle sticks that they keep at their desks and submit to the teacher at the start of the class. The teacher, after posing a relevant question, randomly draws one or two sticks from the class set and asks those students for their responses. This technique helps to keep everyone engaged and on-task (Lemov, 2015).

    The life space interview. Another way to effectively manage disruptive or problem behavior is through a system first developed by Redl (1966), subsequently revised and now referred to as the Life Space Crisis Interview (LSCI) (Long, Fecser, & Brendtro, 1998). The LSCI emphasizes the importance of asking four "internalized" questions: (a) What am I feeling now? (b) What does the student feel, need, want? (c) How is the environment affecting the student?, and (d) How do I best respond? Lastly, the LSCI framework recommends adherence to a specific process when addressing a behavioral crisis (Long, Fecser, & Brendtro, 1998). These steps can best be recalled via the acronym: "I ESCAPE," in which each of the letters represents a step in the process:

I=Isolate the conversation,

E=Explore student point of view,

S=Summarize feelings and content,

C=Connect behavior to feelings,

A=Alternative behaviors discussed,

P=Plan developed/practiced,

E=Enter student back into program.

Long, Fecser and Brendtro (1998) suggest that LSCI be conducted in six steps, the first of which is intervention; the second, appraisal of the incident with input from the stakeholders; third, listening to each individual affected in an unbiased manner; fourth, assessing the incident to ascertain the severity; and, finally, selecting and employing the most effective LCSI technique (Long, Fecser, & Brendtro, 1998).

The following are three, research-based behavioral interventions that have shown to be very effective in helping to reduce maladaptive behavior and increase prosocial responses.

Behavior-specific praise. This approach involves the application of four rules; first, the praise should be instantaneous; second, it should be relevant and meaningful; third, it can only be offered when the target behavior is observed, and it needs to be recurrent (Conroy, Sutherland, Snyder, Al-Hendawi, & Vo, 2009). This is an integral part of the Positive Behavioral Interventions and Supports (PBIS) system currently used in many schools (Positive Behavioral Interventions and Supports, 2018). PBIS best practice requires educators to reward the appropriate behavior by naming it and offering a token that can be used at a later time for a reward (Positive Behavioral Interventions and Supports, 2018).

Behavior momentum. Research suggests that by introducing a student to "easy" tasks first, there is a greater likelihood that the student will more easily complete the more difficult task (Lee, Belfiore, & Gormley, 2008). Using this reasoning, the strategy employs four steps: (a) identify tasks the student finds easy to complete, (b) identify tasks that are difficult for the student, (c) collect data to validate both the "problem" and "easy" tasks, and (d) implement a first/next system of intervention completing an easy task then a more difficult one.

Implementing choice. Kern and Parks (2012) recommend a four-part behavioral strategy that offers the student choices in terms of where, when, and how a desired academic task is accomplished. Since students who exhibit behavioral challenges are seldom, if ever, offered choices, this is a way to empower them while ensuring that the options accomplish the same learning objective (Kern & Parks, 2012).

Mindfulness and Meditation

Since the 1970s research has been conducted to investigate the benefits of meditation in helping to reduce the deleterious effects of anxiety and depression (Schonert-Reichl, Oberle, Lawlor, Thompson, Oberlander, & Diamond, 2015) along with its benefits relative to emotional and psychological health (Langer, Janis, & Wolfer, 1975; Langer, 2005). Flook, Goldberg, Pinger, and Davidson (2015) determined that mindfulness activities help improve social skills, while Norton, Abott, Norberg, and Hunt (2014) found that they helped reduce anxiety and Semple, Lee, Rosa, and Miller (2010) noted that mindfulness helped improve focus and attention.

The practice of "mindfulness" techniques help individuals self-regulate awareness, improve attention and focus, and be more accepting and positive (Bishop et al., 2004; Malow & Austin, 2016). Likewise, mindfulness has been associated with improved resilience, a protective characteristic that helps individuals cope with trauma and disappointment and maintain a level of optimism (Masten, 2001).

Mindfulness activities can involve non-religious meditation, yoga, tai-chi, and Qigong, to name a few. Although little research exists that demonstrates the efficacy of mindfulness practices in helping to reduce teacher stress and as an effective self-care technique, the few studies that have been conducted, show that mindfulness helps teachers manage the demands of teaching by promoting adaptive emotional regulation and coping skills that reduce stress, burnout, and distress while simultaneously increasing energy and providing self-regulatory strategies that can help improve teacher-student interactions and promote learning (Stetka, 2017; Roeser, 2016; Roeser, Skinner, Beers, & Jennings, 2012; Skinner & Beers, 2016).

Other Stress Management Techniques

According to another teacher self-care initiative, Collaboration for Academic, Social, and Emotional Learning (CASEL), a program designed to enhance teachers' social-emotional competence (SEC), teachers need to develop 5 competencies: (a) self-awareness, (b) self-management, (c) social awareness, (d) relationship skills, and (e) responsible decision-making. A recent study conducted by Wong (2017) focused on two of these; specifically, (a) self-awareness and (b) self-management (CASEL, 2108). Wong (2017) recommended and described three programs to enhance teacher self-care: Cultivating Awareness and Resilience in Education, Mindfulness-based Stress Reduction, and Stress Management and Relaxation Techniques for Educators.

The high rate of teacher turnover creates high levels of occupational stress, which can negatively impact the quality of instruction. Cultivating Awareness and Resilience in Education is a mindfulness professional development program designed to promote teachers' social and emotional competence and improve the quality of instruction and the student-teacher relationship (Jennings et al., 2017). The program involves 30 hours of in-person training conducted, typically, over a 4-5-week period designed to help teacher-participants improve their adaptive emotional regulation, increase mindfulness, and reduce psychological distress and the stress created by a sense of time urgency. Jennings et al. (2017) found that participants in their study revealed a reduction in psychological stress indicators, such as improved emotional regulation, increased mindfulness, and less overall psychological distress after their involvement in the study. Teacher-participants' students also displayed significantly better attitudes, classroom climate noticeably improved, there were less disruptive behaviors evident, and students were more engaged and involved in the learning process following the teachers' participation in the CARE program (Jennings et al., 2017).

Two mindfulness programs that seem to show positive results for teachers include the Mindfulness-based Stress Reduction (Kabat-Zinn, 2003) and the Stress Management and Relaxation Techniques for Educators (Roeser, Schonert-Reichl, Jha, Cullen, Wallace, Wilensky, Oberle, Thompson, Taylor & Harrison, 2013). The first is an 8-week course consisting of emotional and somatic practices that involve focused-breathing, body scans, and walking meditation techniques (Kabat-Zinn, 2003). The latter also comprises an 8-week, 20-hour, research-based program that was created for early-childhood, childhood, and adolescent-level teachers. Several studies provide support for the effectiveness in significantly reducing teacher stress and thus helping to diminish teacher burnout (Roeser et al., 2013; Roeser et al., 2012; Roeser, Skinner, Beers, & Jennings, 2012).

Another teacher stress management technique that has achieved successful outcomes is entitled: "The ABCs of Managing Teacher Stress." Developed by Nagel and Brown in 2003, the first letter, "A," in the acronym simply represents the phrase: "acknowledge it [stress]." The "B" represents "Behavior Modification" through meditation and exercise and employs a creative problem-solving process: (a) describe the problem, (b) generate ideas to solve it, (c) select a solution and refine it, (d) implement the solution, and (e) evaluate its efficacy. Finally, the "C" in the acronym stands for "Cognitive Restructuring", which consists of a three-step process: 1. Describe the situation: (e.g., a screaming, disruptive child), 2. Review the original thought this situation induced: (e.g., "This child is loud and obnoxious-a real bother!"), and 3. Restructure the thought so it promotes a prosocial/therapeutic response: (e.g.,

"Perhaps the child is engaged and overly-excited and needs to be taught a more appropriate way to show enthusiasm.") (Nagel & Brown, 2003).

A valuable stress-reducer involves the use of the "I" statement. Simply put, it enables teachers to say what they really mean, without offense or guile, for example, when Mr. Jones is asked by his school's principal if he would consider being the student council faculty advisor, he respectfully replies, "I am very disappointed to have to miss this opportunity this year, but I must decline. At present, I'm finding it a challenge to balance work and home responsibilities. Please check back with me next year, if you need an advisor." Administrators can help to ameliorate teacher stress and subsequent burnout by supporting their teachers and offering after-school programs designed to enhance their psychological and physical well-being, as well as employing experienced peer-mentors to help teach and model stress management techniques (Empowering Education-Social and Emotional Learning Services, 2015).

Positive Self-Affirmations

Self-affirmations are typically written reflections that involve 10-minute writing sessions and target desired values such as the acknowledgment of the need to feel relevant and the importance of being loved and cared-for and the right of everyone to have those needs fulfilled. The benefits of self-affirmations are severally, (a) the perception of self as a "good person" deserving of love and wholesome human interaction, (b) the perception of self as adequate to be considered moral and adaptive, and (c) the perception of self as one who is worthy of esteem or praise (Robinson, 2014).

Morris (2015) offers some suggestions about how teachers can "take care of themselves in wholeness" (n.p.): (a) find some "me time," (b) take walks, (c) keep journals, (d) read for pleasure, (e) reflect, (f) recharge, and (g) respond to themselves. Similarly, Brunette (2004) provides recommendations to enhance teacher self-care: (a) care for yourself, so you can care for others, (b) set healthy boundaries, (c) take frequent breaks, (d) engage in exercise, (e) know your own threshold for stress and don't exceed it, (f) find at least three activities that relieve stress for you and do them consistently, and (g) start your day on a positive note. These relatively simple suggestions will aid teachers in reducing stress and improving their quality of life both in and out of the classroom.

Simple Self-Care Practices that Can Make a Difference

Periodically, teachers may consider changing their methods and techniques - doing so will increase the likelihood that they will feel refreshed and reenergized, and their students will be the beneficiaries of a newfound zest for teaching. Educators can always learn from their students - listening to their ideas are as important as the course curriculum. Students have something worthwhile and unique to offer and will feel valued and respected when the educator listens, earnestly, to their ideas. Teachers should also set aside one day per week to do only what brings them joy; sleep in, go for a walk, read a book, watch a movie, play a game, enjoy the company of friends and family. Educators should try not to work for people who do not believe in them or what they have to offer as a teacher. Personal and professional growth is unlikely in such a negative environment. Finally, teachers must believe in themselves, their craft, and the vital service they provide to the next generation. Educators help to shape their future, arguably, more than any other profession and as such, they must revel in that awareness for at least a moment and take good care of themselves!

Final Thoughts

Unruly students, a perceived lack of control over the work environment, a pervasive sense of disempowerment, a lack of administrative support manifest in an unwillingness to invest resources in relevant and sustained professional development, as well as mounting stress caused by increased responsibilities and the pressures of preparing students for high stakes tests, these are a few of the threats to the emotional and physical well-being of teachers in today's classrooms. These conditions, along with sub-standard pay and a general lack of respect for the profession of teaching, contribute substantively to low teacher self-efficacy and emotional exhaustion, key contributors to teacher attrition. As noted in this chapter, disenchantment with the teaching profession has resulted in a 35% reduction in registrations in teacher preparation programs nationwide, and with an annual attrition rate of 15% (Seidel, 2014), the estimated teacher shortfall for 2018 is 112,000 (Sutcher, Darling-Hammond, & Carver-Thomas, 2016).

For those teachers willing to brave these stressful challenges, the risk of experiencing teacher burnout is very high. In fact, in one western industrialized nation, the teacher burnout rate ranged from 25-35% (Bauer et al., 2006). According to Kenardy et al. (2011), the diagnostics terms for "teacher burnout" are "compassionate fatigue" or "secondary traumatic stress" and some of the symptoms include a decreased concentration and attention, increased irritability or agitation with students, problems planning classroom activities, lessons, and maintaining routines, feeling detached, and experiencing intense feelings of concern about specific students' academic progress and/or emotional well-being.

Aside from leaving the profession, as thousands do, when suffering from these conditions, there is a palliative measure; clearly not a panacea, but a hopeful option for many: teacher self-care practices. Regardless of the technique, it is reassuring to note that "self-care helps teachers remember who they are and where they are and allows them to better care for others [students]. Self-care empowers teachers to cultivate relationships and collegiality, talk openly about teaching, seek mentorship, partnership, and meaningful feedback, and to work with others to support students and create solutions" (Morris, 2015, n.p.). In short, effective teacher self-care techniques can help revitalize a promising career and keep a good teacher in the classroom.

Points to Remember

- *Approximately 35% of new teachers leave the profession within the first three years of employment and between 40 and 50 % of teachers will leave the classroom within their first five years of teaching (Ingersoll, Merrill, & Stuckey, 2014; Riggs, 2013).*

- *The principal reasons that teachers leave the profession include: unruly students, a lack of control over the work environment, a sense of disempowerment, a dearth of administrative support that includes the provision of mentoring and quality as well as a lack of sustained professional development, but another cause of early teacher attrition is attributed to the mounting stress-inducing responsibilities assigned to new and inexperienced teachers (Ingersoll, Merrill, & Stuckey, 2014; Riggs, 2013).*

- *Despite the emphasis on collaboration and "teamwork", teaching continues to be a relatively individualistic profession and teachers continue to be adjudicated as such through the metrics of an APPR, adding to teachers' feelings of isolation.*

- *In their investigation of teacher burnout, Brouwers and Tomic (2000) identified three dimensions: emotional exhaustion (feelings of being emotionally overextended and depleted), depersonalization (a negative, callous, excessively detached response to people who are in one's care), and (c) reduced personal accomplishment (a person's negative self-evaluation relative to the individual's job performance).*

- *As an antidote to teacher burnout and attrition, techniques that increase teacher self-efficacy are recommended (Hawkins, 2017).*

- *Some of the more effective of these techniques include the use of the Life Space Interview, social-emotional competence skills such as mindfulness and similar stress-management interventions, as well as the use of the self-affirmation and other strategies that help to increase teachers' self-efficacy (Redl, 1966; Kabat-Zinn, 2005).*

References

Alkhateeb1, O., Kraishan, O. M., & Salah, R. O. (2015). Level of psychological burnout of a sample of secondary phase teachers in Ma'an Governorate and its relationship with some other variables. *International Education Studies, 8*(6), 56-68. doi:10.5539/ies.v8n6p56

American Federation of Teachers (2015). *Quality of work life survey.* Retrieved from http://www.aft.org/sites/default/files/worklifesurveyresults2015.pdf

Austin, V. L. (2001). Teachers' beliefs about co-teaching. *Remedial and Special Education, 22*(4), 245–255.

Austin, V. L., & Sciarra, D. T. (2016). *Difficult students and disruptive behavior in the classroom: Teacher Responses That Work.* New York: W.W. Norton.

Bandura, A. (1999). Self-efficacy: Toward a unifying theory of behavioral change. In R. F. Baumeister (Ed.), *Key Readings in Social Psychology. The Self in Social Psychology,* 285-298. New York: Psychology Press.

Bauer, J., Stamm, A., Virnich, K., Wissing, K., Miller, U, Wirsching, M., & Schaarschmidt, U. (2006). Correlation between burnout syndrome and psychological and psychosomatic symptoms among teachers. *International Archives of Occupational and Environmental Health.* (79)3, 199-204. DOI: 10.1007/s00420-005-0050-y

Baumeister, R., & Leary, M. R. (1995). The need to belong: desire for interpersonal attachments as a fundamental human motivation. *Psychological Bulletin, 117,* 497–529.

Bergman, P., McLaughlin, M., Bass, M., Pauly, E., & Zellman, G. (1977). *Federal programs supporting educational change: Vol. VII. Factors affecting implementation and continuation.* Santa Monica, CA: RAND. Retrieved from https://www.rand.org/pubs/reports/R1589z7.html

Bishop, S.R., Lau, M., Shapiro, S., Carlson, L., Anderson, N.D., Carmody, J., et al. (2004). Mindfulness: A proposed operational definition. *Clinical Psychology: Science & Practice,* 11, 230-241. doi: 10.1093/clipsy.bph077

Bonhoeffer, D. (1954). *Life together.* New York: Harper Collins.

Brouwers, A. & Tomic, W. (2000). A Longitudinal Study of Teacher Burnout and Perceived Self-Efficacy in Classroom Management. *Teaching and Teacher Education,* 16, 239-253. DOI: 10.1016/S0742-051X(99)00057-8

CASEL. (2018). *SEL Core competencies.* Retrieved from https://casel.org/core-competencies/

Chartock, J. & Wiener, R. (2014). How to save teachers from burning out, dropping out and other hazards of experience. *The Hechinger Report.* http://hechingerreport.org/can-keep-great-teachers-engaged-effective-settle-careers/

Conroy, M.A., Sutherland, K.S., Snyder, A.L., Al-Hendawi, M., and Vo, A. (2009). *Creating a Positive Classroom Atmosphere: Teacher's Use of Effective Praise and Feedback. Beyond Behavior,* 18(2), 18-26. Retrieved from https://eric.ed.gov/?id=EJ869681

Data Works Educational Research (2014). *TAPPLE – How to Check for Understanding.* Retrieved from https://dataworks-ed.com/blog/2014/07/tapple-how-to-check-for-understanding/

Empowering Education-Social and Emotional Learning Services (2015). *I-Statements*. Retrieved from https://empoweringeducation.org/wp-content/uploads/2015/11/I-Statements_final.pdf

Fernet, C., Guay, F., Senecal, C., & Austin, S. (2012). Predicting intraindividual changes in teacher burnout: The role of perceived school environment and motivational factors. *Teaching and Teacher Education, 28*, 514-525. https://www.journals.elsevier.com/teaching-and-teacher-education/

Flook, L., Goldberg, S.B., Pinger, L., & Davidson, R.J. (2015). Promoting prosocial behavior and self-regulatory skills in preschool children through a mindfulness-based kindness curriculum. *Developmental Psychology, 51*(1), 44-51. doi: 10.1037/a0038256

Gladwell, M. (2008). *Outliers: The story of success*. New York: Back Bay Books.

Glasser, W. (1992). *The quality school: Managing students without coercion* (2nd ed.). New York: Harper & Row.

Grant Rankin, J. (2017). First aid for teacher burnout: How you can find peace and success. New York: Routledge.

Guskey, T. R. & Passaro, P. D. (1994) Teacher efficacy: A study of construct dimensions. American Educational Research Journal, 31, 627-645.

Hart, R., Ivtzan, I., Hart D. (2013). Mind the gap in mindfulness research: A comparative account of the leading schools of thought. *Review of General Psychology*, 17(4), 453-466.

Hawkins, K. (2017). *Self-care: The best kind of professional development*. Retrieved from http://corwin-connect.com/2017/07/self-care-best-kind-professional-development/

Haynes, M. (2014, July). On the path to equity: Improving the effectiveness of beginning teachers. *Alliance for Excellence*. Retrieved from http://all4ed.org/reports-factsheets/path-to-equity/

Hofstede, G., Hofstede, G.J., & Minkov, M. (2010). *Cultures and organizations: Intercultural cooperation and its importance for survival* (3rd ed). New York, NY: McGraw-Hill

Ingersoll, R., Merrill, L., & Stuckey, D. (2014). Seven trends: The transformation of the teaching force. CPRE Research Report # RR-80. Philadelphia: *Consortium for Policy Research in Education*. DOI: 10.12698/cpre.2014.rr80

Jennings, P. A., Frank, J. L., Doyle, S., Yoonkyung, O., Rasheed, D., DeWeese, A., & ... Greenberg, M. T. (2017). Impacts of the CARE for Teachers Program on Teachers' Social and Emotional Competence and Classroom Interactions. *Journal of Educational Psychology*, 109(7), 1010-1028. doi:10.1037/edu0000187

Kabat-Zinn J. (2003). Mindfulness-based interventions in context: Past, present, and future. *Clinical Psychology: Science and Practice*, 10:144–156. DOI: 10.1093/clipsy.bpg016

Kenardy J, De Young A, Le Brocque R, March S. (2011). *Childhood trauma reactions: A guide for teachers from preschool to year 12.* http://education.qld.gov.au/studentservices/natural-disasters/resources/child-trauma-handbook.pdf

Kern, L. & Parks, J.K. (2012). *Choice making opportunities for students. Module 4. Virginia Department of Education.* Retrieved from http://ttac-esd.gmu.edu/my_files/Choice_Making_Opportunities_Sup_Doc.pdf

Langer, E.J. (2005). Well-being: Mindfulness versus positive evaluation. In C.R. Snyder & S.J. Lopez (Eds.), *Handbook of Positive Psychology,* 214-230. New York, NY: Oxford University Press.

Langer, E.J., Janis, I., & Wolfer, J. (1975). Reduction of Psychological stress in surgical patients. *Journal of Experimental Social Psychology,* 11, 155-165. doi: 10.1016/S0022-1031(75)80018-7

Lee, D. L., Belfiore, P. J., & Gormley, S. (2008). Riding the wave: Creating a momentum of school success. *Teaching Exceptional Children,* 40, 65-70. DOI: 10.1177/004005990804000307

Lemov, D. (2015). *Teach like a champion: 62 techniques that put students on thee path to college* (2nd ed). San Francisco, CA: Wiley.

Long, N.J., Fecser, F.A., & Brendtro, L.K. (1998). *LSCI: Lifespace crisis interview: New direction for chronic self-defeating behaviors.* Retrieved from https://www.lsci.org/pdf/learn-more/LSCI-Article.pdf

Malow, M. & Austin, V. L. (2016). Mindfulness for students classified with emotional/behavioral disorders. *Insights in Learning Disabilities,* 13(1) 81-94. https://files.eric.ed.gov/fulltext/EJ1103673.pdf

Masten, A.S. (2001). Ordinary magic: Resilience processes in development. *American Psychologist, 56*(3), 227-238. https://www.ncbi.nlm.nih.gov/pubmed/11315249

Merriam-Webster. (2015). *Dictionary: Burnout.* Retrieved from http://www.merriam-webster.com/dictionary/burnout

Morris, S. L. (2015). Care: Whole teachers and whole students in writing classrooms. *Delta Kappa Gamma Bulletin, 82*(1). Retrieved from https://www.questia.com/library/journal/1P3-3971765311/care-whole-teachers-and-whole-students-in-writing

Nagel, L. & Brown, S. (2003). The ABCs of managing teacher stress. *Clearing House, 76*(5), 255-259. Retrieved from http://stressfreeteaching.org/PDF/ABC_managing_stress.pdf

Neufeldnov, S. (2014, November 10). Can a teacher be too dedicated? *The Atlantic.* Retrieved from http://m.theatlantic.com/national/archive/2014/11/can-a-teacher-be-too-dedicated/382563/?singlepage=true

Norton, A.R., Abott, M.J., Norberg, M.M., & Hunt, C. (2015). A systematic review of mindfulness and acceptance-based treatments for social anxiety disorder. *Journal of Clinical Psychology, 71*(4), 283-301. doi: 10.1002/jclp.22144

Palmer, P. J. (1998). *The courage to teach.* San Francisco: Jossey-Bass.

Positive Behavioral Interventions and Supports. (2018). *What is school-wide PBIS?* Retrieved from http://www.pbis.org/school

Redl, F. (1966). *When we deal with children.* New York: The Free Press.

Riggs, L. (2013). Why do teachers quit?: And why do they stay? The Atlantic. Retrieved from https://www.theatlantic.com/education/archive/2013/10/why-do-teachers-quit/280699/

Robinson, S. (2014). A case study of self-affirmations in teacher education. *Journal of Invitational Theory and Practice, 20,* 27-36. Retrieved from https://eric.ed.gov/?id=EJ1051169

Roeser, R. W. (2016). Processes of teaching, learning, and transfer in mindfulness-based interventions (MBIs) for teachers: A contemplative educational perspective. In K. Schonert-Reichl & R. Roeser (Eds.), *The Handbook of Mindfulness in Education: Emerging Theory, Research, and Programs,* 133–149. New York, NY: Springer-Verlag. DOI: 10.1007/978-1-4939-3506-2_10

Roeser, R. W., Benn, R., Akiva, T., & Arel, S. (2012). Mindfulness Training Effects for Parents and Educators of Children With Special Needs. *Developmental Psychology, Vol 48(5),* 1476-1487. doi: 10.1037/a0027537

Roeser, R. W., Schonert-Reichl, K. A., Jha, A., Cullen, M., Wallace, L., Wilensky, R., Oberle, E., Thomson, K., Taylor, C., & Harrison, J. (2013). Mindfulness Training and Reductions in Teacher Stress and Burnout: Results From Two Randomized, Waitlist-Control Field Trials. *Journal of Educational Psychology.* doi: 10.1037/a0032093.

Roeser, R. W., Skinner, E., Beers, J., & Jennings, P. A. (2012). Mindfulness training and teachers' professional development: An emerging area of research and practice. *Child Development Perspectives,* (6) 167–173. DOI: 10.1111/j.1750-8606.2012.00238.x

Ronfeldt, M., Farmer, S. McQueen, K, & Grissom, J. (2015). *Teacher collaboration in instructional teams and student achievement.* doi: 10.3102/0002831215585562

Sawchuk, S. (2015). *Teacher evaluation: An issue overview.* Retrieved from https://www.edweek.org/ew/section/multimedia/teacher-performance-evaluation-issue-overview.html

Schonert-Reichl, K.A., Oberle, E., Lawlor, M.S., Thompson, K., Oberlander, T.F., & Diamond, A. (2015). Enhancing cognitive and social-emotional development through a simple to administer mindfulness-based school program for elementary school children: A randomized control trial. *Developmental Psychology, 51*(1), 52-66. doi: 10.1037/a0038454

Seidel, A. (2014). The teacher dropout crisis. *nprED How Learning Happens.* Retrieved from https://www.npr.org/sections/ed/2014/07/18/332343240/the-teacher-dropout-crisis

Semple, R.J., Lee, J., Rosa, D., & Miller, L.F. (2010). A randomized trial of mindfulness-based cognitive therapy for children: Promoting mindful attention to enhance social-emotional resiliency in children. *Journal of Child and Family Studies,* 19, 218-229. doi:10.1007/s10826-009-9301-y

Shukla, A. & Trivedi, T. (2008). Burnout in Indian teachers. Asia Pacific Education Review, 9(3), 320-334. *Education Research Institute.* Retrieved from https://files.eric.ed.gov/fulltext/EJ835204.pdf

Skinner, E. & Beers, J. (2016). Mindfulness and teachers' coping in the classroom: A developmental model of teacher stress, coping, and everyday resilience. In K. Schonert-Reichl & R. Roeser (Eds.), *The Handbook of Mindfulness in Education: Emerging Theory, Research, and Programs,* 88–118. New York, NY: Springer-Verlag. DOI: 10 .1007/978-1-4939-3506-2_7

Stanley, J. (2014). How unsustainable workloads are destroying the quality of teaching. *Schools Week.* Retrieved from http://schoolsweek.co.uk/how-unsustainable-workloads-are-destroying-the-quality-of-teaching

Stetka, B. (2017). *Where's the proof that mindfulness mediation works?* Retrieved from https://www.scientificamerican.com/article/wheres-the-proof-that-mindfulness-meditation-works1/

Sutcher, L., Darling-Hammond, L., Carver-Thomas, D. (2016). A coming crisis in teaching? Teacher supply, demand, and shortages in the U.S. Retrieved from https://learningpolicyinstitute.org/product/coming-crisis-teaching

Westervelt, E. & Lonsdorf, K. (2016). *What are the main reasons teachers call it quits?* Retrieved from https://www.npr.org/sections/ed/2016/10/24/495186021/what-are-the-main-reasons-teachers-call-it-quits

Wong, P. A. (2017). Mindfulness to Engage in Self-Care: A Pre-Requisite for Teacher Advocacy. *Kentucky English Bulletin, 66*(2), 32-37.

List of Acronyms

ADHD	Attention Deficit Hyperactivity Disorder: A recognized disorder that makes it difficult for students to concentrate and focus.
AIP	Academic Intervention Plan: A written plan that addresses the specific needs of struggling students in all content areas.
BIP	Behavior Intervention Plan: A written plan that addresses the specific needs of students who struggle with appropriate behavior.
CASEL	Collaborative for Academic, Social, and Emotional Learning: An organization whose mission it is to advance social-emotional learning.
CCSS	Common Core State Standards: Math and English language arts standards that have been designed to be of high quality, are aligned both vertically and horizontally between grades, and outline the learning to be mastered at each grade level.
CICO	Check-in/Check-out: positive behavior strategies in which students have a designated person with whom they check-in at arrival and then check-out at dismissal. Through this process the adult is able to gauge student concerns and behaviors and address them before they become an issue during class time.
ESSA	Every Student Succeeds Act: The 2015 reauthorization of the Elementary and Secondary Education Act that defines all educational requirements from the federal government.
ESEA	Elementary and Secondary Education Act: A bill signed in 1965 to address the educational needs of students living in poverty. It emphasized high educational standards, accountability, and equal access to education. The bill has been updated every five years since its' inception.
FAFSA	Free Application for Federal Student Aid: A form college bound student's fill out to qualify for financial aid.
FBA	Functional Behavioral Assessment: a process that identifies behaviors that interfere with a student's education progress.

GED	General Equivalency Diploma: a diploma given to students who pass a test that encompasses four content areas instead of attending secondary school.
GERM	Global Education Reform Movement: A worldwide shift toward standardization, accountability, testing, and privatization brought on by education reform.
IDEA	Individuals with Disabilities Education Act: A four-part piece of legislation that guarantees equal education to all students with disabilities.
IDM	Inquiry Design Model: a blueprint to build inquiry that can be replicated for any number of learning experiences.
IEP	Individualized Education Plan: an educational plan developed by a team of experts to address the needs of a primary, middle, or secondary school student with a documented disability.
IESCAPE	I ESCAPE: an acronym that forms the framework for crisis intervention protocols.
IFSP	Individualized Family Service Plan: A document created by a team of experts, including family, that details special services for a young child from birth to age three who has been identified to have developmental delays.
ILB	Inquiry-based Learning: A student-centered learning approach that begins with a question and a period of investigation of possible solutions and leads to discoveries and new knowledge that is best understood through deep reflection.
LD	Learning Disability: Neurologically-based processing problems that affect the ability to learn basic skills. Students with LD are often as smart or smarter than typical peers.
LRE	Least Restrictive Environment: The opportunity for a student with disabilities to be educated in the same or similar setting to that of typical peers, to the greatest extent possible, and where it is appropriate.
LSCI	Life Space Crisis Interview: A therapeutic verbal strategy used to address a student who has self-defeating behaviors during a crisis situation in hopes of turning the incident into a learning opportunity.

MTSS	Multi-Tiered System of Supports: Synonymous with Response to Intervention (RTI), MTSS is a data-based problem solving support system that uses tiers of service to support students.
NCLB	No Child Left Behind: The 2001 reauthorization of the Elementary and Secondary Education Act that defines all educational requirements from the federal government.
NGSS	New Generation Science Standards: a multi-state effort to update and organize science standards in vertical and horizontal progression; they are content rich and inquiry-based.
ODR	Office Discipline Report: a worksheet that gives a description of inappropriate student behavior, what the adults did to mitigate such behavior, as well as what the consequences were for said behavior. It follows a plan of progressive discipline.
PBIS	Positive Behavioral Interventions and Supports: A system of supports and interventions used by schools to increase positive behaviors and learning communities.
PBL	Problem-based Learning: Similar in many ways to Inquiry-based learning, students examine a real world problem with the goal of explaining or solving the problem.
PjBL	Project-based Learning: Students investigate and respond to an authentic and engaging complex question, problem, or challenge for an extended period of time and must present their findings publicly.
RTI	Response to Intervention: A multi-tiered approach to identifying and supporting students who struggle with academics as well as behaviors within the classroom setting.
SEL	Social-Emotional Learning: A belief that all learning should stem from a base that is strong in social and emotional constructs with a focus on the well-being of children.
TAPPLE	TAPPLE is an explicit instructional strategy that stands for **T**each first, **A**sk a specific question, **P**ause, **P**air-Share, **P**ick a random non-volunteer, **L**isten to the response, provide **E**ffective feedback.
TFA	Teach for America: a non-profit organization who mentors future educators.

About the Primary Authors

Nicholas D. Young, PhD, EdD

Dr. Nicholas D. Young has worked in diverse educational roles for more than 28 years, serving as a principal, special education director, graduate professor, graduate program director, graduate dean, and longtime superintendent of schools. He was named the Massachusetts Superintendent of the Year; and he completed a distinguished Fulbright program focused on the Japanese educational system through the collegiate level. Dr. Young is the recipient of numerous other honors and recognitions including the General Douglas MacArthur Award for distinguished civilian and military leadership and the Vice Admiral John T. Hayward Award for exemplary scholarship. He holds several graduate degrees including a PhD in educational administration and an EdD in educational psychology.

Dr. Young has served in the U.S. Army and U.S. Army Reserves combined for over 33 years; and he graduated with distinction from the U.S. Air War College, the U.S. Army War College, and the U.S. Navy War College. After completing a series of senior leadership assignments in the U.S. Army Reserves as the commanding officer of the 287th Medical Company (DS), the 405th Area Support Company (DS), the 405th Combat Support Hospital, and the 399th Combat Support Hospital, he transitioned to his current military position as a faculty instructor at the U.S. Army War College in Carlisle, PA. He currently holds the rank of Colonel.

Dr. Young is also a regular presenter at state, national, and international conferences; and he has written many books, book chapters, and/or articles on various topics in education, counseling, and psychology. Some of his most recent books include *Stars in the Schoolhouse: Teaching Practices and Approaches that Make a Difference* (in-press); *Guardians of the Next Generations Igniting the Passion for Quality Teaching* (in-press); *Dog Tags to Diploma: Understanding and Addressing the Educational Needs of Veterans, Servicemembers, and their Families* (in-press); *From Cradle to Classroom: A Guide to Special Education for Young Children* (in-press); *Achieving Results: Maximizing Success in the Schoolhouse* (in-press); *Making the Grade: Promoting Positive Outcomes for Students with Learning Disabilities* (in-press); *Paving the Pathway for Educational Success: Effective Classroom Interventions for Students with Learning Disabilities* (2018); *Wrestling with Writing: Effective Strategies for Struggling Students* (2018); *Floundering to Fluent: Reaching and Teaching the Struggling Student* (2018); *Emotions and Education: Promoting*

Positive Mental Health in Students with Learning (2018); *From Lecture Hall to Laptop: Opportunities, Challenges, and the Continuing Evolution of Virtual Learning in Higher Education* (2017); *The Power of the Professoriate: Demands, Challenges, and Opportunities in 21ˢᵗ Century Higher Education* (2017); *To Campus with Confidence: Supporting a Successful Transition to College for Students with Learning Disabilities* (2017); *Educational Entrepreneurship: Promoting Public-Private Partnerships for the 21st Century* (2015); *Beyond the Bedtime Story: Promoting Reading Development during the Middle School Years* (2015); *Betwixt and Between: Understanding and Meeting the Social and Emotional Developmental Needs of Students During the Middle School Transition Years* (2014); *Learning Style Perspectives: Impact Upon the Classroom* (3rd ed., 2014); and *Collapsing Educational Boundaries from Preschool to PhD: Building Bridges Across the Educational Spectrum* (2013); *Transforming Special Education Practices: A Primer for School Administrators and Policy Makers* (2012); and *Powerful Partners in Student Success: Schools, Families and Communities* (2012). He also co-authored several children's books to include the popular series *I am Full of Possibilities*. Dr. Young may be contacted directly at nyoung1191@aol.com.

Elizabeth Jean, EdD

Dr. Elizabeth Jean has served as an elementary school educator and administrator in various rural and urban settings in Massachusetts for more than 20 years. As a building administrator, she has fostered partnerships with various local businesses and higher education institutions. Further, she is currently a graduate adjunct professor at Endicott College and previously taught at Our Lady of the Elms College. In terms of formal education, Dr. Jean received a BS in education from Springfield College; an MEd in education with a concentration in reading from Our Lady of the Elms; and an EdD in curriculum, teaching, learning and leadership from Northeastern University.

Dr. Jean is a primary author on *Stars in the Schoolhouse: Teaching Practices and Approaches that Make a Difference* (in-press); *From Cradle to Classroom: A Guide to Special Education for Young Children* (in-press); *Dog Tags to Diploma: Understanding and Addressing the Educational Needs of Veterans, Servicemembers and their Families* (in-press); *From Lecture Hall to Laptop: Opportunities, Challenges and the Continuing Evolution of Virtual Learning in Higher Education* (2017). She has also written book chapters on such topics as emotional well-being for students with learning disabilities, parental supports for students with learning disabilities, home-school partnerships, virtual education, public and private partnerships in public education, professorial pursuits, technology partnerships between K-12 and higher education, developing a strategic mindset for LD students, the importance of skill and will in developing reading habits for young children, and middle school reading interventions to name a few. Additionally, she has co-authored and illustrated several children's books to include *Yes, Mama* (2018), *The Adventures of Scotty the Skunk: What's that Smell?*, (2014), and the *I am Full of Possibilities* Series. She may be contacted at elizabethjean1221@gmail.com.

Teresa Allissa Citro, **PhD**

Dr. Citro is the Chief Executive Officer, Learning Disabilities Worldwide, Inc. and the Founder and President of Thread of Hope, Inc., She is a graduate of Tufts New England Medical School and Northeastern University, both in Massachusetts. Dr. Citro has co-edited several books on a wide range of topics in special education and she co-authored a popular children's series *I Am Full of Possibilities*. Furthermore, Dr. Citro is the co-editor of two peer review journals to include *Learning Disabilities: A Contemporary Journal and Insights on Learning Disabilities* from *Prevailing Theories to Validated Practices*. She is the mother of two young children and resides in Boston, Massachusetts.

CPSIA information can be obtained
at www.ICGtesting.com
Printed in the USA
BVHW03*1050130518
516110BV00004B/10/P

9 781622 734023